JFLAP

An Interactive Formal Languages and Automata Package

Susan H. Rodger
Duke University

Thomas W. Finley
Cornell University

JONES AND BARTLETT PUBLISHERS

Sudbury, Massachusetts

BOSTON   TORONTO   LONDON   SINGAPORE

World Headquarters

Jones and Bartlett Publishers
40 Tall Pine Drive
Sudbury, MA 01776
978-443-5000
info@jbpub.com
www.jbpub.com

Jones and Bartlett Publishers
 Canada
6339 Ormindale Way
Mississauga, ON L5V 1J2
Canada

Jones and Bartlett Publishers
 International
Barb House, Barb Mews
London W6 7PA
United Kingdom

Jones and Bartlett's books and products are available through most bookstores and online booksellers. To contact Jones and Bartlett Publishers directly, call 800-832-0034, fax 978-443-8000, or visit our website at www.jbpub.com.

Substantial discounts on bulk quantities of Jones and Bartlett's publications are available to corporations, professional associations, and other qualified organizations. For details and specific discount information, contact the special sales department at Jones and Bartlett via the above contact information or send an email to specialsales@jbpub.com.

Production Credits
Acquisitions Editor: Tim Anderson
Producton Director: Amy Rose
Editorial Assistant: Kate Koch
Marketing Manager: Andrea DeFronzo
Composition: Northeast Compositors
Cover Design: Timothy Dziewit
Cover Image: © Scott Bowlin/Shutterstock, Inc.
Printing and Binding: Odyssey Press
Cover Printing: Odyssey Press

Library of Congress Cataloging-in-Publication Data
Rodger, Susan H.
  JFLAP-an interactive formal languages and automata package / Susan H. Rodger, Thomas W. Finley.—1st ed.
   p.cm
  Includes index.
  ISBN-13: 978-0-7637-3834-1 (pbk.)
  1. Formal languages. 2. Machine theory. I. Finley, Thomas W. II. Title.
  QA267.3.R63 2006
  511.3—dc22
                    2005032130

6048

Printed in the United States of America
14 13 12 11 10   10 9 8 7 6 5 4 3 2

To Thomas, Erich, and Markus

— S. H. Rodger

```
K Y H D K I K I N K O I I A G K T I Y K D
B L G K L G F A R O A D G I N I R J R E L
M R J H K D I A R A R A T A L Y M F T K Y
D R N E R K T M A T S K H W G O B B K R Y
R D U N D F F K C K A L A A K B U T C I O
M I O I A J S A I D M J E W R Y R K O K F
W F Y U S C I Y E T E G A U D N M U L W G
N F U C R Y J J T Y N Y H T E O J H M A M
N U E W N C C T H K T Y M G F D E E F U N
A U L W S B T Y M U A I Y K H O N J N H J
T R R L L Y E M N H B G T R T D G B C M S
R Y H K T G A I E R F Y A B N C R F C L J
N L F F N K A U L O N G Y T M B Y L W L U
S R A U E E Y W E L K C S I B M O U K D W
M E H O H U G N I G N E M N L K K H M E H
C N U S C N E Y N I I O M A N W G A W N I
M T A U M K A R E U S H M T S A W R S N W
E W J R W F E E E B A O K G O A E E W A N
F H J D W K L A U M E I A O M G I E G B H
I E U S N W H I S D A D C O G T D R W T B
W F C S C D O I N C N O E L T E I U B G L
```

— T. W. Finley

Contents

Preface

When I first started teaching automata theory in 1989, I taught it the traditional way as it had been taught to me. Students "programmed" finite automata, pushdown automata, and Turing machines by writing them down using pencil and paper, either in formal notation or as a transition diagram. Their answers were almost always wrong, since it was too tedious for them to check. I wanted students to be able to check their answers and interact with these automata. I wanted them to be able to design their own additional problems and be able to receive feedback on them. I began designing a tool for experimenting with pushdown automata, and over the years, with the help of many undergraduate and graduate students, FLAP was created and eventually evolved into JFLAP.

Susan Rodger

This book is a hands-on guide through the Java Formal Language and Automata Package (JFLAP), an interactive visualization and teaching tool for formal languages. This book is intended as a supplement to an undergraduate automata theory course or an undergraduate compiler course. This book is not a textbook! We assume the user is using a textbook along with our book. Our book guides users interactively through many of the concepts in an automata theory course or the early topics in a compiler course, including descriptions of algorithms JFLAP has implemented and sample problems for reinforcement of concepts. However, our book assumes that the user has read briefly about these concepts first in an automata theory textbook or compiler textbook.

JFLAP allows users to create and operate on automata, grammars, L-systems, and regular expressions; the term *structure* is used to refer to any single automaton, grammar, L-system, or regular expression. JFLAP offers the following major groups of operations to apply to structures:

Explore the Language of Structures JFLAP has the ability to simulate input strings on non-deterministic automata, build parse tables and parse trees for grammars, and render successive expansions of L-systems. The automata represented in JFLAP are finite automata (FA), pushdown automata (PDA), and multitape Turing machines. The parsing algorithms in JFLAP are brute-force parsing, LL(1) parsing, and SLR(1) parsing.

Convert Between Equivalent Structures A wide range of conversion abilities is available, including regular expression to FA, nondeterministic FA to deterministic FA (DFA), PDA to grammar, grammar to PDA, DFA to minimized DFA, context-free grammar to Chomsky Normal Form grammar, and others.

Miscellaneous Analysis of Structures JFLAP also offers a few sundry analysis tools to display properties of structures, like highlighting λ-transitions, highlighting nondeterministic states, and determining the equivalence of two FAs.

In addition to designing the structures previously listed, our book guides the user through interactive alternative perspectives that would be difficult to do with pencil and paper. Here we list several examples from the book.

- In Chapter 2 users convert a deterministic finite automaton (DFA) to a minimal DFA. During the conversion, users must determine whether or not two states p and q are distinguishable. With JFLAP users make two copies of the DFA — one with p a start state and the other with q a start state — and run both DFAs on the same set of input strings to determine whether the states are distinguishable.

- In Chapter 6 users parse context-free grammars using a brute-force parser. To determine the language of a grammar, users enter each variable's productions separately (when possible) and determine the language of each variable first, then put them together for the language of the grammar.

- In Chapter 8 users parse a grammar with an SLR(1) parser. They then build an NPDA that models the SLR(1) parsing process for this grammar and run the NPDA with the same strings. The NPDA is likely nondeterministic, so the students guide the run with lookaheads.

JFLAP uses general definitions of its structures to allow it to fit with a range of textbooks. We mention some of these definitions here. Definitions for each structure are in the corresponding chapter. Instructors might prefer to require students to use a subset of the JFLAP definition if that fits with their textbook.

- Finite automata allow users to enter strings of length zero or greater. Instead, an instructor might want to require students to enter strings of length zero or one.

- Pushdown automata can pop zero or more symbols from the stack in each transition. An instructor might want to require students to always pop one symbol.

- Turing machine movements for the tape head are Right, Left, and Stay. An instructor might want to require students to use only Right and Left.

Organization

This book covers topics from a formal languages and automata theory course, with additional topics on parsing and L-systems. We find that undergraduate students need to see an application to understand why this material is important. With SLR(1) parsing, students see the use of DFAs and PDAs. L-systems are included as an alternative grammar that results in interesting visual pictures.

We recommend chapters for an automata theory course and for the first part of a compiler course. Both courses should have students look at the JFLAP Startup section following the Preface before reading the chapters.

For an automata theory course, the minimal coverage would be Chapters 1–6 and 9. Our book covers automata before grammars, so if your textbook covers grammars before automata then for regular languages you should cover Sections 3.1 and 3.2, Chapters 1 and 2, and Sections 3.3 and 3.4, in that order. If context-free grammars are covered before PDA in your textbook, then cover them in the order Section 6.1, Chapter 5, and then Sections 6.2 and 6.3. Optional topics include Chapters 7, 8, 10, and 11. If instructors want to cover SLR(1) parsing only, but not LL(1) parsing, then cover Sections 8.1 and 8.3.

For a compiler course, related chapters on parsing are Chapters 1 and 2, Sections 3.1–3.3, Chapter 5, Sections 6.1 and 6.2, and Chapters 8 and 11. Skip Section 8.2 if you are not covering LL(1) parsing. Chapter 11 is optional but provides some interesting thoughts on how one parses other types of grammars, including the "parse tree" for unrestricted grammars in JFLAP. (This is not really a tree, but rather a directed acyclic graph.)

We now give a brief description of the highlights of each chapter.

Chapter 1, Finite Automata, guides the user through editing and simulating both deterministic and nondeterministic automata.

Chapter 2, NFA to DFA to Minimal DFA, guides the user through transforming an NFA into a DFA and then a minimal state DFA. In the NFA to DFA algorithm, a DFA state represents corresponding states reachable from the NFA. In the DFA to minimal DFA algorithm, states are grouped into sets of indistinguishable states using a tree method.

Chapter 3, Regular Grammars, guides the user through editing and parsing grammars. Its conversion algorithms between FA and right-linear grammars are standard.

Chapter 4, Regular Expressions, has conversion algorithms that use generalized transition graphs (GTG), wherein a transition label can be a regular expression. The regular expression to NFA algorithm starts with a GTG with one transition containing the regular expression and de-expressionifies one operation at a time until the result is an NFA. The FA to regular expression algorithm starts with an FA represented as a GTG with a transition between every pair of states (using $\emptyset$ if there was no transition). The algorithm removes one state at a time, replacing transitions with regular expressions, until there are only two states remaining.

Chapter 5, Pushdown Automata, introduces the editing and simulation of NPDAs.

Chapter 6, Context-Free Grammars, revisits the brute-force parser and goes into detail in terms of how it works. Two algorithms are presented. The CFG to NPDA algorithm uses the model for LL parsing. Students do not need to know LL parsing for this chapter. The NPDA to CFG algorithm can easily result in a rather large grammar with many useless productions, and thus seems magical to students. After the conversion students test the same strings in both the original NPDA and the resulting CFG.

Chapter 7, Transforming Grammars, covers the transformation of a CFG to Chomsky Normal Form. Several transformations occur, including removing λ-productions, unit productions, and useless productions. Students test the same strings in the transformed and original grammars.

Chapter 8, LL and SLR Parsing, describes FIRST and FOLLOW sets that are needed in parsing, and the two parsing methods LL and SLR. For both LL and SLR parsing, students are shown how to convert a CFG to an NPDA for that method, how to build the parse table, and how to compare the NPDA with parsing. In parsing a string, students can view either the derivation or a parse tree.

Chapter 9, Turing Machines, shows how to edit and simulate a one-tape Turing machine first, then expands to multitape Turing machines, including an example of a universal Turing machine.

Chapter 10, L-Systems, describes how to edit L-systems and use them to produce plants, fractals, and other graphical structures.

Chapter 11, Other Grammars in the Hierarchy, describes how to use the brute-force parser to parse strings with unrestricted and context-sensitive grammars, and provides some insight about how to structure these grammars so brute-force parsing is not totally intractable.

JFLAP Software

JFLAP and all files referenced in this book are available at www.jflap.org and are free! We recommend that files be used in conjunction with the text.

Acknowledgments

This book is the result of many years spent developing JFLAP and we would like to thank several people. Thanks to Peter Linz for many conversations and ideas on JFLAP. Thanks to Erich Kaltofen and Mukkai Krishnamoorthy for encouraging me in the early days of JFLAP, and Owen Astrachan in the later days of JFLAP. Thanks to family members for putting up with long absences, including Thomas, Markus, and Erich Narten, and John and Susan Finley. We especially want to thank John and Susan Finley for many hours of proofreading.

Thanks to the many students who have worked on FLAP, JFLAP, or related tools over the years. These include Dan Caugherty, Mark LoSacco, Magda Procopiuc, Octavian Procopiuc, Greg Badros, Ryan Cavalcante, Ted Hung, Eric Gramond, Lenore Ramm, Robyn Geer, Alex Karweit, Anna Bilska, Jason Salemme, Ben Hardekopf, Steve Wolfman, Eric Luce, Ken Leider, Bart Bressler, and Stephen Reading. Thanks to all the people who attended the JFLAP workshop in June 2005 and gave valuable feedback on JFLAP. This includes Michelangelo Grigni, Kelly Shaw, Dwight House, Sandria Kerr, Christopher Brown, Jacquelyn Long, Dawit Haile, Sanjoy Baruah, Costas Busch, Rakesh Verma, Joseph Bergin, Rockford Ross, and Eric Wiebe. And finally, thanks to the over 17,000 users of JFLAP, and to the many of you who have given us feedback over the years.

Susan H. Rodger and Thomas W. Finley

JFLAP Startup

Running JFLAP

Download JFLAP and the files referenced in this book from `www.jflap.org` to get started.

JFLAP is written in Java to allow it to run on a range of platforms. JFLAP requires that your computer have Java SE 1.4 or later installed. JFLAP works with Java 1.5. For the latest version, visit `http://java.sun.com/`. Mac OS X's latest Java release, if not already preinstalled, is available from `http://www.apple.com/java/`, or from Software Update.

With Java SE 1.4 or later installed on your computer, you may attempt to run JFLAP. JFLAP is distributed as an executable .jar (**J**ava **AR**chive) file. JFLAP may be run as either an application or applet. The following table lists how to run the `JFLAP.jar` executable .jar as an application on your platform of choice.

Windows	Double click on `JFLAP.jar`; the file will appear as `JFLAP` if suffix hiding is on.
Unix & Linux	From a shell with the `JFLAP.jar` file in the current directory, enter the command `java -jar JFLAP.jar`.
Mac OS X	The Windows and Unix directions will work on a Mac.

JFLAP Interface Primer

We cover universal elements of the JFLAP interface here. To begin, start JFLAP. When JFLAP has finished loading, a window will appear similar to that shown in Figure 1. This window offers a choice of major structures if you wish to create a new structure; alternatively, the **File** menu allows you to open an existing saved structure or quit JFLAP.

Throughout this book we shall review the creation of these structures. However, right now we are going to open a JFLAP saved file of an existing finite automaton (FA). From the **File** menu, choose **Open**. JFLAP allows users to save and open files that contain a single structure. Select and open the file `ex0.1a`. A new window will appear with an FA.

We refer to all the things you can do to a structure as *operators*. (It is not necessary to understand what the operators are doing at this point; our purpose is to describe JFLAP's interface.)

Figure 1: The window that appears when you start JFLAP.

Operators are typically activated through the menu items. Choose the menu item **Test : Highlight Nondeterminism**. (This activates an operator that shades nondeterministic states in an automaton, in this case q_0 and q_1.) Next, choose the menu item **Test : Highlight λ-Transitions**. (This activates an operator that highlights λ-transitions in an automaton, in this case the arc labeled λ.) We chose these two operators because they require no intervention from the user.

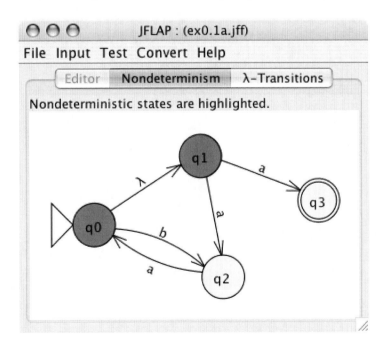

Figure 2: An illustration of the window for a structure, with three tabs active.

The window for a structure consists of a menu bar that contains operators you may apply to the structure, and a *tabbed interface* below the menu bar. Note that JFLAP *keeps everything related to a structure in a single window*, and uses tabs to manage multiple operators active at the same time. The results of the two operators we invoked are displayed in tabs, so there are currently three tabs: **Editor**, **Nondeterminism**, and λ**-Transitions**. In Figure 2, the **Nondeterminism** tab is selected, indicating that the interface for the "highlight nondeterminism" operator is currently active and displayed. To switch to another operator, click on its tab. (Note that you cannot switch to the **Editor** tab at this time. This is because the other two currently active operators depend on the automaton not changing.)

We will now remove the **Nondeterminism** and λ**-Transitions** tabs. To get rid of a tab, select the menu item **File : Dismiss Tab**. This will remove the currently active tab. When it is gone, remove the other tab as well. (JFLAP prevents removal of the **Editor** tab.)

As a last step, peruse the contents of the **File** menu. Use **New** when you want to create a new structure; when **New** is selected, JFLAP will display the window shown in Figure 1 that allows you to choose a type of structure to create. The **Open**, **Save**, and **Save As** menu items allow you to read and write structures to files like any other application that deals with documents. The **Close** item will close the window of the structure. The **Print** item will print the currently active tab. **Quit** will stop JFLAP entirely.

Chapter 1

Finite Automata

A finite automaton is the first type of representation for a regular language that we will examine.

In this chapter we will construct a deterministic finite automaton (DFA) in JFLAP, illustrate several methods of simulating input on that automaton, discuss nondeterministic finite automata (NFAs) in JFLAP, and present simple analyses that JFLAP may apply to automata. We present a standard definition of a DFA in Sections 1.1–1.4, and show in the optional Section 1.5 how JFLAP handles a more general definition of a DFA with multiple character transitions.

1.1 A Simple Finite Automaton

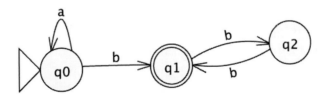

Figure 1.1: A finite automaton (FA), which recognizes the language of any number of a's followed by any odd number of b's.

In this section you will learn how to build automata in JFLAP by way of constructing, with help, the DFA that recognizes the language of strings of any number of a's followed by any odd number of b's (e.g., ab, bbb, $aabbbbb$). This section will teach the essentials of automaton editing in JFLAP: creating and deleting states and transitions, moving existing states, editing existing transitions, and setting states to be initial and final. When you are done, you will have a machine like that pictured in Figure 1.1!

The first step is, of course, to start JFLAP. Once JFLAP is running, you begin building an FA by clicking on the button labeled **Finite Automaton**. A window will appear with (from top to bottom) a menu, a tab that says **Editor**, a tool bar, and a large blank area at the bottom.

1

1.1.1   Create States

All automata require a set of states. Before you can create states you must first activate the State Creator tool: click on the ⊚ button below the window's menu bar. This button will now appear shaded to indicate that tool is active.

The large blank area below the tools, called the *canvas*, is where the automaton is created and edited. Now that the State Creator tool is active, click on the canvas to create a state. A state will appear under the location where you clicked. As you will see, states in JFLAP are yellow circles with some identifying text inside. Click three more times in three other locations to create three more states. There will now be four states on the canvas, with the text q_0, q_1, q_2, and q_3 to identify each of them.

1.1.2   Define the Initial State and the Final State

All automata require an initial state and a set of final states. In this automaton we will make q_0 the initial state, and q_1 the single final state. Select the Attribute Editor tool, by clicking the ↖ button. Two of this tool's many functions are to define an initial state and to define the set of final states. (This tool's other functions are described in Section 1.1.5.)

Now that the Attribute Editor tool is selected, right-click on q_0 (or, control-click if you are a Macintosh user with a single mouse button). A pop-up menu above the state will appear with several items, including two items **Final** and **Initial**. Select the item **Initial**. The state q_0 will now have a white arrowhead appear to its left to indicate it is the initial state. Similarly, right-click on the state q_1, and select the item **Final**. The state q_1 will now have a double outline instead of a single outline, indicating that this state is a member of the set of final states.

You may find it necessary to set a final state as nonfinal. To illustrate how, right-click on q_1 once you have marked it as final. Notice that the item **Final** now has a check mark next to it. Select the item **Final** again. This will toggle q_1 out of the set of final states. Before you proceed, you must of course put q_1 in the set of final states again!

1.1.3   Creating Transitions

We will now create transitions. In this machine, three transitions are necessary: three on b from q_0 to q_1, q_1 to q_2, and back again from q_2 to q_1, and a loop transition on a for state q_0. We will create others for illustrating some special features, and for later illustration of the Deleter tool.

To create these transitions, select the Transition Creator tool, denoted by the ↗ icon. The first transition we are going to create is the b transition from q_0 to q_1. Once the Transition Creator tool is selected, press the mouse cursor down on the q_0 state, drag the mouse cursor to the q_1 state, and release the mouse button. A text field will appear between the two states. Type "b" and press return. A new b transition from q_0 to q_1 will appear. By the same method, create the two b transitions from q_1 and q_2 and from q_2 and q_1.

> **Tip** | As an alternative to pressing return, you can stop editing a transition merely by doing something else like clicking in empty space (but not on a state!), or creating another transition by dragging between two other states. If you wish to cancel an edit of a transition, press Escape.

The next transition is q_0's loop transition on a. Creating loop transitions on a state is just like other transitions: you press the mouse on the start state and release the mouse on the end state. However, because the start and end states are the same for a loop transition, this is the same as clicking on the state. So, click on state q_0, and enter "a" and press return, just as you did for the b transitions.

Lastly, create three transitions from q_0 to q_3, the first on the terminal a, another on b, and a third on c. Notice that JFLAP stacks the transition labels atop each other.

> **Tip** | If you are in the process of editing a transition from a state q_i to a state q_j and you wish to create another transition from state q_i to state q_j without having to use the mouse, press Shift-Return. This creates a new transition from q_i to q_j in addition to ending your editing of the current transition.

1.1.4 Deleting States and Transitions

You probably noticed that the automaton built requires three states, not four. This fourth state q_3 and the transitions going to it are unneccessary and can be removed. Deleting objects has a tool all its own: click the ♣ button to activate the Deleter tool.

First, we want to remove the transition on b from q_0 to q_3. To delete this transition, click on the b. The b transition will be gone, leaving the a and c transitions. You can also click on the transition arrow itself to delete a transition: click on the arrow from q_0 to q_3, and notice that the a transition disappears. The c transition remains. When you click on the arrow, the transition with the label closest to the arrow is deleted.

Deleting states is similar. Click on the state q_3. The state q_3 will disappear, and notice that the c transition is gone as well. Deleting a state will also delete all transitions coming from or going to that state. You should now be left only with the other three states and the transitions between them.

1.1.5 Attribute Editor Tool

We already used the Attribute Editor tool ↖ in Section 1.1.2, but it has many other functions related to modification of attributes of existing states and transitions. Select the Attribute Editor tool ↖ once again as we walk through examples of its use.

Setting states as initial or final

This tool may set states as initial or final states as described in Section 1.1.2.

Moving states and transitions

When you initially placed the states for the FA built earlier you may not have arranged them in a logical order. To move a state, press on the state and drag it to a new location. Dragging a transition will likewise move its two associated states. Attempt this now by dragging states and transitions.

Editing existing transitions

To edit an existing transition, simply click on it! Try clicking the transition from q_0 to q_1. The same interface in which you initially defined this transition will appear on the transition and allow you to edit the input characters read by that transition.

Labels

When you set the state q_0 as the initial state and the state q_1 as a final state, perhaps you noticed the menu item **Change Label**. Right-click on q_2 and select **Change Label**. A dialog box will appear, asking for a label. When processing input, while the machine is in state q_2, we shall have processed an even number of b's, so enter "even # of b's". A box will appear under the state with this label. By a similar token, label q_1 "odd # of b's". To delete an existing label from a state choose the menu item **Clear Label** from the same menu. Alternatively, the menu item **Clear All Labels** will delete all labels from all states.

If you right-click in empty space, a different menu will appear, with the item **Display State Labels**. This will initially have a check mark next to it to indicate that it is active. Select it. The labels will become invisible. Hover the mouse cursor over q_2; after a short time, a tool-tip will appear to display the label **even # of b's**. Right-click in empty space once more, and reactivate **Display State Labels**; the labels will appear again.

Automatic layout

Right-click in empty space again. Notice the menu item **Layout Graph**. When selected, JFLAP will apply a graph layout algorithm to the automaton. While usually not useful for automata you produce yourself, many of JFLAP's algorithms automatically produce automata, often with large numbers of states. If you find JFLAP's first attempt at automatic layout inappropriate, this may alleviate the tedium of moving those states yourself.

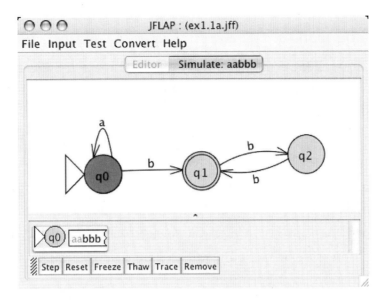

Figure 1.2: In the midst of the simulation of *aabbb* on our FA.

Tip In addition to activating a tool by clicking on its button in the toolbar, there are also shortcut keys available for quickly switching tools. For example, hover the mouse over the State Creator tool ⊙; after a little while a tool-tip will appear with the text **(S)tate Creator**. The parentheses enclosing the **S** indicate that this is the shortcut key for the State Creator tool. Note that in spite of appearances, shortcut keys are really lower case, so do not press Shift when typing the shortcut key for a tool!

1.2   Simulation of Input

In this section we cover three of JFLAP's methods to simulate input on an automaton: stepping with closure, fast simulation, and multiple simulation. The fourth, stepping by state, is discussed briefly in Section 1.3.

1.2.1   Stepping Simulation

The stepping simulation option allows you to view every configuration generated by an automaton in its attempt to process an input string. Figure 1.2 shows a snapshot of a stepping simulation of the input string *aabbb* on the automaton you built in Section 1.1, also stored in file `ex1.1a`. The top portion of the window displays the automaton, with the state in the active configuration shaded darker. The portion below the automaton displays the current configuration. In Figure 1.2, notice the configuration is in state q_0, and that the first two characters *aa* are grayed-out, indicating that they have been read, while the three characters *bbb* are not grayed-out, indicating that they remain to be read.

Try stepping

We shall walk through the process of stepping through input in an automaton. First, select the menu item **Input : Step with Closure**. A dialog box will ask for input for the machine: enter "aabbb" and press Return or click **OK**.

Your window will now appear similar to Figure 1.2. The single configuration displayed will be on the initial state q_0, and have the unprocessed input *aabbb*.

The tool bar at the bottom is your interface to the simulator. Click **Step**. The old configuration on q_0 has been replaced with a new configuration, again on the state q_0, but with the character *a* read. Notice that the first character *a* in the input has been lightened a bit to indicate that it has been read. Click **Step** twice more, and it will go from q_0 to q_0 again, and then to q_1, with the input *bb* remaining.

Some of the operations in the tool bar below the configuration display act only on selected configurations. Click on the configuration; this will select it (or deselect it if it is already selected). A selected configuration is drawn shaded. Click **Remove**. Unfortunately, this deletes the only configuration! The simulator is useless. Oops! Click the **Reset** button; this will restart the simulation, so you can try again.

With the simulation back to its original state, click **Step** repeatedly (five times) until all the input is read. The configuration at this point should be drawn with a green background, indicating that it is an *accepting configuration*, and that the machine accepts the input. FA configurations are *accepting configurations* if all the input is read and it is in a final state. The configuration's input is entirely gray, indicating that all the input has been read.

One can **Trace** a configuration to see its ancestry from the initial configuration. (Do not select a configuration; press **Trace** instead. An error message indicates that **Trace** requires a selected configuration!) Now select the single configuration, and click the **Trace** button. A window will show the ancestry of this configuration, starting with the initial configuration on top and the selected configuration on the bottom. When you've had a chance to look over the trace of the configuration, close this window.

To return to the editor, choose **File : Dismiss Tab** to dismiss the simulator.

Failure

On the flip side of an accepting configuration is a *rejected configuration*. A rejected configuration is one which (1) does not lead to any more configurations and (2) is not accepting. Run a stepping simulation again, except this time with the input *aabb*. Since this has an even number of *b*'s the machine will not accept it. Click **Step** repeatedly, and note that eventually the configuration will turn red. This indicates that it is a rejected configuration.

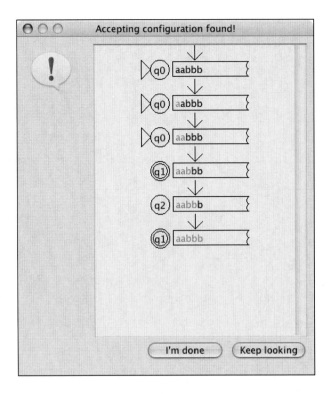

Figure 1.3: The result of performing a fast simulation of *aabbb* on the automaton.

1.2.2 Fast Simulation

Stepping through simulation of input is fine, but **Fast Run** will reveal if the automaton accepts a string and, if it does, the series of configurations leading to that string's acceptance without the bother of having to repeatedly step through the machine watching for accepting configurations.

Choose **Input : Fast Run**. When prompted for input, enter the same "aabbb" string. The result after JFLAP determines that the machine accepts this input is shown in Figure 1.3. The trace of configurations, from top to bottom (i.e., from initial to accepting configuration), is displayed. Alternatively, if the machine did not accept this input, JFLAP would report that the string was not accepted.

Notice the two buttons near the bottom of the dialog box. **I'm Done** will close the display. **Keep Looking** is useful for nondeterministic machines and is covered later in Section 1.3.2.

1.2.3 Multiple Simulation

The third method for simulating input on an automaton is **Multiple Run**. This method allows one to perform multiple runs on a machine quickly. Select **Input : Multiple Run** now. (Your display will not resemble Figure 1.4 exactly, but do not worry!) The automaton is displayed to the left, and on the right is an empty table where you may enter inputs for multiple runs. One enters inputs in the **Input** column. Select the upper-left cell of this table, enter the input "aabbb", then

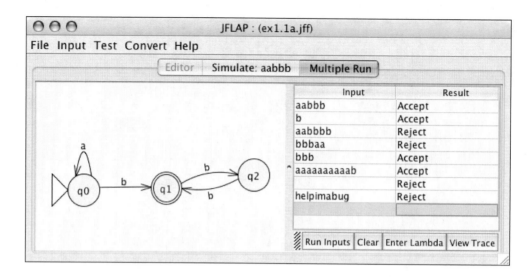

Figure 1.4: An example of simulating multiple entries. The second-to-last input is the empty string, entered with **Enter Lambda**.

press return. Notice that instead of one row there are now two: the table will grow to accommodate more entries as you enter them.

Continue entering various inputs you wish to test on the machine; whichever you choose is up to you. If you wish to make a lambda entry—that is, test to see if the automaton accepts the empty string—then *while entering an input*, click the **Enter Lambda** button near the bottom of the window, and that input field will hold the empty string. When you have entered all inputs and wish JFLAP to simulate all these strings, click **Run Inputs**. Notice that the **Result** column is now full of **Accept** and **Reject** entries, indicating whether an input was accepted or not. **View Trace** will show the trace of the last configuration generated for each selected run in the table. **Clear** will clear the table of all inputs.

> **Tip** ‖ For convenience, the multiple run simulator will remember all inputs entered by the user between machines. For example, suppose you have one automaton, and perform multiple runs on that machine. If you later perform multiple run simulation on a different automaton those same inputs will appear.

1.3   Nondeterminism

In this section we will talk about NFAs in JFLAP, using the automaton pictured in Figure 1.5 as our example.

Either of two conditions imply that an FA is nondeterminstic. The first condition is, if the FA has two transitions from the same state that read the same symbol, the FA is considered an NFA.

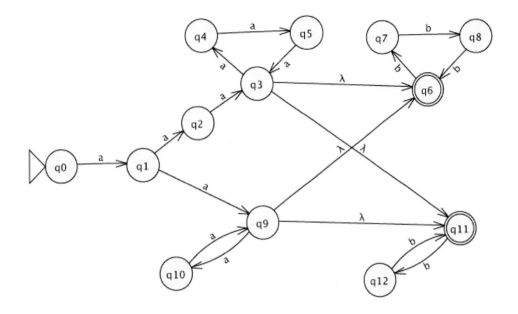

Figure 1.5: An NFA that accepts the language of a series of a's followed by a series of b's, where the number of a's is nonzero and divisible by 2 or 3, and the number of b's is divisible by 2 or 3.

For example, q_1 of the FA in Figure 1.5 has two outgoing transitions on a. The second condition is: if the FA has any transitions that read the empty string for input, the FA is nondeterministic.

1.3.1   Creating Nondeterministic Finite Automata

Creating an NFA is much the same as creating a DFA. Select **File : New**, and then select **Finite Automaton** to get a new window. In this window we will create the automaton shown in Figure 1.5, that accepts the language $a^n b^m$, where $n > 0$ and is divisible by 2 or 3 and $m \geq 0$ and is divisible by 2 or 3. The first step is to create the thirteen states of the automaton, and to make q_0 the initial state and make q_6 and q_{11} the final states.

Note that JFLAP numbers states in the order that you create them: the first state is q_0, the second q_1, and so on. It is important to respect this order: the following discussion assumes that you create the states in such an order that they are numbered as they are in Figure 1.5.

Notice the four transitions in Figure 1.5 with a λ (the Greek letter lambda). These λ-*transitions* are transitions on the empty string. To enter a λ-transition, create a transition, but leave the field empty. When you finish editing, a transition with the label λ will appear. Create the four λ-transitions from q_3 and q_9 to q_6 and q_{11}.

Once you have created the λ-transitions, create the other transitions on the symbols a or b.

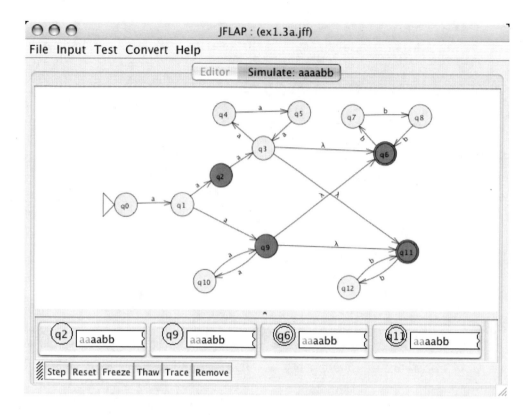

Figure 1.6: Step with closure simulation of *aaaabb* on our NFA after two steps.

1.3.2   Simulation

During simulation, input on a deterministic machine will produce a single path of configurations, while input on a nondeterministic machine may produce multiple paths of configurations. JFLAP's simulators have features to deal with this possibility.

Stepping simulation: Step with Closure

Select the menu item **Input : Step with Closure** and input the string "aaaabb", that is, four a's followed by two b's. This is a string that will eventually be accepted since the number of a's is nonzero and divisible by 2 and the number of b's is divisible by 2. After you enter this input, you should see the familiar step simulator, with a starting configuration on q_0 with all the input remaining to be processed. Click **Step** once to move this configuration to q_1. However, if you click **Step** a second time you will see a rather unfamiliar sight, as shown in Figure 1.6.

Notice that there are four configurations in your simulator. This is because your machine is nondeterministic: The last configuration was on q_1 with the unread input *aaabb*, and q_1 has a transitions to q_2 and q_9. However, what two configurations on q_6 and q_{11}? These configurations are due to the λ-transitions. When a configuration proceeds to a state q_i, **Step with Closure** creates configurations not only for q_i, but for all states reachable on λ-transitions from q_i. The set of states reachable from q_i on λ-transitions is called the *closure* of q_i. So, when the configuration in q_9 with the remaining input *aabb* was created, configurations for q_6 and q_{11} were created as well because the closure of q_9 includes q_6 and q_{11}.

As you may have figured out, of these two paths of configurations, the only one that will eventually lead to an accepting configuration is the configuration on q_9. Click on this configuration to select it. With the configuration selected, click **Freeze**. The configuration will appear tinted light ice blue! Now try stepping again: While the other configurations move on (and are rejected), that configuration will not progress! Frozen configurations do not progress when the simulator steps. With that configuration still selected, click **Thaw**. **Thaw** "unfreezes" selected configurations. Click the **Step** button once more, and the now unfrozen configuration will continue, and one of its nondeterministic paths will be accepted.

Select the accepting configuration and click **Trace** to view the series of configurations that led to the accepting configuration. Notice that there is a configuration from q_{10} directly to q_{11}, even though there is no transition from q_{10} to q_{11}. In stepping by closure one does not explicitly traverse λ-transitions in the same sense that one traverses regular transitions: Instead, no configuration was ever generated for q_9, and the simulator implicitly traversed the λ-transition.

When you have finished, dismiss the simulator tab.

Stepping simulation: Step by State

Select the menu item **Input : Step by State**, and input the string "aaaabb". In stepping by state, the closure is not taken, so the simulator explicitly traverses λ-transitions. If you step twice, you will have configurations in q_2 and q_9, but not the configurations in q_6 and q_{11} that we saw when stepping by closure.

Notice that the unread input on the q_9 configuration is *aabb*. If you step again, the configuration on q_9 will split into three configurations, two of which are on q_6 and q_{11}. The λ-transition was taken explicitly over a step action. If you continue stepping until an accepting configuration is encountered and run a trace, the configuration after q_{10} is on q_9, which then proceeds to q_{11} after explicitly taking the λ-transition.

Though stepping by state is in some ways less confusing, stepping with closure is often preferred because it guarantees that each step will read an input symbol.

Fast simulation

The fast simulator has some additional features specifically for nondeterminism. Select **Input : Fast Run**, and enter the string "aaaaaabb". Once you enter this, JFLAP will display one trace of accepting configurations.

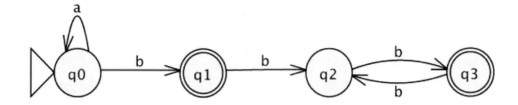

Figure 1.7: Another FA, which also recognizes the language of the automaton in Figure 1.1.

The button **Keep Looking** is useful for nondeterministic machines, where multiple branches of configurations may accept the same input. Note that there are six a's. Since six is divisible by both two and three, there will be two paths of configurations that accept this input: one path leads through state q_3 (which verifies that the number of a's is divisible by three), and another path leads through state q_9 (which verifies that the number of a's is divisible by two). The trace through either q_3 or q_9 should be visible now. Click **Keep Looking**, and it will search for and display the trace through the other state. Click **Keep Looking** again. JFLAP will display a message, **2 configurations accepted, and all other possibilities are exhausted**, which indicates that no other accepting configurations are possible.

Multiple simulation

Nondeterministic machines may produce multiple configuration paths per run. However, the multiple run simulator's ability to view traces of selected runs will present only a single trace for each run. Specifically, this feature displays only the trace of the *last* configuration generated for a run. This means that for an accepting run JFLAP displays the trace of the first accepting configuration encountered, and further for a rejecting run displays the trace of the last configuration rejected, which may not provide enough information. Viewing a run in the stepwise simulator can give a more complete picture if you want to debug a nondeterministic machine.

1.4   Simple Analysis Operators

In addition to the simulation of input, JFLAP offers a few simple operators from the **Test** menu to determine various properties of the automaton.

1.4.1   Compare Equivalence

This operator compares two finite automata to see if they accept the same language. To illustrate how this works, we shall load an automaton that recognizes the same language as the automaton we have abused throughout much of this chapter: the automaton shown in Figure 1.7, stored in file ex1.4a. Open this file. Also, open the file ex1.1a; this contains the automaton of Figure 1.1.

You will now have two windows, one with the original automaton of Figure 1.1 (presumably titled **ex1.1a**), the other with the automaton of Figure 1.7 (presumably titled **ex1.4a**). Choose the menu item **Test : Compare Equivalence** from the **ex1.4a** window. A prompt will appear where you may choose from the names of one other automaton (i.e., the title of another automaton's window) from a list. After you select the original automaton's window's name (again, presumably **ex1.1a**), click **OK**. You will then receive a dialog box telling you that they are equivalent! Dismiss this dialog. Edit the Figure 1.7 automaton so that the b transition from q_0 to q_1 is instead an a transition (so that the automaton now recognizes strings with any nonzero number of a's and an even number of b's), or make whatever other change is to your liking so that the automaton no longer recognizes the same language as the original. Repeat the test for equivalence, and this time you will receive a notice that it does not accept the same language.

Close the two files, but do not save the changes from the modified **ex1.4a**.

1.4.2   Highlight Nondeterminism

This operator will show the user which states in an automaton are nondeterministic states. Consider again the automaton in Figure 1.5, stored in the file **ex1.3a**. Load this file. The state q_1 is obviously nondeterministic, and JFLAP considers all states with outgoing λ-transitions to be nondeterministic states, so q_3 and q_9 are nondeterministic. Select **Test : Highlight Nondeterminism**: a new view will display the automaton with these states highlighted.

1.4.3   Highlight λ-Transitions

This operator will highlight all λ-transitions. Here we use the same automaton we built in Section 1.3.1, the automaton shown in Figure 1.5 and stored in the file **ex1.3a**. Load this file if it is not already present. When you select **Test : Highlight λ-Transitions**, a new view will display the automaton with the four λ-transitions highlighted.

1.5   Alternative Multiple Character Transitions[*]

JFLAP provides a more general definition of an FA, allowing multiple characters on a transition. This can result in simpler FAs. Pictured in Figure 1.8 is a five-state NFA that accepts the same language as the thirteen-state NFA in Figure 1.5. Notice that the six transitions that are not λ-transitions are on multiple symbols, for example, aaa from q_0 to q_1. A configuration may proceed on an n character transition of $s_1 s_2 \ldots s_n$ if the next unread input symbols are s_1, s_2, and so on through s_n.

We will now run a simulation on this NFA. Load the file **ex1.5a**, select **Step With Closure**, and enter the same *aaabb* string we used in Section 1.3.2. After you enter the input, you will see

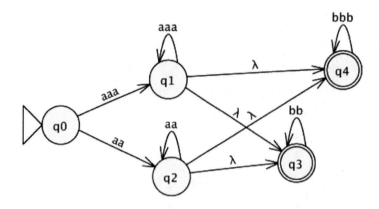

Figure 1.8: An NFA equivalent to that of Figure 1.5.

the familiar step simulator, with a starting configuration on q_0 with all the input remaining to be processed. Click **Step** once and you will see six configurations! There are two configurations for q_3, one closure from q_1 and one closure from q_2. Note that these two configurations have different amounts of remaining input since the transitions to q_1 and q_2 process a different amount of input. Similarly, there are two configurations for q_4. Stepping twice more results in acceptance in q_3.

By allowing multiple character transitions, the first condition for FA nondeterminism in Section 1.3 changes. The first condition is now the following: if the FA has two transitions from the same state that read strings A and B, where A is a prefix of B, the FA is considered an NFA. For example, note that q_0 is a nondeterministic state: it has two transitions, one from aaa and the other from aa; aa is a prefix of aaa, so the FA is nondeterministic. The NFA would use both of these transitions while simulating the string $aaaabb$.

1.6   Definition of FA in JFLAP

JFLAP defines a finite automaton M as the quintuple $M = (Q, \Sigma, \delta, q_s, F)$ where

    Q is a finite set of states $\{q_i | i$ is a nonnegative integer$\}$

    Σ is the finite input alphabet

    δ is the transition function, $\delta : D \to 2^Q$ where D is a finite subset of $Q \times \Sigma^*$

    $q_s \in Q$ is the initial state

    $F \subseteq Q$ is the set of final states

    Users reading only Sections 1.1–1.4 will want to use a simpler definition of δ. In that case, for a DFA δ is the transition function $\delta : Q \times \Sigma \to Q$, and for an NFA δ is the transition function $\delta : Q \times \Sigma \cup \{\lambda\} \to 2^Q$.

For those users reading Section 1.5, note that JFLAP allows for multiple characters on a transition. These multiple character transitions complicate the definition of the transition function's domain: the set $Q \times \Sigma^*$ is of infinite cardinality, though the transition function requires a finite domain. Σ^* means a string of 0 or more symbols from the input alphabet.

1.7 Summary

In Section 1.1 you learned how to create a deterministic finite automaton (DFA) in JFLAP. The editor for an automaton has a tool bar along the top portion of the window, and the automaton display on the bottom portion of the window. You create states with the ⊙ tool, create transitions with the ↗ tool, delete states and transitions with the ✱ tool, and edit attributes (position, labels, setting final and initial) of existing states and transitions with the ↖ tool.

In Section 1.2 you learned how to simulate input on automata. Each simulator accepts an input string and determines if the automaton accepts that input. The step simulator is useful if you are interested in seeing every configuration generated by a machine as it attempts to read your input. The fast simulator is useful if you are interested only in those configurations that led to an accepting configuration. The multiple input simulator is useful if you are interested in running many inputs on an automaton quickly.

In Section 1.3 you learned about creating and simulating input on a nondeterministic finite automaton (NFA). Leaving the field blank when creating a transition will produce a λ-transition. While simulating input, the step simulator may display multiple configurations at once as the machine follows different paths attempting to read the input. The fast simulator can search for multiple branches of nondeterminism accepting the same input.

In Section 1.4 we presented three analysis operators available from the **Test** menu. **Compare Equivalence** checks if two finite automata accept the same language. **Highlight Nondeterminism** highlights nondeterministic states, and **Highlight λ-Transitions** highlights λ-transitions.

In Section 1.5 we presented an alternative definition of an FA that allows for multiple characters on a transition. This can lead to an FA with a smaller number of states.

In Section 1.6 we presented JFLAP's formal definition of a finite automaton, which corresponds to Section 1.5. We also presented a simpler definition corresponding to Sections 1.1–1.4.

1.8 Exercises

1. Build FAs with JFLAP that accept the following languages:

   (a) The language over $\Sigma = \{a\}$ of any odd number of a's.

   (b) The language over $\Sigma = \{a\}$ of any even number of a's.

   (c) The language over $\Sigma = \{a, b\}$ of any even number of a's and any odd number of b's.

   (d) The language over $\Sigma = \{a, b\}$ of any even number of a's and at least three b's.

(e) The language over $\Sigma = \{a, b\}$ where the number of a's and b's are both either even or odd.

2. We present here a series of FAs where the author of each FA has made an incorrect claim about the language it recognizes. For each FA, we list the file name where the FA is stored and the *claimed* language it recognizes. For each FA you must: (i) Produce six strings that are either in the indicated language but are not accepted by the FA, or that are accepted by the FA and are not in the language; simulate these strings on the FAs as well. (ii) Modify the FA so that it actually recognizes the language we claim it does. (iii) Simulate those six strings again to show that they are now either accepted or rejected if they either are or are not in the language respectively. It helps to use the fast simulator so that your test strings are saved from (i) to (iii).

   (a) The FA in `ex1.6a` recognizes the language of any string over the alphabet $\Sigma = \{a, b\}$ with exactly two b's.

   (b) The FA in `ex1.6b` recognizes the language of any string of a's of some length divisible by 2 or 3.

   (c) The FA in `ex1.6c` recognizes the language of any string over the alphabet $\Sigma = \{a, b, c\}$ with at least three b's or at least three c's.

   (d) The FA in `ex1.6d` recognizes the language of any string over the alphabet $\Sigma = \{a, b, c\}$ with at least two b's or at least three c's.

3. We present here a series of FAs. We then describe the language we *want* the FA to recognize. You must describe the changes necessary to make the FA recognize the desired language. Edit the FA to make these modifications in JFLAP, and run several simulations of strings in (and out) of the language to determine if they are accepted or rejected.

   (a) The FA in `ex1.6e` accepts the language of any odd number of a's. We want the language of any even number of a's.

   (b) The FA in `ex1.1a` accepts the language of any number of a's followed by any odd number of b's. We want the language of any nonzero number of a's followed by any odd number of b's.

   (c) The FA in `ex1.6f` accepts the language over $\Sigma = \{a, b, c\}$ of a followed by any odd number of b's followed by c, repeated any number of times. We now want instead the FA where instead of one c, there can be any even number of c's.

   (d) Now, we want the *DFA* that accepts the language of Exercise 3c!

4. Consider the five regular language definitions given below under the alphabet $\Sigma = \{a, b\}$:

    (a) Where aa is not a substring.

    (b) Where aa and aaa are not substrings.

    (c) Where aa and aba are not substrings.

    (d) Where aa and $abaa$ are not substrings.

    (e) Where aaa and aab are not substrings.

    Separate these five languages into groups that you believe all accept the same language. Build the five automata that recognize these languages, and use JFLAP to confirm your suspicion that they are or are not the same language.

5. Consider the five regular language definitions given below under the alphabet $\Sigma = \{a\}$:

    (a) $\{a^\ell | \ell \equiv 0 \pmod 6, \ell \not\equiv 0 \pmod 4\}$

    (b) $\{a^\ell | \ell \equiv 0 \pmod 3, \ell \not\equiv 0 \pmod 2\}$

    (c) $\{a^\ell | \ell \equiv 0 \pmod 2, \ell \equiv 0 \pmod 3, \ell \not\equiv 0 \pmod 4\}$

    (d) $\{a^\ell a^\ell | \ell \equiv 0 \pmod 3, \ell \not\equiv 0 \pmod 2\}$

    (e) $\{a^\ell | \ell \equiv 0 \pmod 3, \ell \not\equiv 0 \pmod 6\}$

    Separate these five languages into groups that you believe all accept the same language. Build the five automata that recognize these languages, and use JFLAP to confirm your suspicion that they are or are not the same language.

6. Consider the set of 17 strings

$$S = \{bid, pad, hin, bat, pin, pit, hid, han, pid,$$
$$pan, hat, ban, bad, bit, pat, hit, had\}$$

    If S had one more string, you could build a DFA with only eight transitions that recognizes the language S. What is this string?

7. (a) Suppose we have $\Sigma = \{0, 1\}$ as our input alphabet and we want to accept the language of strings $a_0 b_0 c_0 a_1 b_1 c_1 \ldots a_n b_n c_n$ such that the binary sum $\begin{array}{r} a_n \ldots a_1 a_0 \\ +\quad b_n \ldots b_1 b_0 \\ \hline c_n \ldots c_1 c_0 \end{array}$ is correct, carries and all. Is the language regular? If not, why not? If it is, build a DFA that recognizes the language in JFLAP.

(b) Repeat part (a), but with the language of strings $a_n b_n c_n \ldots a_1 b_1 c_1 a_0 b_0 c_0$.

(c) Repeat part (a), but with the language of strings $a_0 \ldots a_n b_0 \ldots b_n c_0 \ldots c_n$.

8. Given two FAs A with language L_A and B with language L_B, you can use JFLAP's **Compare Equivalence** operator to determine whether or not $L_A = L_B$. Can you devise a general method using JFLAP to determine whether $L_A \subseteq L_B$ (i.e., B accepts every string A accepts) using **Compare Equivalence**? (Yes, part of your instructions may, indeed must, involve editing A or B. Your method must produce the right answer for any two FAs!)

Chapter 2

NFA to DFA to Minimal DFA

This chapter shows how each NFA can be converted into an equivalent DFA, and how each DFA can be reduced to a DFA with a minimum number of states. Although an NFA might be easier to construct than a DFA, the NFA is usually not efficient to run, as an input string may follow several paths. Converting an NFA into an equivalent DFA ensures that each input string follows only one path. The NFA to DFA algorithm in JFLAP combines similar states reached in the NFA into one state in the DFA. The DFA to minimum state DFA algorithm in JFLAP determines which states in the DFA have similar behavior with respect to incoming and outgoing transitions and combines these states, resulting in a minimal state DFA.

2.1 NFA to DFA

In this section we use JFLAP to show how to convert an NFA into an equivalent DFA. The idea in the conversion is to create states in the DFA that represent multiple states in the NFA. The start state in the DFA represents the start state in the NFA and any states reachable from it on λ. For each new state in the DFA and each letter of the alphabet, one determines all the reachable states from the corresponding NFA states and combines them into a new state for the DFA. This state in the DFA will have a label that will contain the state numbers from the NFA that would be reachable in taking the same path.

2.1.1 Idea for the Conversion

Load the NFA in file ex2.1a as shown in Figure 2.1. We will refer to this example in explaining the steps in converting this NFA to a DFA.

First examine the choices that occur when the NFA processes input. Select **Input : Step with Closure** and enter the input string "aabbbaa" and press return. Clicking **Step** once shows that processing a can result in arriving in both states q_0 and q_1. Clicking **Step** six more times shows

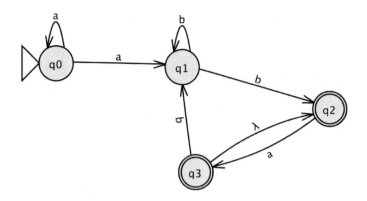

Figure 2.1: Example from file ex2.1a.

that there are always three configurations (one of which is rejected), and results in two paths of acceptance in states q_2 and q_3.

The states in the constructed DFA will represent combined states from the NFA. For example, processing an a resulted in either state q_0 or q_1. The DFA would have a state that represents both of these NFA states. Processing $aabbbaa$ resulted in reaching final states q_2 and q_3. The DFA would have a state that represented both of these NFA states. Dismiss the tab for the step run (select **File : Dismiss Tab**) to go back to the NFA editor.

2.1.2   Conversion Example

Now we will convert the NFA to a DFA (select **Convert : Convert to DFA**), showing the NFA on the left and the first state of the DFA on the right. The initial state in the DFA is named q_0 and has the label 0, meaning it represents the q_0 state from the NFA.

> **Tip** ‖ The NFA may be tiny. Adjust the size in one of two ways: either resize the window,
> or drag the vertical bar between the NFA and the DFA to the right. In addition, the
> states in the DFA can be dragged closer to each other, resulting in larger states.

We will now add the state that is reachable from q_0 on the substring a. Select the Expand Group on Terminal tool ⬚. Click and hold the mouse on state q_0, drag the cursor to where you want the next state, and release it. When prompted by **Expand on what terminal?**, enter "a" and press return. When prompted by **Which group of NFA states will that go to on a?**, enter the numbers of the states that are reachable from q_0 on an a. In this case enter "0,1". (These NFA states could also be entered with a blank separator and with or without the q, such as "q0,q1".) The new state q_1 appears in Figure 2.2.

Use the Attribute Editor tool you learned about in Chapter 1 to move states around if you don't like their placement.

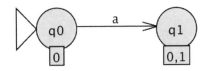

Figure 2.2: Expansion of state q_0 on a.

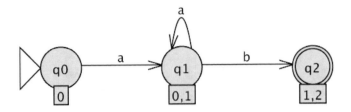

Figure 2.3: Expansion of a and b from state q_1.

Try expanding DFA state q_0 on the terminal b. Since there are no paths from NFA state q_0 on a b, a warning message is displayed.

Next expand the DFA state q_1 on the terminal a. Note that DFA state q_1 represents both states q_0 and q_1 from the NFA. In the NFA, state q_0 on an a reaches states q_0 and q_1, and state q_1 on an a reaches no state. The union of these results $(0, 1)$ are the states reachable by DFA state q_1, which happens to be the DFA state q_1. Upon the completion of the expansion a transition loop labeled a is added to DFA state q_1. Now expand DFA state q_1 on b. The result of these two expansions is shown in Figure 2.3. Why is DFA state q_2 a final state? If a DFA state represents any NFA state that is a final state, then the substring processed is accepted on some path, and thus the DFA state also must be a final state. NFA state q_2 is a final state, so DFA state q_2 (representing NFA states q_1 and q_2) is a final state.

Expand DFA state q_2 on a. This state is represented by NFA states q_1 and q_2. NFA state q_1 does not have an a transition. NFA state q_2 on an a reaches state q_3 and due to the λ-transition also reaches state q_2.

Note ‖ In using the Expand Group Terminal tool, if the destination state already exists, then drag to the existing state and you will be prompted only for the terminal to expand. Thus, to add a loop transition, just click on the state.

Expand DFA state q_2 on b by clicking on state q_2. You are prompted for the b, but not the states reachable, as that is interpreted as your selected state (itself in this case). The resulting DFA is shown in Figure 2.4.

There is another way to expand a state—the State Expander tool ⌁. When one selects this tool and clicks on a state, all arcs out of the state are automatically expanded. In Figure 2.5 state q_3 was selected and expanded on both a and b, resulting in a new state q_4.

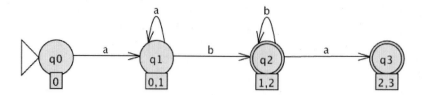

Figure 2.4: Expansion of a and b from state q_2.

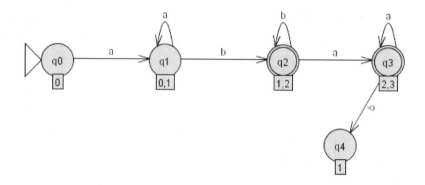

Figure 2.5: State Expander tool applied to state q_3.

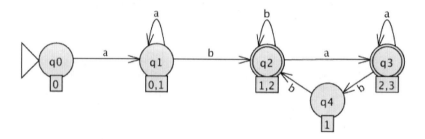

Figure 2.6: The completed DFA.

Is the DFA complete? Select the **Done?** button. If the DFA is not complete, a message indicating items missing is displayed. At this time, one transition is missing.

Expand DFA state q_4 on b by going back to the Expand Group on Terminal tool. Note that q_4 on b goes to the existing DFA state q_2. Click on state q_4, drag to state q_2, and release. You will be prompted for the terminal only.

Is the DFA complete? Select the **Done?** button. The DFA is complete and is exported to a new window. The complete DFA is shown in Figure 2.6. Alternatively, the **Complete** button can be selected at any time during the construction process and the complete DFA will be shown.

The constructed DFA should be equivalent to the NFA. To test this, in the DFA window select **Test : Compare Equivalence**. Select file ex2.1a, the name of the NFA, and then press return. The two machines are equivalent.

2.1.3 Algorithm to Convert NFA M to DFA M'

We describe the algorithm to convert an NFA M to a DFA M'. We first define the *closure* of a set of states to be those states unioned with all states reachable from these states on a λ-transition.

1. The initial state in M' is the closure of the initial state from M.

2. For each state q' in M' and each terminal x do the following:

   (a) States q and r are states in M. For each state q that is in state q', if q on an x reaches state r on an x, then place state r in new state p'.

   (b) $p' = \text{closure}(p')$

   (c) If another state is equivalent to state p' (represents the same states from M), then set p' to the state already existing.

   (d) Add the transition to M': q' to p' on an x.

3. Each state q' in M' is a final state if it contains a final state from M.

2.2 DFA to Minimal DFA

In this section we show how to convert a DFA to a minimal state DFA. Consider two states p and q from a DFA, each processing a string starting from their state. If there is at least one string w such that states p and q process this string and one accepts w and one rejects w, then these states are *distinguishable* and cannot be combined. Otherwise, states p and q "act the same way," meaning that they are *indistinguishable* and can be combined.

2.2.1 Idea for the Conversion

Load the DFA in Figure 2.7 (file `ex2.2a`). We will refer to this example to explain the steps to convert this DFA to a minimal state DFA.

We would like to examine pairs of states to see if they are distinguishable or not. To do this we will need two separate windows for this DFA. JFLAP lets you open only one copy of each file, so if you try to open the same file again, JFLAP will show just the one window. Instead we will make a duplicate copy of this file by saving it with a different name (select **File : Save as** and type the filename "ex2.2a-dup"). The current window is now associated with the duplicate file. Load the original file `ex2.2a` again and it will appear in a separate window (possibly on top of the first window). Move the two windows so you can see both of them.

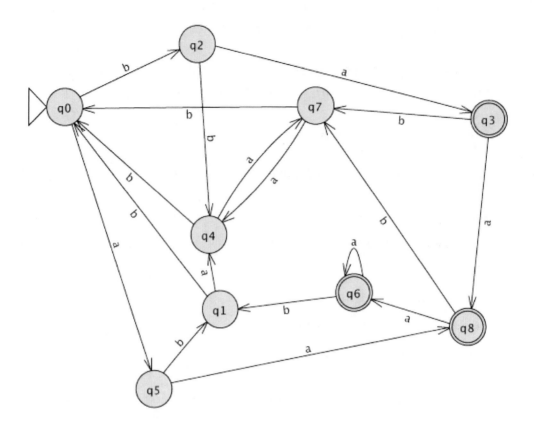

Figure 2.7: Example from file `ex2.2a`.

We will examine the two states q_0 and q_1 to see if they are distinguishable. In one of the windows, change the start state to q_1. Examine the two DFA. Are there any strings that one DFA accepts and the other DFA rejects?

We will examine several strings to see if there is any difference in acceptance and rejection. In both DFA windows, select **Input : Multiple Run**. In both windows, enter the following strings and any additional ones you'd like to try: "a", "aab", "aaaab", "baa", "baaa", and "bba". Select **Run Inputs** and examine the results. Do the strings have the same result in both DFAs? There is at least one string in which the result is **Accept** for one DFA, and **Reject** in the other DFA. Thus the two states q_0 and q_1 are distinguishable and cannot be combined.

Now we will examine the two states q_2 and q_5 to see if they are distinguishable. Dismiss the tab in both windows to go back to the DFA window. In one window change the start state to q_2, and in the other window change the start state to q_5. Select **Input : Multiple Run** again. Notice that the strings from the last run still appear in the window. Select **Run Inputs** to try these same strings. Type in additional strings and try them as well. Are these states distinguishable or indistinguishable? They are distinguishable if there is one string that accepts in one and does not accept in the other. All strings must be tested to determine if the states are indistinguishable. Clearly it is impossible to test *all* strings, so a reasonable test set should be created.

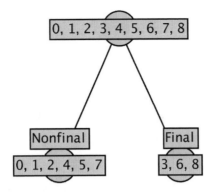

Figure 2.8: Initial split of final and nonfinal states.

2.2.2   Conversion Example

We go through an example of converting a DFA to a minimum state DFA. Remove the previous windows (without saving them) and load the file `ex2.2a` again, which should have the start state q_0. Select **Convert : Minimize DFA**. The window splits into two showing the DFA on the left and a tree of states on the right.

We assume that all states are indistinguishable to start with. The root of the tree contains all states. Each time we determine a distinction between states, we split a node in the tree to show this distinction. We continue to split nodes until there are no more splits possible. Each leaf in the final tree represents a group of states that are indistinguishable.

The first step in distinguishing states is to note that a final and a nonfinal state are different. The former accepts λ and the other does not. Thus the tree has already split the set of states into two groups of nonfinal and final states as shown in Figure 2.8.

For additional splits, a terminal will be selected that distinguishes the states in the node. If some of the states in a leaf node on that terminal go to states in one leaf node and other states on that same terminal go to states that are in another leaf node, then the node should be split into two groups of states (i.e., two new leaf nodes).

Let's first examine the leaf node of the nonfinal states (0, 1, 2, 4, 5, 7). What happens for each of these states if they process a b? State q_0 on a b goes to state q_2, state q_1 on a b goes to state q_0, and so on. Each of these states on a b goes to a state already in this node. Thus, b does not distinguish these states. In JFLAP, click on the tree node containing the nonfinal states. (Click on the circle, not the label or the word Nonfinal.) The states in this node are highlighted in the DFA. Try to split this node on the terminal b. Select **Set Terminal** and enter b. A message appears informing you that b does not distinguish these states.

Again select **Set Terminal** and enter the terminal a. Since a does distinguish these states, the node is split, resulting in two new leaf nodes. The set of states from the split node must be entered into the new leaf nodes, into groups that are indistinguishable. A state number can be entered by

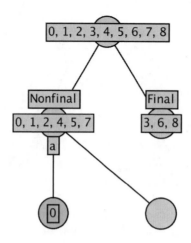

Figure 2.9: Split node on a.

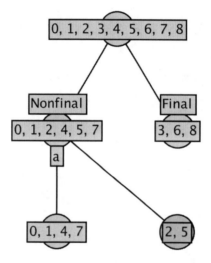

Figure 2.10: Node (0, 1, 2, 4, 5, 7) split on a.

first selecting the leaf node it will be assigned to, and then clicking on the corresponding state in the DFA. Click on the left leaf node and then click on state q_0 in the DFA. The state number 0 should appear in the leaf node, as shown in Figure 2.9.

State q_0 on an a goes to state q_5, which is in the node we are splitting. Note that states q_1, q_4, and q_7 on an a also go to a state in the node we are splitting. Add all of them to the same new leaf node as 0 by clicking on these states in the DFA. The remaining states, q_2 and q_5 on an a, go to a final state, thus distinguishing them. Click on the right new leaf node, and then click on states q_2 and q_5 to enter them into this node, resulting in the tree shown in Figure 2.10. To see if we have done this correctly, click on **Check Node**. Figure 2.10 shows the resulting tree after splitting this node on a.

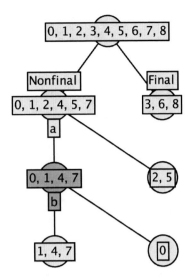

Figure 2.11: The completed tree of distinguished states.

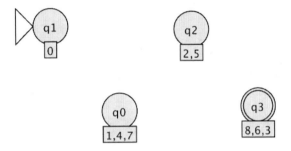

Figure 2.12: The states for the minimum DFA.

We must continually try to split nodes on terminals until there is no further splitting. Each time we split a node, we have created new groups that might now allow another group to be split that could not be split before.

Next we try to split the leaf node with states $0, 1, 4$, and 7. Which terminal do you try? In this case either a or b will cause a split. We will try a. Select **Set Terminal** and enter a. Enter the split groups. State q_0 on an a goes to state q_5, which is in leaf node group 2, 5, and states q_1, q_4, and q_7 on an a go to states in the leaf node we are splitting. Let's enter these states a different way. Select **Auto Partition** and the states will automatically be entered in as shown in Figure 2.11.

When the tree is complete (as it is now, convince yourself that none of the leaf nodes can be further split), then the only option visible is **Finish**. Select **Finish** and the right side of the window is replaced by the new states for the minimum DFA. There is one state for each leaf node from the tree (note the labels on the states correspond to the states from the original DFA), as shown in Figure 2.12. You may want to rearrange the states using the **Attribute Editor**.

Now add in the missing arcs in the new DFA using the **Transition Creator** tool. In the original DFA there is an a from state q_0 to state q_5, so in the new DFA a transition is added

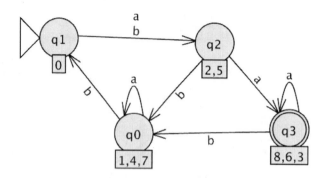

Figure 2.13: The minimum DFA.

from state q_1 (representing the old state q_0) to state q_2 (representing the old state q_5). Selecting **Hint** will add one transition for you and selecting **Complete** will complete the DFA, as shown in Figure 2.13. Selecting **Done?** will export the new DFA to its own window.

The minimum state DFA should be equivalent to the original DFA. Test this using the **Test : Compare Equivalence** option.

> **Note** When you select a node and select **Set Terminal**, the node you select is split and two children appear. It is possible that the node to be split might need more children; that is, there may be 3 or more distinguished groups split on this terminal. In that case, you must add the additional leaf nodes by selecting the **Add Child** option for each additional child desired.

2.2.3   Algorithm

We describe the algorithm to convert a DFA M to a minimal state DFA M'.

1. Create the tree of distinguished states as follows:

   (a) The root of the tree contains all states from M

   (b) If there are both final and nonfinal states in M, create two children of the root—one containing all the *nonfinal* states from M and one containing all the *final* states from M.

   (c) For each leaf node N and terminal x, do the following until no node can be split:

      i. If states in N on x go to states in k different leaf nodes, $k > 1$, then create k children for node N and spread the states from N into the k nodes in indistinguishable groups.

2. Create the new DFA as follows:

   (a) Each leaf node in the tree represents a state in the DFA M' with a label equal to the states from M in the node. The start state in M' is the state that contains the start

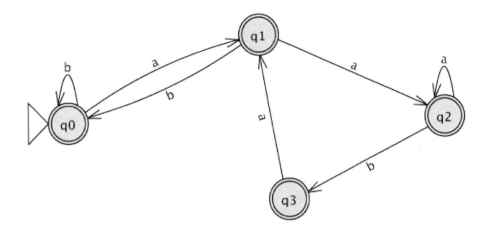

Figure 2.14: DFA from file `ex2.3a`.

state from M in its label. A state in M' is a final state if it contains a final state from M in its label.

(b) For each arc in M from states p to q, add an arc in M' from the state that has p in its label to the state that has q in its label. Do not add any duplicate arcs.

2.3 Exercises

1. Convert the NFAs in the given files into DFAs.

   (a) `ex2-nfa2dfa-a`

   (b) `ex2-nfa2dfa-b`

   (c) `ex2-nfa2dfa-c`

   (d) `ex2-nfa2dfa-d`

   (e) `ex2-nfa2dfa-e`

   (f) `ex2-nfa2dfa-f`

2. Consider the language $L = \{w \in \Sigma^* \mid w \text{ does not have the substring } aabb\}$, $\Sigma = \{a, b\}$.

   Load the DFA in file `ex2.3a` shown in Figure 2.14. This DFA recognizes L.

   Also load the file `ex2.3b`. It is the NFA shown in Figure 2.15 that attempts to recognize L, but fails.

   Give an input string that shows why this NFA is not equivalent to this DFA.

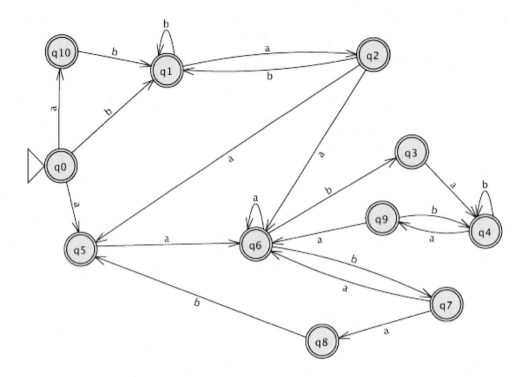

Figure 2.15: NFA from file `ex2.3b`.

3. Consider the DFA in file `ex2-dfa2nfa`. This DFA was converted from an NFA and the labels show the states of the original NFA. That NFA did not have any λ-transitions. Create the original NFA.

4. Convert the DFAs in the given files into minimal state DFAs.

   (a) `ex2-dfa2mindfa-a`

   (b) `ex2-dfa2mindfa-b`

   (c) `ex2-dfa2mindfa-c`

   (d) `ex2-dfa2mindfa-d`

   (e) `ex2-dfa2mindfa-e`

5. Consider the DFA in file `ex2.3c`. Explain why it is not a minimal DFA.

6. Consider the DFA in file `ex2-dfa2mindfa-test`. States q_2 and q_8 are distinguishable. Make a copy of this file and make q_2 the start state in one and q_8 the start state in the other. Give five input strings that are accepted by both of these DFAs and one input string that distinguishes the two DFAs, thus distinguishing states q_2 and q_8 in the original DFA. You can confirm your answer by running the DFAs on the input strings.

Chapter 3

Regular Grammars

In this chapter we go beyond JFLAP's handling of automata and look at regular grammars. Regular grammars are equivalent in power to the FAs we have studied, and are another representation of regular languages. We enter a right-linear grammar into JFLAP, and show how to parse strings on that grammar and convert that grammar into an equivalent FA. We also show how to convert an FA to a right-linear grammar.

3.1   Grammar Editing

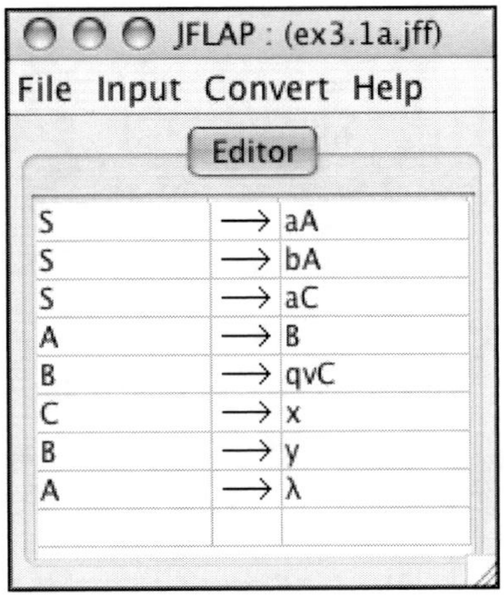

Figure 3.1: The editor for a grammar where a right-linear grammar has been entered.

We shall now enter a right-linear grammar, a type of regular grammar. You may recall that in a *right-linear grammar* all productions must have at most one variable in the right-hand side, and this variable must be to the right of any terminals. For example, if we consider uppercase letters as variables and lowercase letters as terminals, $A \rightarrow abcB$, $A \rightarrow \lambda$, $A \rightarrow B$, and $A \rightarrow def$ could all be productions in a right-linear grammar. However, $A \rightarrow Babc$, $A \rightarrow BC$, and $A \rightarrow abcBC$ could not be productions in a right-linear grammar.

31

Note	There are two types of regular grammars: right-linear and left-linear. In a left-linear grammar all productions must have at most one variable in the right-hand side, and this variable must be to the *left* of any terminals. JFLAP handles both of these types in addition to many other classes of grammars, and does not restrict the user during editing: it is up to the user to make sure that the grammar meets the restrictions of the type of grammar they are attempting to enter.

Start JFLAP. When you are at the list of choices of structure for creating a new document, choose **Grammar**. A window similar to that shown in Figure 3.1 will appear, though without any productions entered.

There are some necessary notes specific to JFLAP's representation of grammars:

- Symbols in the grammar are always represented as single characters.

- A symbol in the grammar is a variable if and only if it is an uppercase letter; otherwise it is a terminal. For Example, JFLAP considers 4, q, and # terminals, and T, W, and F variables.

- When entering a grammar you do not enter the start variable explicitly. Rather, the start variable is assumed to be the variable in the left side of the first production.

Consider the grammar of Figure 3.1 with this in mind. The set of variables is $\{S, A, B, C\}$, the start variable is S, and the set of terminals is $\{a, b, q, v, x, y\}$. The last production $A \to \lambda$ is the only λ-production in the grammar.

Now enter the grammar of Figure 3.1 into your window. Each row in the table corresponds to a production, where you enter the left side of a production in the left cell and the right side of a production in the right cell. Click on the left cell to select it and type "S". Next, click on the right cell to select it and type "aA". You have now entered the production $S \to aA$. Notice that the table automatically extends itself: The table will grow when you edit the last row. On the next row, enter the production $S \to bA$. In addition to clicking on cells to select them, you may also use the tab key: click on the left cell of this row and enter "S", but instead of clicking on the right cell, type the tab key twice to select the right cell and type "bA". Press tab again; the left cell of the next row will be selected, and you may enter another production! Continue entering productions up to the seventh production, the $B \to y$ production.

On the last row you will enter the production $A \to \lambda$, a λ-production. To do this, enter A into the left cell, but leave the right cell blank. The right field is really empty, but will display with a λ to signify that it is a λ-production.

Note	Entering grammars into JFLAP is the same whether you are entering regular grammars (as we do in this chapter) or any other class of grammar.

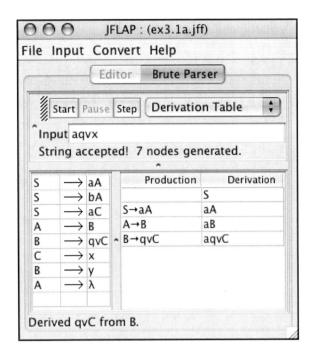

Figure 3.2: This shows the brute-force parser after a string has been entered and the derivation table expanded.

3.2 Brute-Force Parser

As with finite automata, there are a number of actions that you can apply to a regular grammar. Peruse the menus' contents, but do not select any items. While the contents of the **File** and **Help** menus remain the same, the **Input** and **Convert** menus have markedly different items! JFLAP customizes the operators you may apply to a system based on its type. Obviously, **Minimize DFA** cannot be applied to a grammar; by the same token, **LL(1) Parse** cannot be applied to an FA.

In this section, we shall use the **Brute Force Parse** operator on the right-linear grammar we built in Section 3.1. In a nutshell, JFLAP's parsers attempt to find a sequence of substitutions in the grammar that derive a given string, called a *sentence*, from the start variable. The brute-force parser is JFLAP's most naïve parser and works merely by repeatedly replacing symbols starting with the start variable until it just happens to stumble on the string the user entered. After deriving the sentence from the start variable with the grammar, the parser allows the user to step through replacements of variables by productions, showing the intermediate steps of the derivation. These intermediate steps are called *sentential forms* and include variables as well as terminals, whereas the final sentence and final step of the derivation contains only terminals.

If you do not have the grammar of Section 3.1 open in JFLAP, load the file ex3.1a. Choose **Input : Brute Force Parse** from the menu. You will see a view similar to that of Figure 3.2. The top portion of the window contains controls and your interface with the parser. The bottom-left portion displays the grammar. The bottom-right portion displays the grammar expansion to whatever string you input.

JFLAP allows you to view the derivation of a string graphically and nongraphically. The graphic view is the default, but we want the nongraphic view. Click the button **Noninverted Tree**, and you will see a pop-up menu with another option, **Derivation Table**. Select **Derivation Table**. The window will more closely resemble that shown in Figure 3.2.

Enter "bab" in the text field next to the **Input** label; this is the string you wish the parser to attempt to generate with the grammar.

Press Return, or press the **Start** button near the top tool bar. The parser will attempt to parse the string. After searching for a short time, the message **String rejected** will appear, to indicate that JFLAP has concluded that it is impossible to generate *bab* with our grammar.

Now replace your previous input with "aqvx", and again press Return (or again press **Start**). This time, JFLAP will be able to successfully generate your input string *aqvx* with the grammar. JFLAP will display the message **String accepted** below the **Input** field.

Since the parse was successful, we may view the derivation. In the bottom-right table you see the first sentential form, **S**, in the "Derivation" column. To view successive sentential forms, press the **Step** button. The first step will expand S by the production $S \to aA$ into aA. At the bottom of the window it says **Derived** aA **from** S; the table the production used in the expansion is shown in the **Production** column, and the resulting sentential form is shown in the **Derivation** column. If you press **Step** again, the A will be expanded to B by $A \to B$ so that aA becomes aB. If you press **Step** again, the sentential form aB will be expanded by $B \to qvC$ to $aqvC$. Lastly, pressing **Step** again will expand the sentential form $aqvC$ by $C \to x$ to the sentence $aqvx$. The derivation is now complete, as shown in Figure 3.2.

3.3   Convert a Right-Linear Grammar to an FA

This section describes JFLAP's conversion of a right-linear grammar into an equivalent FA. The grammar and the generated FA will recognize the same regular language.

The idea behind the conversion from a right-linear grammar to an FA is that variables in a right-linear grammar can be functionally similar to states in an FA. As an example, consider again the grammar from Figure 3.1, saved in the file ex3.1a, and consider again parsing the string *aqvx* with that grammar as we did in Section 3.2. We started the derivation with the variable S, similar

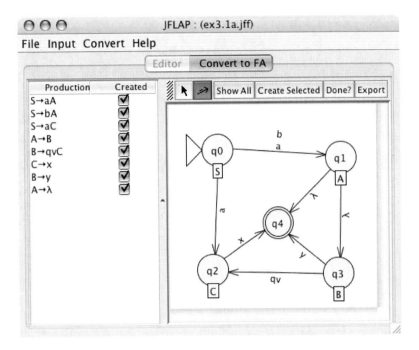

Figure 3.3: The finished conversion of the grammar of Figure 3.1 to an FA.

to having a configuration in the initial state S with no input read. When we expand on the production $S \to aA$, it is similar to reading a and moving to state A. The next derivation step on the production $A \to B$ is similar to moving from state A to state B without reading any input, i.e., a λ-production from state A to state B. The next derivation step on the $B \to qvC$ production is similar in an FA to reading qv from the input and moving from state B to state C. Lastly, the expansion on the $C \to x$ production is similar to reading x and moving into a final state, at which point the derivation is complete since there are no more variables.

Put more generally, a production $A \to \alpha B$ is rather like a transition in an FA from a state A to a state B on the string α. A production $A \to \beta$ is rather like a transition in an FA from a state A to a final state on the string β.

Figure 3.3 shows the finished conversion of the right-linear grammar to an FA. Select the menu item **Convert : Convert Right-Linear Grammar to FA** from the grammar in the file ex3.1a.

We now will go through the steps in the conversion of the right-linear grammar from Section 3.1 into an FA. Figure 3.3 shows the generated FA. Load the grammar from Section 3.1 if it is not currently loaded, and select the menu item **Convert : Convert Right-Linear Grammar to FA**. Your window should appear similar to Figure 3.3, with the grammar displayed to the left (but with no boxes checked yet) and an automaton editor displayed to the right (but with no transitions).

Notice that every state except the final state is labeled with a single variable from the grammar; a state labeled with A indicates that this state corresponds to the variable A in the grammar.

Your goal is to create the FA's transitions. Each transition you create corresponds to a single production. The first production we will convert is $S \to aA$: Create a transition from state S to state A on the terminal a. When you create this transition, note that the box in the **Created** column next to $S \to aA$ is now checked. Next we want to create the $C \to x$ production. This production has no variables in the right side; any derivation on this production must be the final derivation, so this is akin to moving to the final state in an FA. Create a transition on x from the C state to the final state. The next production we will convert is $A \to B$. That production has no terminals, so neither shall the transition: create a λ-transition from state A to state B. The next production we will convert is $B \to qvC$, with the two terminals qv. Create a transition on qv from state B to state C.

To illustrate the converter's error handling, attempt to enter a wrong transition: create a transition on xyz from A to S. There is no production $A \to xyzS$, so this transition is not in the FA. When you stop editing the transition a dialog box will appear to tell you that the transition is not in the converted grammar.

Click on the **Done** button above the automaton editor. You are not done, and a dialog will appear saying that **4 more transitions must be added**. Next, examine the table in the left portion of the window. Four of the eight productions should have their corresponding transitions created in the automata. In the table, click on a row of a converted production to select it. Notice that in the automaton editor the transition corresponding to that transition now appears highlighted in red! Next, select the row for the production $S \to bA$; its corresponding transition does not exist yet. Once this row is selected, click the **Create Selected** button above the automaton editor. The corresponding transition from S to A on b will appear. Three more transitions remain. Next, click the **Show All** button above the automaton editor, and those three transitions will be created. The **Show All** button will complete the conversion entirely.

Since you have finished the conversion, press the **Export** button. Your finished DFA will appear in a new FA window.

> Note ‖ If you want an FA with at most one symbol on each transition, you can modify the FA after it has been exported. For each transition that has n symbols, add $n - 1$ states between those two states and add a path of n transitions through these new states such that each transition reads exactly one symbol. For example, in the example we just converted, add one state q_5 between q_3 and q_2, a transition on q from q_3 to q_5, a transition on v from q_5 to q_2, and remove the transition qv.

3.3.1   Algorithm to Convert a Right-Linear Grammar to an FA

1. Start with a right-linear grammar $G = (V, T, S, P)$; V is the set of variables, T is the set of terminals, S is the start variable, and P is the set of productions.

2. Produce an FA $M = (Q, \Sigma, \delta, q_0, F)$ with $|Q| = |V| + 1$, so there is one more state in M than there are variables in G. The initial state is q_0. Let $\Sigma = T$, and let $F = \{q_f\}$ so that q_f is the only final state. $|\delta| = |P|$, so there are exactly as many transitions as productions (we describe δ in step 4).

3. Suppose the existence of a bijective mapping $\sigma : V \to (Q - F)$, where $\sigma(S) = q_0$. That is, (a) each variable corresponds to a unique nonfinal state in the FA so that for any variable A, $\sigma(A) = q_A$ is the corresponding state in the FA, (b) the grammar's start variable corresponds to the FA's initial state, and (c) no variable corresponds to the final state.

4. For each production $p \in P$:

    (a) If p is of the form $A \to \alpha B$, where $A, B \in V$ and α is a possibly empty string of terminals, add a transition to M from $\sigma(A)$ to $\sigma(B)$ on α.

    (b) If p is of the form $A \to \beta$, where $A \in V$ and β is a possibly empty string of terminals, add a transition to M from $\sigma(A)$ to q_f on β to δ.

3.4   Convert an FA to a Right-Linear Grammar

This section describes JFLAP's converter to produce a right-linear grammar that generates the same languages that a given FA recognizes.

The idea behind the conversion of an FA to a right-linear grammar follows nearly identical logic to converting a right-linear grammar to an FA, as described at the beginning of Section 3.3. The same analogy between states and variables, and transitions and productions, is made. The converter first assigns to each state a variable, with the converter assigning the start variable S to the initial state of the automata. In the former conversion, recall that a production $A \to xyzB$ would result in a transition from state A to state B on xyz; in this new conversion, a transition from state A to state B on xyz results in a production $A \to xyzB$.

The one caveat comes from the final state. In the *previous* conversion from a right-linear grammar to an FA, unlike all other states the final state did not correspond to a variable in the grammar. The final state was the destination for transitions resulting from productions with no variable on the right-hand side, that is, productions that imply the end of a string. However, a general FA differs: It may have transitions from a final state to a different state. Being in the final state does not necessarily mean that we have reached the end of the string. This means that in the conversion to a grammar, a final state must correspond to a variable since further expansion of the string is possible. On the other hand, a configuration in the final state *could* indicate that we have reached the end of the string. Therefore, for every final state with a corresponding variable F, we must include the production $F \to \lambda$.

3.4.1 Conversion

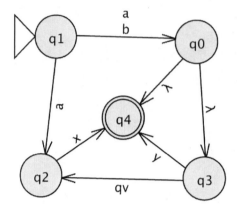

Figure 3.4: The starting FA we are converting to a right-linear grammar.

Open the file `ex3.4a`, which holds the FA pictured in Figure 3.4. This FA was the result of the example conversion described in Section 3.3. We are going to convert this FA back to a right-linear grammar.

Choose the menu item **Convert : Convert to Grammar**. Your window will resemble Figure 3.5, though without any productions in the right portion of the window. Note the new labels on the states in the left portion of the window: When you choose to convert to a grammar, each state is assigned a unique variable, displayed in a label for the state.

The method for conversion is fairly simple. Each transition and each final state corresponds to a production in the grammar. When you click on a transition or final state, its production will be shown in the right portion of the window.

Try clicking on the transition on a from q_1 to q_0. Since the variable for state q_1 is S and the variable for q_0 is A, the corresponding production displayed will be $S \to aA$. Next, click the λ-production from q_0 to q_3. The state q_0's variable is A and q_3's variable is C, and since λ represents the empty string the corresponding production is $A \to C$; C prefixed by the empty string is C, after all.

Next click on the final state q_4. As mentioned before, the production for a final state is a λ-production on its variable, to indicate that the derivation of a string over this grammar could end with this variable. The state q_4's variable is D, so the production will be $D \to \lambda$.

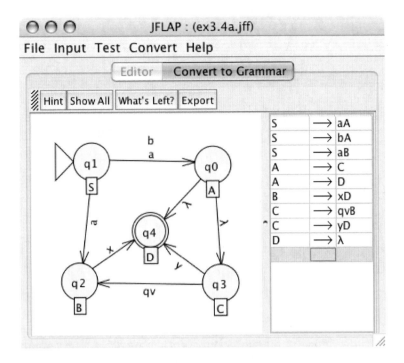

Figure 3.5: The finished conversion of the FA of Figure 3.4 to a right-linear grammar.

Tip	Select one of the productions in the table to the right. The corresponding transition, or final state, for that production will be highlighted.

The **Hint** button near the top of the window will show a production for an item that has not yet been added to the table. Click **Hint**. A production will be added to the grammar, and the FA transition, or final state, to which it corresponds will be highlighted in the left table.

To highlight all objects remaining in the automaton that have not yet had their production created, click the **What's Left** button. The grammar should now have four of the productions. There are nine items in the FA to convert, so five items should be highlighted in the FA. To simply create them all with no more fanfare, click the **Show All** button: all productions remaining will be added to the grammar.

Now that you have finished the conversion, press the **Export** button. The right-linear grammar produced by the conversion will appear in a new window.

3.4.2 Algorithm to Convert an FA to a Right-Linear Grammar

1. Start with an FA $M = (Q, \Sigma, \delta, q_i, F)$; Q is the set of states, Σ is the alphabet, δ describes M's transitions, q_i is the initial state, and F is the set of final states.

2. Produce a grammar $G = (V, T, S, P)$ with $|V| = |Q|$ so there are as many variables in G as states in M. Let $T = \Sigma$. Also, $|P| = |\delta| + |F|$, so there are exactly as many productions as transitions and final states (we populate P in step 4).

3. Suppose the existence of a bijective mapping $\tau : Q \to V$, where $\tau(q_i) = S$. That is, (a) each state corresponds to a unique variable in the grammar, and (b) the FA's initial state corresponds to the grammar's start variable.

4. The set of productions $P = P_t \cup P_f$, where:

   (a) $\delta' = \{(q_i, q_j, \alpha)\}$ for all $q_i, q_j \in Q$, and all $\alpha \in \Sigma^*$ for which there is a transition from q_i to q_j on α; δ' lists all transitions of M. Then, $P_t = \{(\tau(q_i) \to \alpha\tau(q_j)) \mid \forall\, (q_i, q_j, \alpha) \in \delta'\}$. Put another way, for every transition from q_i to q_j on α, for the variable $A = \tau(q_i)$ corresponding to q_i and the variable $B = \tau(q_j)$ corresponding to q_j, add the production $A \to \alpha B$ to the grammar.

   (b) $P_f = \{(\tau(q_f) \to \lambda) \mid \forall\, q_f \in F\}$. Put another way, for every final state q_f, for its corresponding variable $C = \tau(q_f)$, add the production $C \to \lambda$.

3.5   Definition of Regular Grammar in JFLAP

JFLAP defines a regular grammar G as a quadruple $G = (V, T, S, P)$ where

- V is the finite set of variables, which JFLAP restricts to a subset of the uppercase alphabetic letters;

- T is the finite set of terminals where $T \cap V = \emptyset$, which JFLAP restricts to a subset of all characters that are not uppercase alphabetic letters;

- $S \in V$ is the start variable; and

- P is the finite set of productions. $P \subset \{A \to T^*B \mid A, B \in V\} \cup \{A \to T^* \mid A \in V\}$ for a right-linear grammar, or $P \subset \{A \to BT^* \mid A, B \in V\} \cup \{A \to T^* \mid A \in V\}$ for a left-linear grammar. $P \neq \emptyset$.

One does not explicitly set the start variable in JFLAP; rather, the left side of the first production in the list of productions is assumed to be the start variable.

3.6   Summary

In Section 3.1 we learned that users enter grammars into JFLAP via a table. The left column of the table holds the left sides of productions, and the right column holds the right sides of productions. Each character corresponds to a single symbol in the grammar. JFLAP considers uppercase alphabetic characters as variables and all other characters as terminals.

A user may use one of JFLAP's parsers to detect whether and determine how a grammar derives a particular string. Section 3.2 taught how to use JFLAP's brute-force parser. The brute-force parser is JFLAP's most naïve parser; it works by exhaustively replacing symbols until it stumbles upon the string you are attempting to derive, or until it decides such a derivation is impossible.

In Section 3.3 we explored a converter of JFLAP's that produces an FA equivalent to a given right-linear grammar. The basic idea is that in a right-linear grammar, variables are functionally similar to states and productions are functionally similar to transitions. The user edits the FA by adding transitions to the FA that correspond to the productions in the grammar, until all productions have a corresponding transition.

In Section 3.4 we learned about JFLAP's converter that produces a right-linear grammar equivalent to a given FA. Similar to the previous converter, this converter works on the principle that states and variables, and transitions and productions, are functionally similar. However, because of the possibility in an FA of the existence of transitions *from* a final state in addition to possibly seeing the end of a string, we also produce λ-productions for each final state.

Section 3.5 presented JFLAP's formal definition of a regular grammar.

3.7 Exercises

1. Load the regular grammars in the given files. For each grammar list five strings they accept, five strings they do not accept, and give a description in words of the language they represent.

   (a) `ex3.reggrm-a`

   (b) `ex3.reggrm-b`

   (c) `ex3.reggrm-c`

   (d) `ex3.reggrm-d`

   (e) `ex3.reggrm-e`

   (f) `ex3.reggrm-f`

2. Create right-linear grammars that generate the following languages. *Hint: Test input strings that should be accepted and rejected.*

   (a) $\Sigma = \{a, b\}$. The language is strings with an even number of a's that have exactly one b. For example, accepted strings include *aba*, *b*, *aaaabaa*, and *aaaba*, and rejected strings include *abab* and *aaab*.

(b) $\Sigma = \{a, b\}$. The language is strings with an even number of a's followed by three or fewer b's. For example, accepted strings include aab, bbb, $aaaabb$, and $aaaa$, and rejected strings include $aabbbb$ and $aabaab$.

(c) $\Sigma = \{a, b\}$. The language is strings in which each b cannot be adjacent to another b. For example, accepted strings include aba, b, $aabaaabaa$, and $baaaba$, and rejected strings include $aaabba$ and $babb$.

(d) $\Sigma = \{a, b\}$. The language is strings in which the number of a's is a multiple of three. For example, accepted strings include $ababa$, bb, aaa, and $aababb$, and rejected strings include $aababa$ and $aaaaba$.

(e) $\Sigma = \{a, b\}$. The language is strings in which every a must have a b adjacent to it on both sides. For example, accepted strings include $bababab$, bab, $bbab$, and $babbbabb$, and rejected strings include $abab$ and $baab$.

(f) $\Sigma = \{a, b\}$. The language is strings in which every other a starting with the first a must immediately be followed by a b. For example, accepted strings include $babaab$, bab, $abaabbabab$, and $abbaab$, and rejected strings include $ababa$ and aab.

3. The collegiate parasite Carl S. Student wants his parents to buy him a car. His father produces a "transcript string" of all the grades Carl has ever received in his entire life, an arbitrarily long single string made up of symbols from $\Sigma = \{a, b, c, d, f\}$ in no particular order. An a is a high grade and an f is failure. His father produces a simple criterion: if Carl received fewer than four d grades, he shall get a car, otherwise he shall not. An f grade counts as a single d grade.

His father asks you to design a right-linear grammar where the grammar generates the transcript string if and only if Carl gets the car. *Hint: You can check if a right-linear grammar generates a string with the brute-force parser, or by converting the grammar to an FA and checking if the FA accepts the string.*

(a) Design a right-linear grammar to the above specifications.

(b) Carl's initial reaction to this was to provide a succinct, heartfelt plea for his father to adopt less draconian methods, indirectly appealing to notion that the alienating presence of the generational gap between father and son may have led to the father to be unduly harsh. Specifically: "Mellow out, old dude." The father then decides to make an f grade count as two d's. Adopt the grammar accordingly.

(c) With slightly more tact, Carl was able to successfully argue with his father that an a grade should mitigate a d grade. Why can this language not be expressed with a right-linear grammar?

4. Consider the grammars in the given files. Determine if the grammar is regular. If it is not regular, convert it to a regular grammar that represents the same language. *Hint: Test input strings that should be accepted and rejected in both grammars.*

   (a) `ex3.isregular-a`

   (b) `ex3.isregular-b`

   (c) `ex3.isregular-c`

   (d) `ex3.isregular-d`

   (e) `ex3.isregular-e`

5. Convert the following right-linear grammars to FAs. The last three have productions with multiple terminals.

   (a) `ex3.rg2fa-a`

   (b) `ex3.rg2fa-b`

   (c) `ex3.rg2fa-c`

   (d) `ex3.rg2fa-d`

   (e) `ex3.rg2fa-e`

   (f) `ex3.rg2fa-f`

6. Convert the following FAs to regular grammars. The last two have transitions with multiple terminals.

   (a) `ex3.fa2rg-a`

   (b) `ex3.fa2rg-b`

   (c) `ex3.fa2rg-c`

   (d) `ex3.fa2rg-d`

   (e) `ex3.fa2rg-e`

   (f) `ex3.fa2rg-f`

   (g) `ex3.fa2rg-g`

7. Consider the simple right-linear grammar in the file `ex3.6a`.

   (a) Use the brute-force parser to parse the string *aaaaaa* on the grammar. There are many ways to generate this string, with various combinations of expansions on the productions $S \rightarrow aS$ and $S \rightarrow aaS$. What do you notice about the productions used in the derivation? Repeat the experiment with *aaaaaaaaaa* (ten *a*'s). Do you notice the same phenomenon?

(b) We now want to count the number of ways to generate some of these strings; the brute-force parser will find only one, but we convert the grammar to an equivalent FA and use the fast simulator. Convert the right-linear grammar to an FA. Let a^ℓ be the string of a's of length ℓ. Run the fast simulator described in Section 1.2.2 on the strings $a^0 = \lambda$, $a^1 = a, \ldots$, through $a^6 = aaaaaa$, and count the number of ways the fast simulator finds to accept each of these strings. Remember, you can keep pressing **Keep Looking** until the final summary message appears saying how many accepting configurations it found.

(c) Let A_n be the number of ways the FA can accept (equivalently, that the grammar can generate) the string a^n. We have $A_0, A_1, \ldots, A_6$. Present a recursive formula for A_n, that is, determine a formula for A_n in terms of values of A_i, where $i < n$. *Hint: Use a counting argument. If we use the production $S \to aaS$, how many ways are there to generate the rest of the string without the aa?*

(d) Load the right-linear grammar in the file `ex3.6b`. Let B_n be the number of ways to generate a^n with this new grammar. Using your knowledge in determining a recursive formula for A_n, determine a recursive formula for B_n. *Hint: If you convert this to an FA, the number of accepting configurations during simulation of a^n is the same as the number of ways to generate a^n. For various a^n, do a fast simulation as described in Section 1.2.2 to count accepting configurations. You can manually find specific B_n this way until you see the pattern.*

8. Consider the conversion of a right-linear grammar to an FA. Sometimes the conversion of a right-linear grammar will result in a DFA, and sometimes it will result in an NFA, depending on the structure of the grammar. In this problem we explore theoretical properties of JFLAP's converter of right-linear grammars to FAs.

   (a) In Chapter 1 we explored a DFA that accepted the language over $\Sigma = \{a, b\}$ of any number of a's followed by any odd number of b's. Can you create a right-linear grammar that generates this language *and* converts directly to a DFA? If you can, create the grammar with JFLAP and convert it to a DFA.

   (b) Consider a second language, the language over $\Sigma = \{a, b, c\}$ of any number of a's followed by any odd number of b's, and finally suffixed with a single c. Can you create a right-linear grammar that generates this language *and* converts directly to a DFA? If you can, create the grammar with JFLAP and convert it to a DFA.

   (c) What is the general characteristic of a language for which one may construct a right-linear grammar that converts directly to a DFA? *Hint: The string aabbb is in the first language. Does any other string in that language start with aabbb? The string aabbbc is in the second language. Does any other string in the language start with aabbbc?*

Chapter 4

Regular Expressions

In this chapter we introduce a third type of representation of regular languages: regular expressions (REs). We describe how to edit REs, convert an RE to an equivalent NFA, and convert an FA to an equivalent RE, and then give JFLAP's formal definition of an RE.

4.1   Regular Expression Editing

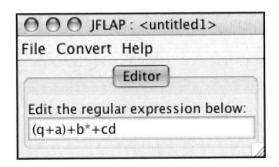

Figure 4.1: The editor for REs where the RE $(q+a) \ldots + b^*+cd$ has been entered.

In this section we learn how to edit REs. Start JFLAP; if it is already running, choose to create a new structure via the menu item **File : New**. Select **Regular Expression** from the list of new structure choices. A window will appear that is similar to Figure 4.1. Since an RE is essentially a string, JFLAP's RE editor consists of a small text field in the middle of the window.

JFLAP's REs use three basic operators. To clarify, these are not operators in the JFLAP sense, but rather the mathematical sense (e.g., pluses and minuses). The three operators in order of decreasing precedence are: the Kleene star (represented by the asterisk character *), the concatenation operator (implicit by making two expressions adjacent), and the union operator (also called the "or" operator, represented by the plus sign +). You may use parentheses to specify the order

45

of operations. Lastly, the exclamation point (!) designates the empty string, and is an easy way to enter λ.

A few examples of REs will help clarify JFLAP's operators' precedence. The expression $a+b+cd$ describes the language $\{a, b, cd\}$, whereas $abcd$ describes the singleton language $\{abcd\}$. The expression $a(b+c)d$ describes the language $\{abd, acd\}$, whereas $ab+cd$ describes the language $\{ab, cd\}$. The expression abc^* describes the language $\{ab, abc, abcc, abccc, \ldots\}$, whereas $(abc)^*$ describes the language $\{\lambda, abc, abcabc, abcabcabc, \ldots\}$. The expression $a+b^*$ describes the language $\{a, \lambda, b, bb, bbb, \ldots\}$, whereas $(a+b)^*$ describes the language $\{\lambda, a, b, aa, ab, ba, bb, aaa, aab, \ldots\}$. The expression $(!+a)bc$ describes the language $\{bc, abc\}$; recall that ! is the user's way of entering λ.

In this chapter we restrict ourselves to languages over lowercase letters, but JFLAP allows any character except *, +, (,), or ! as part of an RE's language. Specifically, beware that the space key is a perfectly legal character for a language. For example, a * where a space follows the a (so a is followed by any number of spaces) is distinct from a^* (any number of a's). *Note that none of the regular expressions in this chapter or its exercises have spaces in them, so do not type them in.*

We are going to enter the RE $(q+a)+b^*+cd$, a very simple RE that indicates that we want a string consisting of either q or a, or of any number of b's, or the string cd. Type this RE into the text field.

4.2   Convert a Regular Expression to an NFA

Since REs are equivalent in power to FAs, we may convert between the two. In this section we will illustrate the conversion of an RE to an NFA. For this example we use the RE defined in Figure 4.1, the expression $(q+a)+b^*+cd$, also stored in file ex4.1a. In the window with the RE, select the menu item **Convert : Convert to NFA** to start the converter.

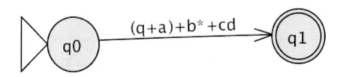

Figure 4.2: The starting GTG in the conversion.

For the purpose of the converter, we use a *generalized transition graph* (GTG), an extension of the NFA that allows *expression transitions*, transitions that contain REs. In a GTG, a configuration may proceed on a transition on a regular expression R if its unread input starts with a string $s \in R$; this configuration leads to another configuration with the input s read. We start with a GTG of two states, and a single expression transition with our regular expression from the initial to the final state. The idea of the converter is that we replace each transition with new states connected by transitions on the operands of that expression's top-level operator. (Intuitively, the *top-level operator* is the operator in an expression that must be evaluated last. For example, in $ab+c$, the top-level operator is $+$ since the concatenation operator has higher priority and will be evaluated before the $+$.) We then connect these operands with λ-transitions to duplicate the functionality of the lost operator. In this way, at each step we maintain a GTG equivalent to the original RE. Eventually all operators are removed and we are left with single character and λ-transitions, at which point the GTG can be considered a proper NFA.

Tip ‖ You may use the Attribute Editor tool ➤ at any point to move states around. In addition to moving states manually, with this tool the automatic graph layout algorithm may be applied, as described in Section 1.1.5.

4.2.1 "De-oring" an Expression Transition

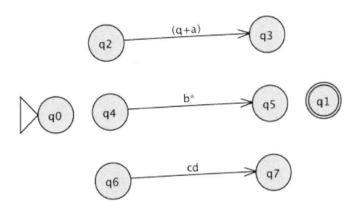

Figure 4.3: The GTG after "de-expressionifying" the first transition, but before we add the supporting λ-transitions.

To start converting, select the De-expressionify Transition tool ⟐. With this tool active, click on the $(q+a)+b^*+cd$ transition. The GTG will be reformed as shown in Figure 4.3. Note that the transition has been broken up according to the top-level $+$ union operator, and that the operands that were being "ored" have now received their own transitions. The De-expressionify Transition tool ⟐ determines the top-level operator for an expression, and then puts the operands of that operator into new expression transitions.

Note the labels near the top of the converter view: **De-oring $(q+a)+b^*+cd$**, and **6 more λ-transitions needed**. These labels give an idea of what you must do next.

In this case, you must produce six λ-transitions so that these new six states (q_2 through q_7) and their associated transitions act like the $+$ union operator that we have lost. To add these transitions, select the Transition Creator tool ↗. To approximate the union functionality, you must add six λ-transitions, three from q_0 to q_2, q_4, and q_6, and three more to q_1 from q_3, q_5, and q_7. Intuitively,

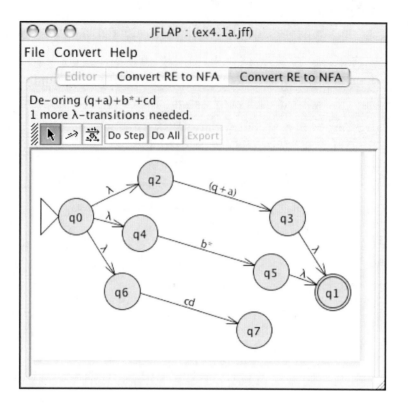

Figure 4.4: The converter window in the midst of "de-oring" the first transition. All the λ-transitions for this de-oring have been added, except the transition from q_7 to q_1.

in going from q_0 to q_1, a simulation may take the path through the $(q+a)$ expression transition *or* the b^* expression transition *or* the cd expression transition. In short, these λ-transitions help to approximate the functionality of the lost $+$ operator on these operands. Use the Transition Creator tool ⤳ to create these. All transitions are λ-transitions, so JFLAP does not bother asking for labels. As you add transitions, the label at the top of the window decrements the number of transitions needed. Figure 4.4 shows an intermediate point in adding these transitions, with only the transition from q_7 to q_1 not created. When you finish adding these transitions to the GTG, JFLAP allows you to "de-expressionify" another transition.

4.2.2 "De-concatenating" an Expression Transition

Once you finish "de-oring" the first transition, you have three expression transitions. We will reduce cd next; the top-level operator for this expression is the concatenation operator. Select the De-expressionify Transition tool ⚒ once more, and click on the cd transition. In Figure 4.5 you see the result. Note that JFLAP informs us that we are **De-concatenating cd** and that we have **3 more λ-transitions needed**; similar to de-oring, de-concatenating requires the addition of λ-transitions to approximate the lost concatenation operator.

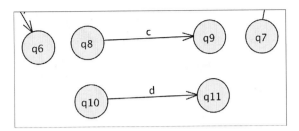

Figure 4.5: The beginning of de-concatenating the expression transition cd. States and transitions extraneous to the de-concatenating are cropped out.

We require three λ-transitions: one from q_6 to q_8, another from q_9 to q_{10}, and a last one from q_{11} to q_7. Configurations on q_6 will have to satisfy the c expression (between q_8 and q_9), and then satisfy the d expression (between q_{10} and q_{11}) before proceeding to q_7. This arrangement is functionally equivalent to c concatenated with d.

A remedy of errors

Select the Transition Creator tool ![tool icon]. Instead of adding the right transitions, let's add an incorrect transition! Create a transition from q_6 to q_{10}. With this transition, the configuration can proceed from q_6 to the d portion, bypassing c. This is incorrect. A dialog box will report **A transition there is invalid**, and the transition will not be added.

Although checking for wrong transitions is universal to the converter no matter what operator you are splitting on, the de-concatenating process has some additional restrictions. Add a transition from q_{11} to q_7. This is perfectly valid! However, JFLAP reports in a dialog, **That may be correct, but the transitions must be connected in order**. In this case, this means you must first connect q_6 to q_8, and then q_9 to q_{10}, and only then may you connect q_{11} to q_7. Add these transitions now.

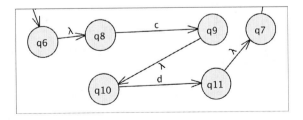

Figure 4.6: The finished de-concatenating of the expression transition cd.

The relevant portion of the automaton will resemble Figure 4.6. Since you have finished the de-concatenation of *cd*, you may now reduce another expression transition. Select the De-expressionify Transition tool again. Recall that the converter recursively breaks down expression transitions until they are either one character or λ-transitions. If you click on the *c* transition, the message **That's as good as it gets** appears to inform you that you needn't reduce that transition.

4.2.3 "De-staring" a Transition

We will reduce the b^* transition next. With the De-expressionify Transition tool active, click the b^* transition. Kleene stars may have only one operand, in this case *b*. As we see in Figure 4.7, the *b* has been separated into a new portion of the automaton. JFLAP tells us that we are **De-staring** b^* and that there are **4 more λ-transitions needed**.

Similar to concatenations and ors, we must add λ-transitions to duplicate the functionality of the Kleene star. The four transitions that JFLAP wants are from q_4 to q_{12} and q_{13} to q_5 (to allow configurations to read a *b* from their input), and another from q_4 to q_5 (to allow zero *b*'s to be read), and the last from q_5 to q_4 (to allow for repeat reading of *b*). Select the Transition Creator tool, and add these transitions so the relevant portion of the GTG resembles Figure 4.8.

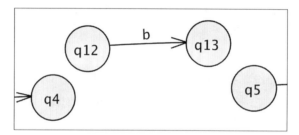

Figure 4.7: The beginning of de-staring the expression transition b^*. States and transitions extraneous to the de-staring are cropped out.

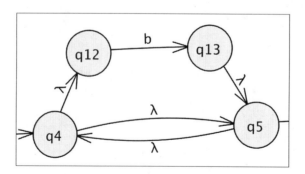

Figure 4.8: The finished de-staring of the expression transition b^*.

4.2.4 Surrounding Parentheses

The only remaining existing transition incompatible with an NFA is the $(q+a)$ transition, which has surrounding parentheses. The parentheses are the top-level operator since they indicate that their contents must be evaluated first, and only when that evaluation finishes do the parentheses finish evaluating. However, when the parentheses surround the entire expression, they are completely unnecessary. Activate the De-expressionify Transition tool 🜊, and click on the $(q+a)$ transition. The surrounding parentheses will disappear, leaving you with $q+a$. No λ-transitions are needed.

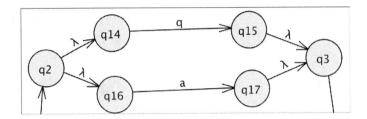

Figure 4.9: The finished de-oring of the expression transition $q+a$.

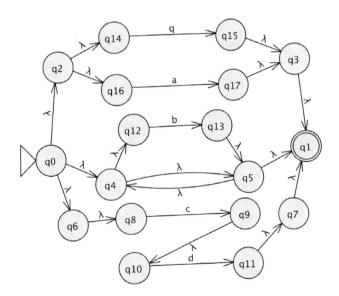

Figure 4.10: The NFA that recognizes the language $(q+a)+b^*+cd$.

To finish, use the De-expressionify Transition tool 🜊 tool once more to break $q+a$ by the + operator. Connect λ-transitions similar to the procedure described in Section 4.2.1, so that the relevant section of the GTG resembles Figure 4.9, and overall the automaton resembles Figure 4.10. The GTG is now a proper NFA, so the conversion to an NFA is finished! You may press the **Export** button to put the automaton in a new window.

4.2.5   Automatic Conversion

Dismiss the **Convert RE to NFA** tab now. Once you have returned to the RE editor, select the menu item **Convert : Convert to NFA**. We shall convert the same RE again, but we'll do it automatically this time!

Once you see the converter view with the GTG as pictured in Figure 4.2, press **Do Step**. A step in this conversion is the reduction of a single expression transition. There is only one expression transition, the $(q+a)+b^*+cd$ transition, so that is reduced and the requisite λ-transitions are added without intervention from the user.

The second option is **Do All**; this is functionally equivalent to pressing **Do Step** until the conversion finishes. This is useful if you want the equivalent NFA immediately. Press **Do All**; the finished NFA will appear in the window, ready to be exported.

4.2.6   Algorithm to Convert an RE to an NFA

1. Start with an RE R.

2. Create a GTG G with a single initial state q_0, single final state q_1, and a single transition from q_0 to q_1 on the expression R.

3. Although there exists some transition $t \in G$ from states q_i to q_j on the expression S longer than one character, let ϕ be the top-level operator of the expression S, and let $[\alpha_1, \alpha_2, \ldots, \alpha_\psi]$ be the ordered list of operands of the operator ϕ (since parenthetical and Kleene star operators take exactly one operand $\psi = 1$ in those cases).

   (a) If ϕ is a parenthetical operator, replace t with an expression transition on α_1 from q_i to q_j.

   (b) If ϕ is a Kleene star operator (*), create two new states q_x and q_y for G, remove t, and create an expression transition on α_1 from q_x to q_y, and create four λ-transitions from q_i to q_x, q_y to q_j, q_i to q_j, and q_j to q_i.

   (c) If ϕ is a union operator (+), remove t, and for each k from 1 through ψ (i) create two new states q_{x_k} and q_{y_k}, (ii) create an expression transition on α_k from q_{x_k} to q_{y_k}, and (iii) create two λ-transitions, from q_i to q_{x_k} and from q_{y_k} to q_j.

   (d) If ϕ is a concatenation operator, remove t, and for each k from 1 through ψ (i) create two new states q_{x_k} and q_{y_k}, (ii) create an expression transition on α_k from q_{x_k} to q_{y_k}, and

(iii) if $k > 1$ create a λ-transition from $q_{y_{k-1}}$ to q_{x_k}. Finally, create two λ-transitions, one from q_i to q_{x_1} and another from q_{y_ψ} to q_j.

4. The GTG is now a proper NFA. The conversion is finished.

4.3   Convert an FA to a Regular Expression

The conversion of an FA to an RE follows logic that is in some respects reminiscent of the RE to NFA conversion described in Section 4.2. We start with an FA that we consider a GTG for the purposes of conversion. We then remove states successively, generating equivalent GTGs until only a single initial and single final state remain. JFLAP then uses a formula to express the simplified GTG as a regular expression.

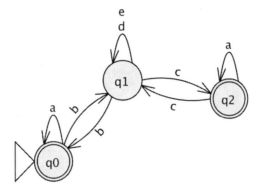

Figure 4.11: The FA we convert to an RE.

In this walk-through we convert the automata pictured in Figure 4.11 to a regular expression. This automata is stored in the file `ex4.3a`. Open this automata. Choose the menu item **Convert : Convert FA to RE** to begin converting. Your window will resemble Figure 4.12.

4.3.1   Reforming the FA to a GTG

The algorithm to convert an FA to an RE requires first that the FA be reformed into a GTG with a single final state, an initial state that is not a final state, and exactly one transition from q_i to q_j for every pair of states q_i and q_j (i may equal j).

Reform FA to have a single noninitial final state

There are two things wrong with our FA's final states: there are two final states, and one of them is also the initial state. We must reform the automaton so that it has exactly one final state and ensure that that final state is not the initial state. To do this JFLAP first requires that a new state be created: select the State Creator tool ⑨, and click somewhere on the canvas to create a new state. (Similar to the conversion from an RE to an NFA, this converter also displays directions above the editor. At this stage it tells you **Create a new state to make a single final state**.)

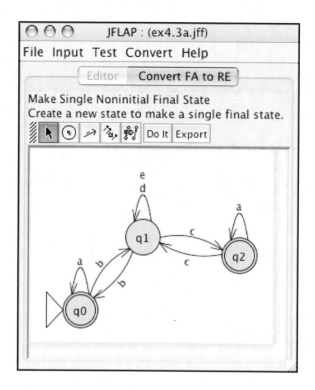

Figure 4.12: The starting window when converting an FA to an RE.

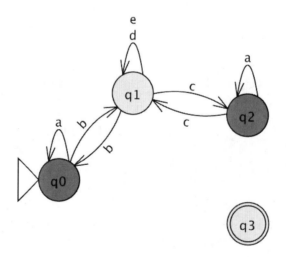

Figure 4.13: The FA after a new final state is created.

Once this new state is created, the FA will resemble Figure 4.13. Note that this new state is the final state, and those states that were previously final states are now regular states and have been highlighted. JFLAP directs you to **put λ-transitions from old final states to new**. Select the Transition Creator tool and create transitions from each of the highlighted states to the new final states. JFLAP assumes that every transition is a λ-transition and does not query for the

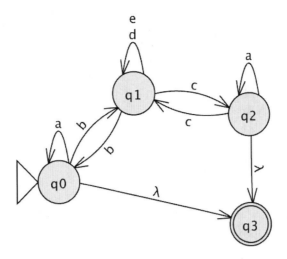

Figure 4.14: The FA after the λ-transitions have been made from the old final states to the new final state.

transition label. As you create each λ-transition, the source state will be de-highlighted. When you finish, your FA will resemble Figure 4.14.

Collapse multiple transitions

One of the requirements of this algorithm is that for every pair of states q_i and q_j there must be exactly one transition from q_i to q_j. Half of this requirement is that there cannot be more than one transition from q_i to q_j. Consider the two loop transitions for q_1 on d and e. We can satisfy the requirement by replacing these two transitions with the single expression transition $d+e$, which indicates that we may proceed on either d or e.

Select the Transition Collapser tool ⚡, and click on either the d or e. When you click on a transition that goes from q_i to q_j, this tool reforms all transitions from q_i to q_j into a single transition where the labels of the removed transitions are separated by $+$ operators. The new transition will be either $d+e$ or $e+d$, either of these is equivalent, of course, but for the sake of this discussion's simplicity we assume the result was $d+e$. With this step, our GTG is no longer a proper FA. The GTG is shown in Figure 4.15.

In general, if more than one pair of states have more than one transition, use the Transition Collapser tool ⚡ on their transitions as well.

Add empty transitions

Recall once more that every pair of states q_i and q_j must have exactly one transition from q_i to q_j. This means that if no transition exists, an *empty transition* (on the empty set symbol $\emptyset$) must

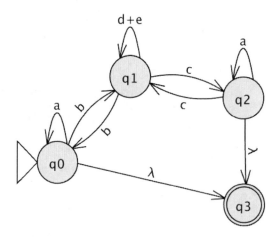

Figure 4.15: The GTG after the d and e
loop transitions on q_1 are combined into
$d+e$.

be created! Select the Transition Creator tool 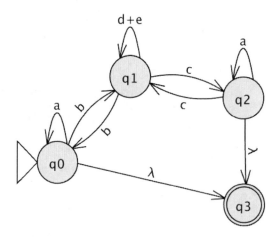 again, and create a transition from q_0 to q_2. A
transition on $\emptyset$ will appear.

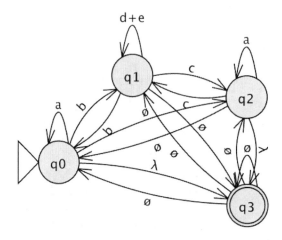

Figure 4.16: The FA after the addition of
empty transitions.

The essential distinction between GTGs and FAs is that FA transitions describe a single string,
while GTG transitions describes sets of strings. In this particular case, we are creating transitions
on the empty set of strings, hence transitions on $\emptyset$. Similar to the earlier creation of λ-transitions,
JFLAP assumes you are creating empty transitions. As you proceed, JFLAP will inform you how
many more empty transitions are required. Seven are required in all: from q_0 to q_2, q_1 to q_3, q_2 to
q_0, q_3 to q_0, q_3 to q_1, q_3 to q_2, and a loop transition on q_3 (q_3 to q_3). When you finish, your GTG
will resemble Figure 4.16.

4.3.2 Collapse Nonfinal, Noninitial States

Now we have a GTG with a single final state, an initial state that is not a final state, and for every pair of states q_i and q_j there is exactly one transition from q_i to q_j. The next step is to iteratively remove every state in the GTG except the final state and the initial state. As each state is removed, we adjust the transitions remaining to ensure the GTG after the state removal is equivalent to the GTG before the state removal.

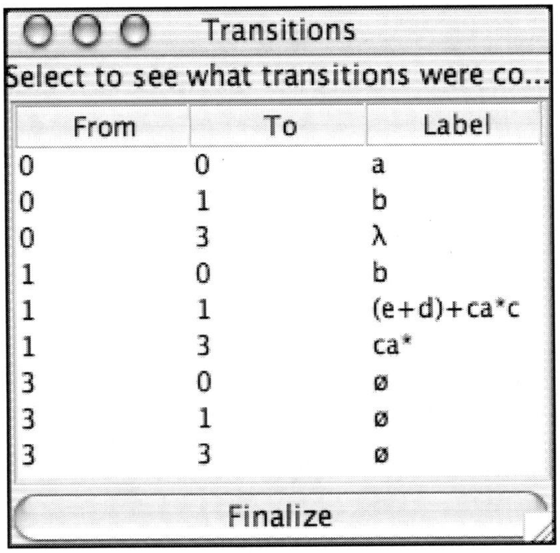

From	To	Label
0	0	a
0	1	b
0	3	λ
1	0	b
1	1	(e+d)+ca*c
1	3	ca*
3	0	∅
3	1	∅
3	3	∅

Transitions — Select to see what transitions were co...

Finalize

Figure 4.17: The window that shows the replacement transitions when removing a state.

The states can be collapsed in any order. However, to understand the following discussion, you will need to collapse states in the given order. Select the State Collapser tool. Once selected, click first on state q_2. A window like the one shown in Figure 4.17 appears that informs you of the new labels for transitions before the collapse occurs. Let r_{ij} be the expression of the transition from q_i to q_j. The rule is, if we are removing q_k, for all states q_i and q_j so that $i \neq k$ and $j \neq k$, r_{ij} is replaced with $r_{ij} + r_{ik}r_{kk}^*r_{kj}$. In other words, we compensate for the removal of q_k by encapsulating in the walk from q_i to q_j the effect of going from q_i to q_k (hence r_{ik}), then looping on q_k as much as we please (hence r_{kk}^*), and then proceeding from q_k to q_j (hence r_{kj}). Lastly, note that $\emptyset$ obeys the following relations: if r is any regular expression, $r + \emptyset = r$, $r\emptyset = \emptyset$, and $\emptyset^* = \lambda$.

Select the row that describes the new transition from q_1 to q_1 (the loop transition on q_1), $d+e+ca^*c$. The transitions from which this new transition is composed are highlighted in the GTG. There are two paths that must be combined into one expression transition, the walk from q_1 to q_1, $d+e$, and the alternative walk from q_1 to q_1 that goes through q_2, ca^*c. More formally, $r_{1,1} = d+e$, $r_{1,2} = r_{2,1} = c$, and $r_{2,2} = a$, so the new transition is $r_{1,1} + r_{1,2}r_{2,2}^*r_{2,1} = d+e+ca^*c$ as JFLAP indicates.

The rules for operations on the empty set are more unfamiliar. Select the row that describes the new transition from q_0 to q_1. There are two paths that must be combined into one expression transition, the walk from q_0 to q_0, b, and the alternative walk from q_0 to q_1 that goes through q_2, $\emptyset a^*c$. More formally, $r_{0,1} = b$, $r_{0,2} = \emptyset$, $r_{2,2} = a$, and $r_{2,1} = c$, so the new transition is $r_{0,1} + r_{0,2}r_{2,2}^*r_{2,1} = b + \emptyset a^*c$. The concatenation of any expression with the empty set is the empty set, so $\emptyset a^*c = \emptyset$, so $b + \emptyset a^*c = b + \emptyset$. The union of the empty set with any expression is that expression, so $b + \emptyset = b$, which is the new expression from q_0 to q_1.

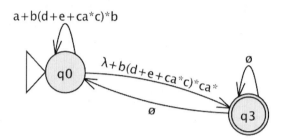

Figure 4.18: The finished GTG after the removal of q_2 and q_1.

Inspect all the other replacements to see if you can figure out the formula, and then reduce it to the label shown in Figure 4.17. Then click **Finalize**. The transitions listed will be replaced, and q_2 will be removed. Repeat this process with q_1. Note there are only four replacements, and some of the labels are quite long. (You might have to resize the window to see the complete labels.) When q_1 is removed, your GTG will resemble Figure 4.18.

4.3.3   Regular Expression Formula

At this point your GTG should have two states—one final and one initial—and resemble Figure 4.18. Let r_{xy} be the expression of the transition from q_x to q_y. For a GTG in this form, where q_i is the initial state and q_j is the final state, the equivalent RE r is given by equation 4.1.

$$r = \left(r_{ii}^*r_{ij}r_{jj}^*r_{ji}\right)^* r_{ii}^*r_{ij}r_{jj}^* \tag{4.1}$$

The conversion is now finished, and JFLAP displays the RE of equation 4.2, derived from equation 4.1.

$$\left(a+b\left(d+e+ca^*c\right)^*b\right)^*\left(\lambda+b\left(d+e+ca^*c\right)^*ca^*\right) \tag{4.2}$$

At this point, you may press **Export** to put the finished RE in a new window.

> **Note** │ If for your input FA any of these steps are unnecessary, JFLAP will skip over them. In the extreme case, if you have an FA with two states (one initial, the other final), and with four transitions (a loop on the initial, a loop on the final, another from the initial to final, and a last one from the final to the initial), JFLAP will skip everything and display the finished RE!

4.3.4 Algorithm to Convert an FA to an RE

1. Start with an FA, though we consider it a GTG G for the purpose of the algorithm.

2. Let F be the set of G's final states, and q_0 be its initial state. If $|F| > 1$ or $F = \{q_0\}$, create a new state q_f, produce λ-transitions for every $q_i \in F$ from q_i to q_f, and make q_f the only final state.

3. Let S be the set of G's states. For every $(q_i, q_j) \in S \times S$, let $L = \{\ell_1, \ell_2, \dots, \ell_n\}$ be the set of expressions of transitions from q_i to q_j. Let $e = \emptyset$ if $|L| = 0$ and $e = \ell_1 + \ell_2 + \cdots + \ell_n$ otherwise, and replace all transitions from q_i to q_j with a single transition from q_i to q_j on the expression e.

4. Let T be the set of G's nonfinal, noninitial states. Let r_{xy} be the expression of the transition from q_x to q_y. For every $q_k \in T$, for every $(q_i, q_j) \in (T - \{q_k\}) \times (T - \{q_k\})$ replace r_{ij} with $r_{ij} + r_{ik} r_{kk}^* r_{kj}$, and finally remove q_k from G. (Note: If r is any regular expression, $r + \emptyset = r$, $r\emptyset = \emptyset$, and $\emptyset^* = \lambda$.)

5. G now has two states: the initial state q_0 and single final state q_f. The equivalent regular expression is $r = \left(r_{00}^* r_{0f} r_{ff}^* r_{f0} \right)^* r_{00}^* r_{0f} r_{ff}^*$.

4.4 Definition of an RE in JFLAP

Let Σ be some alphabet. The set of all possible regular expressions is given by R.

$$R = \{\emptyset, \lambda\} \cup \Sigma \cup \{ab | a, b \in R\} \cup \{a + b | a, b \in R\} \cup \{a^* | a \in R\} \cup \{(a) | a \in R\}$$

4.5 Summary

In Section 4.1 we learned how to edit regular expressions (REs). JFLAP respects the following operators in order of decreasing precedence: the Kleene star (the * character), concatenation (implicit by making two expressions adjacent), and lastly, union (the + character). Parentheses may be used to specify the order of operations. The character ! is used to enter the empty string. All other characters may be used as alphabet symbols, including spaces.

In Section 4.2 we learned how to use JFLAP to convert an RE to an NFA. We use the idea of a generalized transition graph (GTG), which is essentially an FA that allows regular expressions in transitions (called expression transitions). The converter starts with a two-state GTG, with a transition on the starting regular expression from the initial to final state. While there are expression transitions, JFLAP will break the transition into subcomponents that contain the operands of the top-level operator of the expression; the user is responsible for connecting the subcomponents with λ-transitions to duplicate the lost functionality of the operator. The converter finishes when all transitions are single-character or λ-transitions.

In Section 4.3 we learned how to use JFLAP to convert an FA to an RE. We start by considering the FA as a GTG, and reforming the GTG so it has a single final state and a nonfinal initial state, and so that for any two states in the GTG there is exactly one transition from the first state to the second state. We then successively remove all states but the final and initial state; with each removal JFLAP adjusts the remaining transitions to duplicate the functionality of the lost state and its transitions so that each GTG is equivalent to the original FA. Eventually, only the initial and final states remain, to which JFLAP applies a known formula to derive the final RE equivalent to the FA.

In Section 4.4 we presented JFLAP's formal definition of an RE.

4.6   Exercises

1. Using JFLAP, first convert the following REs to NFAs. Then run the multiple run tester and list six input strings that are in the language.

   (a) $abc+a^*$

   (b) a^*b^*+c

   (c) $(ab+\lambda)b$

   (d) $(a+c)a^*$

   (e) $(a+bc+d)$

   (f) $(cd+b)^*$

   (g) $(a+b)^*cd$

2. Write a regular expression for each of the following languages. Enter it in JFLAP, quickly convert it to an NFA (select **Do All**), and then use the multiple run window to verify the strings below. You should check additional strings as well.

(a) $\Sigma = \{a, b\}$. The language is strings with an even number of a's followed by an odd number of b's. For example, accepted strings include *aab*, *b*, *aaaab*, and *aaaabbb*, and rejected strings include *aba* and *aaab*.

(b) $\Sigma = \{a, b\}$. The language is strings with an even number of a's that have exactly one b. For example, accepted strings include *aba*, *b*, *aaaabaa*, and *aaaba*, and rejected strings include *abab* and *aaab*.

(c) $\Sigma = \{a, b\}$. The language is strings with zero or more a's followed by three or fewer b's. For example, accepted strings include *aab*, *bbb*, *aaaabb*, and *aaaa*, and rejected strings include *aabbbb* and *aabaab*.

(d) $\Sigma = \{a, b\}$. The language is strings in which every a must have a b adjacent to it on both sides. For example, accepted strings include *bababab*, *bab*, *bbab*, and *babbbabb*, and rejected strings include *abab* and *baab*.

(e) $\Sigma = \{a, b\}$. The language is strings in which every pair of adjacent a's is followed by a b. For example, accepted strings include *bababab*, *baab*, *aabbaab*, and *aaba*, and rejected strings include *aaab* and *baaa*.

(f) $\Sigma = \{a, b\}$. The language is strings in which every a is followed by an odd number of b's. For example, accepted strings include *bb*, *bbbab*, *abbbab*, and *babbbababbb*, and rejected strings include *ba*, *abbab*, and *bbbabb*.

(g) $\Sigma = \{a, b\}$. The language is strings in which every group of adjacent b's is divisible by two or three. For example, accepted strings include *bbabb*, *bbbbbb*, *abbba*, and *bbbbaabbba*, and rejected strings include *ba*, *abbab*, and *bbbbb*.

3. Revisit the example in Section 4.3 with `ex4.3a` in which q_2 is removed first. In the process of removing q_2, how many new labels are empty transitions? Now redo the example and remove q_1 first. In the process of removing q_1, how many new labels are empty transitions?

4. Convert the following FAs to REs.

   (a) `ex4.nfa2re-a`

   (b) `ex4.nfa2re-b`

   (c) `ex4.nfa2re-c`

   (d) `ex4.nfa2re-d`

   (e) `ex4.nfa2re-e`

   (f) `ex4.nfa2re-f`

   (g) `ex4.nfa2re-g`

   (h) `ex4.nfa2re-h`

5. Load file `ex4.1a` and convert it to an FA. Then convert the FA back into a regular expression by first converting it to a DFA, then a minimial state DFA, and then a regular expression. The original RE and the resulting RE are different. Explain.

6. Load file `ex4.3a` and convert it to an RE. Then convert the resulting RE to a FA, then a DFA, and then a minimal state DFA. What do you observe about the original DFA and the resulting minimal state DFA?

Chapter 5

Pushdown Automata

A pushdown automaton (PDA) is the first type of representation for a context-free language (CFL) that we will examine.

In this chapter we will construct a pushdown automaton (PDA), simulate input on that automaton, discuss strategy in constructing nondeterministic pushdown automata (NPDA), and then give JFLAP's formal definition of a PDA.

5.1 A Simple Pushdown Automaton

Constructing a PDA is similar to constructing an FSA, as you did in Chapter 1; the main difference is in the transitions. A PDA has additional memory in the form of a stack. Symbols can be pushed onto and off of the stack. A transition must now encode two inputs (what must be read from input and the top of the stack before you can take this transition) and one output (what must be pushed onto the stack if you decide to take this transition).

A transition for a PDA is defined in JFLAP as $X, Y; Z$ where X represents the input symbols to be processed, Y represents the stack symbols that must be on the stack and are popped off the stack, and Z represents the stack symbols that are pushed onto the stack. Note that the comma separates the two inputs (what must be matched if this transition is to be taken) and the semicolon separates the inputs from the output.

For example, the transition $a, ab; cd$ from state q_1 to q_2 would be represented in JFLAP as shown in Figure 5.1. This transition is interpreted as "if a is the next symbol in the input and ab (with a on top of b) is on the top of the stack, then process the input symbol a, pop ab off the stack, and push cd (first push d, then c) onto the stack."

63

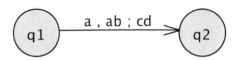

Figure 5.1: A transition on a PDA.

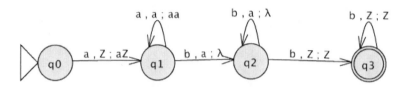

Figure 5.2: A simple PDA.

Figure 5.3: The transition text fields.

5.1.1   Building the NPDA

Let's now create the NPDA shown in Figure 5.2. Start JFLAP and click on the button labeled **Pushdown Automaton**. The **Editor** tab that appears looks identical to the editor for the FSA. There will be only a few differences.

Start by creating four states using the State Creator tool ⓐ. Add transitions by selecting the Transition Creator tool ⤳ and add a transition from q_0 to q_1 (click on q_0 and drag to q_1). When you release the mouse note that three adjacent text fields appear. For the DFA there was only one text field. In the PDA there are three inputs that must be entered: input symbol(s), stack symbol(s) to pop, and stack symbol(s) to push, as shown in Figure 5.3. We want to enter the transition $a, Z; aZ$. Type "a" and press Tab. Note that the a is entered and the next field is ready for input. Type "Z" (note that this is the capital letter Z), press Tab, type "aZ", and press Enter. Note that the comma and semicolon are automatically added to the transition.

Add the remaining five transitions (leave a field blank for λ); make q_0 the initial state and q_3 the final state.

5.1.2   Simulation of Input

What is the language represented by this PDA? Let's step through a simulation of an input string. Select **Input : Step with Closure** and enter the input string *aaabbbbb*. The initial configuration is shown in Figure 5.4 and includes the current state q_0, the input string, and the stack (shown below the input string). The stack is always "empty" when a trace starts. The stack actually has

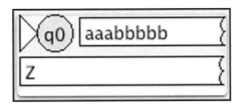

Figure 5.4: The initial configuration.

a bottom-of-stack marker Z (the capital letter Z) so there is a symbol to test to see if the stack is empty or not. Be careful! The Z can be removed, but if you do, you cannot check to see if the stack is empty.

Click **Step** and the first a in the input string has been processed (it is now shaded gray), the Z was popped off the stack, but then put back on with an a on top of it. The transition from q_0 to q_1 could also have been written as $a, \lambda; a$. (See Section 5.3 for different definitions of PDAs.)

Click **Step** two more times and there will be a total of three a's on top of the stack; one for each a in the input string. Click **Step** three more times, and each a is matched with a b. For each b grayed-out an a is popped off the stack.

There are still two more b's to be processed. Click **Step** two more times and the b's are processed and the string is accepted.

What is the language accepted by this PDA? Try testing additional strings if you don't see it right away. For example, does this PDA accept *bbaaa*, *aabb*, *aaabb*, *ababb*, and *bbb*? Don't forget that you can test many input strings at the same time by selecting the multiple simulation input method.

The language accepted by this PDA is those strings with a's first followed by b's such that there is at least one a and there are more b's than a's. Another way to write this is $\{a^n b^m \mid n > 0$ and $n < m\}$. This example is also stored in the file `ex5.1`.

5.2 Nondeterministic PDA

A PDA is nondeterministic if there is a state with more than one choice of transition for its move. Remember that an FSA is nondeterministic if there is a state with either a λ-transition or two outgoing transitions from the same state with the same symbol. For an NPDA to be nondeterministic, there is a state with either a λ-transition $(\lambda, \lambda; \lambda)$ or two outgoing transitions from the same state with the same symbols for the input symbol and the symbols to pop. For example, the two transitions $a, b; \lambda$ and $a, a; \lambda$ outgoing from the same state do not make a PDA nondeterministic since the symbol to pop from the stack is different. The two transitions $a, ba; b$ and $a, ba; \lambda$ outgoing from the same state do make a PDA nondeterministic.

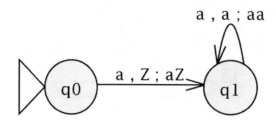

Figure 5.5: Push all the a's on the stack.

We will build in stages an NPDA using JFLAP that accepts the language $\{a^n b^m \mid n > 0, n \leq m \leq 3n\}$. First think about how you would build a deterministic PDA for this language. Is it possible? For each a processed, you must know how many b's (1, 2, or 3) will be processed. But you do not know the number of b's per a unless you can examine the whole string. A PDA can examine and process only one input symbol at a time. Thus, no deterministic PDA can be built that accepts this language. We must build an NPDA. In this NPDA there will be choices of paths that can be taken, such that for a valid input string, one of those paths will lead to acceptance.

Let's now build the NPDA. First let's discuss the possible strings in the language. They include $aabb$, $aabbb$, $aabbbb$, $aabbbbb$, and $aabbbbbb$. All the a's come first and for each a there must be one to three b's. It is also a good idea to discuss strings not in the language. They include bba (a's not first), bab (a's not first), $abbbb$ (too many b's), aa (there must be at least one b), and bb (there must be at least one a).

Since all the a's come first, create states that push all the a's onto the stack. This NPDA is shown in Figure 5.5.

How do we continue so that for each a there will be one to three b's? After all the a's are pushed on we must have three paths that pop one a and end up at the same point: one path for reading one b, one path for reading two b's, and one path for reading three b's. These three paths are added in Figure 5.6, with all three paths ending at q_2. Note in each path that only one a is popped from the stack.

At the point where the three paths end, we need to have three loops: one for matching one a with one b, one for one a with two b's, and one with one a with three b's. These three loops are added in Figure 5.7. Note that only two transitions were added, as one transition can be used for the loop for two b's and three b's.

When the stack is empty, the string is accepted if all the input has been processed. Add one final state and arc as shown in Figure 5.8. This example is also stored in file ex5.2.

Which states are nondeterministic? In JFLAP select **Test : Highlight Nondeterminism** to show which states are nondeterministic.

There are several path choices in this NPDA. Let's simulate a string on the NPDA. Select **Input : Step with Closure** and enter the input string $a^4 b^{10}$.

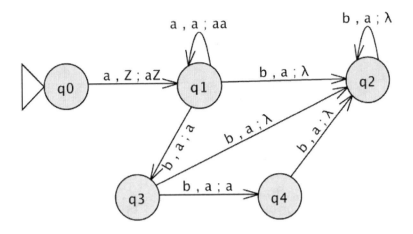

Figure 5.6: Pop one *a* and process 1, 2, or 3 *b*'s.

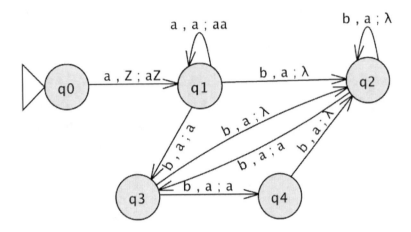

Figure 5.7: Three loops added.

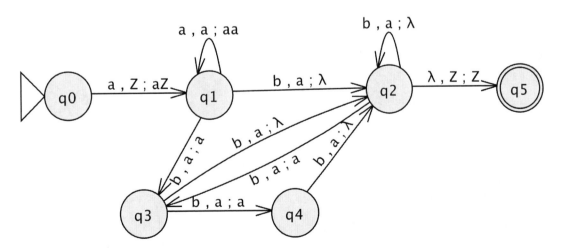

Figure 5.8: A nondeterministic PDA.

With nondeterminism, the number of configurations can grow at a rapid rate. Click on **Step** nine times and see all the configurations! It is helpful in tracing NPDAs to remove configurations

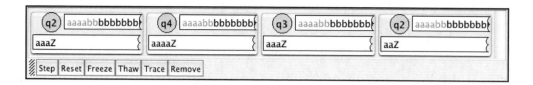

Figure 5.9: Possible configurations after six steps.

you think are unlikely to succeed, and freeze selected configurations so you can focus on a smaller number of configurations.

Let us restart the trace by clicking on **Reset**. Click on **Step** four times and all the a's are pushed onto the stack. Click on **Step** two more times and there are now four possible configurations, as shown in Figure 5.9.

Can any of these configurations no longer possibly succeed? The rightmost configuration has already pushed two a's off the stack and there are eight b's left, so this configuration will eventually lead to failure since there are more than three b's for each remaining a. Although JFLAP will automatically remove this configuration later when it fails, it can be removed now by selecting it first and then selecting **Remove**. This will reduce the number of configurations later to examine as this configuration would have generated several more configurations, all that would eventually fail. Continue stepping through, trying to keep the number of choices down by removing or freezing some configurations. There are several possible solutions, as there are several combinations of matching two of the a's with three b's each and two of the a's with two b's each.

5.3   Definition of an NPDA in JFLAP

JFLAP gives a general definition of an NPDA M to be defined as a septuple $M = (Q, \Sigma, \Gamma, \delta, q_s, Z, F)$ where:

   Q is a finite set of states $\{q_i | i \text{ is a nonnegative integer}\}$

   Σ is the finite input alphabet

   Γ is the finite stack alphabet

   δ is the transition function, $\delta : Q \times \Sigma^* \times \Gamma^* \rightarrow$ finite subsets of $Q \times \Gamma^*$

   $q_s \in Q$ is the initial state

   Z is the start stack symbol (must be capital Z)

   $F \subseteq Q$ is the set of final states

The definition of δ in JFLAP is general to allow JFLAP to work with many definitions of an NPDA. Zero or more symbols can be read as input, zero or more symbols can be popped from the stack, and zero or more symbols can be pushed onto the stack. In defining an NPDA you do not need to define the input symbols and stack symbols explicitly, but they are determined based on the labels you enter in the transactions. The bottom-of-stack marker is set in JFLAP to Z and cannot be changed. JFLAP assumes this marker is the only symbol on the stack when a simulation begins.

You might want to restrict the definition of δ for a particular NPDA to a subset of what JFLAP allows. For example, consider the following restrictions: Require the input symbol to be either a single symbol or λ and require exactly one symbol to be popped from the stack. In that case, the definition of δ would be:

$$\delta : Q \times (\Sigma \cup \{\lambda\}) \times \Gamma \to \text{finite subsets of } Q \times \Gamma^*$$

If you want to use this definition of δ, then when you build your NPDA with JFLAP make sure all the transitions follow this restricted rule. JFLAP does not check this for you.

Here is an example showing the nonpictorial representation of the NPDA M in Figure 5.2. Using the formal definition of an NPDA in JFLAP, $M = (Q, \Sigma, \Gamma, \delta, q_s, Z, F)$ where:

$$Q = \{q_0, q_1, q_2, q_3\}$$

$$\Sigma = \{a, b\}$$

$$\Gamma = \{a, Z\}$$

$$\delta = \{(q_0, a, Z, q_1, aZ), (q_1, a, a, q_1, aa), (q_1, b, a, q_2, \lambda), (q_2, b, a, q_2, \lambda), (q_2, b, Z, q_3, Z), (q_3, b, Z, q_3, Z)\}$$

$$q_s = q_0$$

$$F = \{q_3\}$$

The δ moves are described as five-tuples where the first field is the state the transition originates in, the second field is the input symbol(s) to process, the third field is the stack symbol(s) to pop, the fourth field is the state at which the transition ends, and the fifth field is the stack symbol(s) to push onto the stack.

5.4 Summary

In Section 5.1 we learned how to edit and simulate an NPDA. The main difference between editing an NPDA and an FSA is the label on a transition. The transition format is $X, Y; Z$ where X represents the input symbols to be processed, Y represents the stack symbols that must be on the stack and are popped off the stack, and Z represents the stack symbols that are pushed onto the stack. The configuration of an NPDA includes the current state, the current input left to be processed, and the current stack contents. A special symbol, capital Z, is the bottom-of-stack marker.

In Section 5.2 we built an NPDA for the language $\{a^n b^m \mid n > 0, n \leq m \leq 3n\}$, a language that cannot be recognized by a deterministic PDA. We then traced it with the string $a^4 b^{10}$ and saw how quickly the nondeterminism led to an exponential number of configurations.

In Section 5.3 we presented JFLAP's formal definition of an NPDA. JFLAP's definition is general so that it accomodates many definitions of a PDA. For example, you may prefer to use the definition in which a single symbol is always popped from the stack. (Popping multiple symbols or λ is not allowed.)

5.5   Exercises

1. Load the following files containing NPDAs. For each NPDA, list five strings that are accepted, list five strings that are not accepted, and determine the language represented.

   (a) `ex5.5a`

   (b) `ex5.5b`

   (c) `ex5.5c`

   (d) `ex5.5d`

   (e) `ex5.5e`

   (f) `ex5.5f`

2. Modify the NPDA from Section 5.1 to accept the following languages.

   (a) $\{a^n b^m \mid n > 0 \text{ and } n = m\}$

   (b) $\{a^n b^m \mid n > 0 \text{ and } m = 2n\}$

   (c) $\{a^n b^m \mid n > 0 \text{ and } n > m\}$

3. Generate a set of strings for testing the NPDA from Section 5.2 that will convince you this NPDA is correct. You should create a minimal set of strings that covers all cases of strings that are accepted and not accepted.

4. The following NPDAs are incorrect. Load the files and determine why they do not represent the corresponding language. List strings they should accept and do not, or strings they should not accept but do. Then correct the NDPA.

   (a) `ex5.5wrong-a` should represent the language $\{a^n b^m c^p \mid n < m+p, n > 0, m > 0, p > 0\}$.

   (b) `ex5.5wrong-b` should represent the language $\{(ab)^n c^n \mid n \geq 0, m \geq 0\}$.

   (c) `ex5.5wrong-c` should represent the language $\{(a)^n b^m c^n \mid n \text{ is odd}, n > 0, m > 0\}$.

(d) `ex5.5wrong-d` should represent the language $\Sigma = \{a, b\}, \{w \in Sigma^* \mid n_b(w) > 2 * n_a(w)\}$.

5. Write NPDAs to accept the following languages.

   (a) $\{a^n b^m \mid n > 0, n < m < 4n\}$

   (b) $\{a^n b^m \mid m > 0, m \leq n \leq 3m\}$

   (c) $\{a^n b^m \mid n > 0, n = 2m, \text{ and } n \bmod 3 = 0\}$

   (d) $\{a^n b^m c^p \mid p = n + m, n > 0, m > 0, p > 0\}$

   (e) $\{a^n b^m c^p \mid p = n + m, p \text{ is odd}, n > 0, m > 0, p > 0\}$

Chapter 6

Context-Free Grammars

A context-free grammar (CFG) is another representation for a context-free language (CFL). CFGs are less restrictive on the right side of productions than regular grammars, so CFGs are able to generate a proper superset of the languages generated by regular grammars.

In this chapter we use JFLAP to construct and parse context-free grammars. We also show examples of context-free grammars and NPDAs that are equivalent by using JFLAP to convert a CFG into an equivalent NPDA and to convert an NPDA into an equivalent CFG.

6.1   Creating and Parsing Context-Free Grammars

In this section we will cover CFGs and show how to parse them in JFLAP. Then we will look at a simple, yet inefficient, parsing method. In Chapter 8 we will study more efficient parsing methods.

6.1.1   Entering a CFG in JFLAP

Section 3.1 described how to use the grammar input window. We will use the same grammar editor for inputting a CFG. Start JFLAP and choose **Grammar**. Input the grammar shown in Figure 6.1 or load the file ex6.1a.

S	$\longrightarrow$	aSb
S	$\longrightarrow$	bB
B	$\longrightarrow$	bbB
B	$\longrightarrow$	λ

Figure 6.1: A simple CFG.

A context-free grammar G is defined using the four-tuple $G = (V, T, S, P)$, where V is a set of variables, T is a set of terminals, S represents the start variable, and P is a set of productions. Productions are in the form $A \to x$, where A is a single variable and x is a string of zero or more terminals and variables.

In JFLAP, these parts are represented as stated in Chapter 3.1. Symbols in the grammar are always represented as single characters, variables are represented by uppercase letters, terminals are represented as any symbol that is not an uppercase letter, and the start variable S can be any variable. JFLAP assumes the start variable is the variable in the left side of the first production shown. For example, in Figure 6.1, the variables are $\{S, B\}$, the start variable is S, the terminals are $\{a, b\}$, and there are four productions shown.

6.1.2 Parsing with the Brute-Force Parser

What is the language of the grammar in Figure 6.1? Let's derive some strings using the brute-force parser we used in Chapter 3. Select **Input : Brute Force Parse**. Click the pop-up menu **Noninverted Tree** and select **Derivation Table**. Enter the string "aaabbbbbb" in the text field labeled **Input**. Press Return, or click on the **Start** button. Repeatedly click **Step** until the string is derived. The productions used are shown on the left under the heading **Productions** and the sentential forms in the derivation are shown on the right under the heading **Derivation**, as shown in Figure 6.2.

Now we know one string in the language of this grammar. One way to figure out a description of all the strings in the language is to think about what type of string each variable can derive. We introduce the term V *production* where V is a variable to mean a production with V on the left side. What can the variable S derive? By looking at the first three sentential forms in the derivation of $aaabbbbbb$ in Figure 6.2, S can derive $\{aSb, aaSbb, aaaSbbb, \ldots\}$. By thinking about all the S productions, we can see other sentential forms S could derive, such as $\{bB, abBb, aabBbb, \ldots\}$, and come to the conclusion that S can derive $\{a^n bBb^n \mid n \geq 0\}$. If you focus on the variable B, what can it derive? Let's force B to be the start symbol by moving the first production past the last

Production	Derivation
	S
S→aSb	aSb
S→aSb	aaSbb
S→aSb	aaaSbbb
S→bB	aaabBbbb
B→bbB	aaabbbBbbb
B→λ	aaabbbbbb

Figure 6.2: A derivation of *aaabbbbbb*.

production and entering $B \rightarrow B$ as the first production. Enter in a few input strings to determine what B can derive. B can derive the strings $\{\lambda, bb, bbbb, bbbbbb \ldots\}$, or rather $(bb)^*$, an even number of b's. The combination of what S and B can derive implies the language of this grammar is $\{a^n b(bb)^* b^n \mid n \geq 0\}$.

After experimenting with the B productions, be sure to put the grammar back into its original form.

> **Tip** ‖ In JFLAP you can determine the strings a particular variable A can derive by making A the start symbol. Enter the first production at the end of the production list to save it, and then enter $A \rightarrow A$ as the first production.

> **Note** ‖ JFLAP only parses input strings, which are formed of terminals. If you enter a sentential form with a variable for the **Input**, JFLAP gives an error message.

6.1.3   Parse Tree

A parse tree is a visualization of a derivation. Each production in the derivation is visualized as nodes in a tree: the symbols on the right side of the production are children and the symbols on the left side of the production are variables. For example, the production $B \rightarrow bbB$ would be visualized as the tree in Figure 6.3. A parse tree for an input string starts with the start variable as the root of the tree, and for each production that is applied, the corresponding variable node in the tree is expanded. The tree is complete when all the leaves in the tree are terminals or λ. Thus, the leaves read from left to right reproduce the input string.

In the grammar from Figure 6.1, we saw the derivation of the string $aaabbbbbb$. Now let's see the same derivation as a parse tree. Click on **Start** again to restart the parse, then click on **Derivation Table** and select **Noninverted Tree**. The start variable is shown as a node. Click on **Step** once and S is expanded into aSb. Note in the bottom left of the window that a message appears informing you of the production that was used, **Derived aSb from S**. Click on **Step** repeatedly until the parse tree is complete. The completed parse tree is shown in Figure 6.4.

> **Note** ‖ In JFLAP's parse trees, variables are shown as green nodes and terminals are shown as yellow nodes.

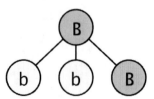

Figure 6.3: A derivation visualized as a tree.

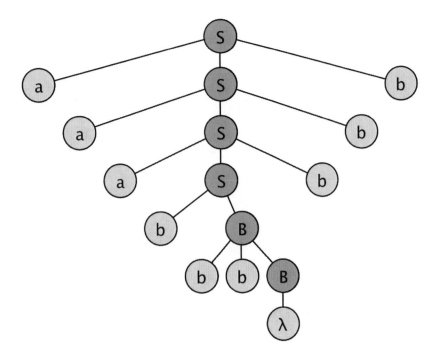

Figure 6.4: A parse tree of *aaabbbbbb*.

Parse trees show the productions that are used in the derivation, but they do not keep the order the productions were applied in if there is more than one variable to be replaced. We will see this in a later example.

6.1.4 How Brute-Force Parsing Works

How does brute-force parsing determine a derivation for an input string? The Brute-Force Parsing Algorithm is so named because it takes a brute-force approach by trying all possible derivations. Internally to JFLAP (and not shown), it builds a tree of possible sentential forms, called a derivation tree. In this derivation tree the nodes are sentential forms, with the start variable as the root of the tree.

For example, consider the grammar from Figure 6.1 (load file ex6.1a if it is not loaded). Start the brute-force parser, enter the input string *aabbb*, and click **Start**. Note the message below the input string that says **String accepted! 5 nodes generated**. The derivation tree for this string (JFLAP does not display this tree) is shown in Figure 6.5. The tree starts with the start variable and generates all possible sentential forms after one production replacement (*aSb* and *bB*). Since the sentential form *bB* starts with *b* and the string we are trying to derive starts with *a*, the node *bB* does not need to be expanded further (illustrated by the line drawn underneath it). All valid nodes are then expanded by one more production producing *aaSbb* and *abBS* (not valid), one more time producing *aaaSbbb* (not valid) and *aabBbb*, and finally *aabbb* (circled since it is the input string!) and *aabbbBbb* (not valid). The message above **5 nodes generated** gives you an idea of

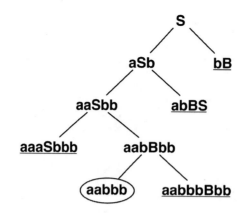

Figure 6.5: A derivation tree of *aabbb*.

how large the derivation tree is, since JFLAP does not display it. In this case the '5' represents the five nodes that were not immediately rejected as being impossible.

How efficient is brute-force parsing? Trying every possible combination works fine if the grammar has few choices, but it could be extremely inefficient. JFLAP tries to prune the tree to cut down on its size in several ways. JFLAP eliminates those sentential forms whose currently derived terminals are incompatible with the target string, those sentenial forms it has already seen, and those sentential forms whose length of non-λ-deriving variables and terminals is greater than the length of the target string. Even with JFLAP's pruning, parsing can still take a long time. Dismiss the tab and go back to the grammar and add the production $S \rightarrow SS$ to the grammar. Then select the brute-force parser again. Enter the string *aabbb*. This string was accepted before, so it should be accepted again. It is, but this time there are 62 nodes in the tree instead of five! Figure 6.6 shows the first two levels of this derivation tree and illustrates how rapidly it is growing. Note that the node labeled SS derives six nodes after an additional step; however, two of them are SSS, so JFLAP combines them into one node.

Enter in another input string *aaabbbbbb* and click **Start**. This string was accepted before and should be accepted now. Under the **Input** label you will see a message **Parser running. Nodes generated** and a number followed by a second number in parentheses. The first number is the current number of nodes in the parse tree that have not been rejected yet, and the second number

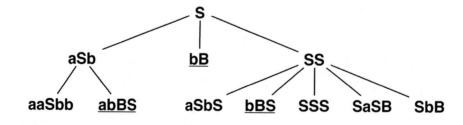

Figure 6.6: Start of the derivation tree of *aabbb* after adding $S \rightarrow SS$.

is the number of nodes on the current level that are being examined. This number can be quite large! As you can see, the parsing is taking a long time due to the additional production and choices available. The parsing of this string will probably take too long, so you should try another string. To stop the parsing, click on **Pause**. If you really want to continue with this string, you can click **Resume**.

6.2 Converting a CFG to an NPDA

In this section we will use JFLAP to show how to convert a CFG to an equivalent NPDA with exactly three states using the LL parsing method. LL parsing will be explained in more detail in Chapter 8. The details of LL parsing are not needed for this conversion.

The idea behind the conversion from a CFG to an equivalent NPDA is to derive the productions through the stack. The conversion starts by pushing the start variable on the stack. Whenever there is a variable on the top of the stack, the conversion replaces the variable by its right side, thus applying a production toward deriving the string. Whenever a terminal is on top of the stack, the conversion pops the symbol off and makes sure that the current input symbol is the same. Thus the terminals on the stack are popped off in the same order they appear in the input string. If the stack is emptied, then all the variables were replaced and all the terminals matched, so the string is accepted.

6.2.1 Conversion

We will convert the CFG in Figure 6.1 (also in file `ex6.1a`) to an NPDA. Open the grammar if it is not already open and select **Convert : Convert CFG to PDA (LL)**. You will see a view much like that in Figure 6.7. On the left is the CFG and on the right is the incomplete NPDA with three states. There are four transitions that have already been added to the NPDA. The transition from q_0 to q_1 pushes the start variable on the top of the stack. There is one transition from q_1 to q_1 for each terminal in the language. This transition ensures that when a symbol is read in the input, it must appear on top of the stack. The final transition from q_1 to q_2 ensures that the stack is empty before accepting. The transitions that correspond to the productions in the CFG are missing.

The goal for an input string is the following: If q_2 is reached, then all the symbols in the input string were pushed on the stack using the productions in the grammar and popped off the stack in the same order they appear in the input string. We have already added the "popped off" loop transitions on q_1. We must now add the "pushed on" loop transitions on q_1 for each production to get the terminals on the stack. For each production, the left side of the production is popped and the right side of the production is pushed.

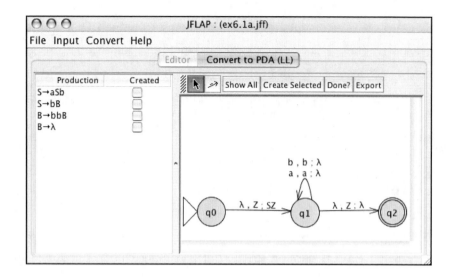

Figure 6.7: Start of conversion of a CFG to an NPDA.

Tip | If you don't like the layout of the NPDA, use the Attribute Editor tool ⬆ to rearrange the states.

In JFLAP, each production $A \rightarrow BCD$ will be replaced by a loop transition on state q_1 with the label $\lambda, A; BCD$. Add the missing transitions. Select the Transition Creator tool ↗ and click on state q_1. Input the transition $\lambda, S; aSb$ corresponding to the production $S \rightarrow aSb$. Since you created the transition corresponding to $S \rightarrow aSb$, the box to the right of this production is checked.

There is an alternative way to enter labels. Select a production whose corresponding transition has not yet been created and then click on **Create Selected**. JFLAP will add the corresponding transition. Add the remaining transitions. The resulting NPDA is shown in Figure 6.8. Select

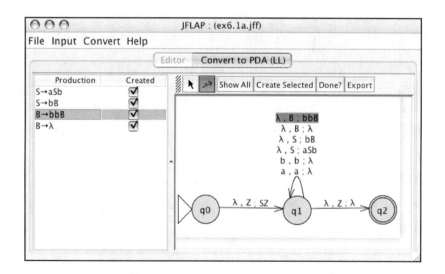

Figure 6.8: Completion of converting a CFG to an NPDA.

Export, and the NPDA will be placed into a new window. To see that the NPDA accepts the same strings as the CFG, run the same input string *aaabbbbbb* on the NPDA. Try other strings on both the CFG and the NPDA to convince yourself.

6.2.2 Algorithm

We describe the algorithm to convert a CFG G into an equivalent NPDA M.

1. Start with a CFG $G = (V, T, S, P)$.

2. Create an NPDA $M = (Q, \Sigma, \Gamma, \delta, q_s, Z, F)$ with three states such that $Q = \{q_0, q_1, q_2\}$, $q_s = q_0$; $F = \{q_2\}$, $\Sigma = T$, and $\Gamma = V \cup T \cup \{Z\}$.

3. Create a starting transition, $\delta(q_0, \lambda, Z) = (q_1, SZ)$.

4. Create an ending transition, $\delta(q_1, \lambda, Z) = (q_2, Z)$.

5. For each terminal $a \in T$, create the transition $\delta(q_1, a, a) = (q_1, \lambda)$.

6. For each production $A \rightarrow BCD \in P$, create the transition $\delta(q_1, \lambda, A) = (q_1, BCD)$.

6.3 Converting an NPDA to a CFG

We now show how to convert an NPDA to a CFG. The idea behind the conversion from an NPDA into an equivalent CFG is to convert each transition into one or more productions that mimic the behavior. To simplify the process JFLAP will require that the NPDA be in a certain format. If it is not, the user must convert the NPDA into the appropriate format. All transitions in the NPDA must pop exactly one symbol and push exactly zero or two symbols. In other words, with each transition the stack will increase its size by one or decrease its size by one. There are no restrictions on the number of terminals read on any transition. The NPDA must have one final state and at least one transition into the final state that pops Z off the stack.

For those transitions that pop one symbol and push no symbols, one production is generated to mimic this behavior. For those transitions that pop one symbol and push two symbols, a lot of productions are generated to indicate possible ways these two symbols that are pushed could eventually be popped off the stack. Many useless productions will be generated in addition to the correct productions.

6.3.1 Conversion

We will convert the NPDA in Figure 6.9 to an equivalent CFG. Load the NPDA from file `ex6.3a` and select **Convert : Convert to grammar**.

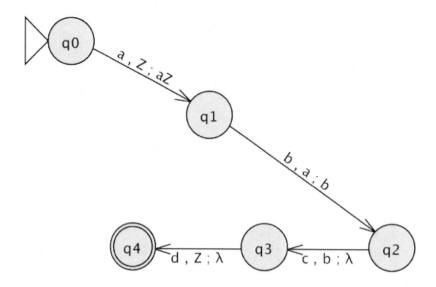

Figure 6.9: A simple NPDA.

Oops! An error message appears, as shown in Figure 6.10. The NPDA is not in the correct format. The error message states that the transition from q_1 to q_2 is supposed to pop one symbol (it does) and push 0 or 2 symbols (it pushes only one). We must replace the transition with one state and two correctly formatted transitions. These two transitions simulate the deleted transition by pushing an additional symbol on the stack in the first transition and then popping that symbol off the stack in the second transition.

Figure 6.11 shows the NPDA with the transition $b, a; b$ from before replaced with new state q_5 and two transitions. The first new transition $b, a; xb$ pops the a off the stack and pushes the b onto

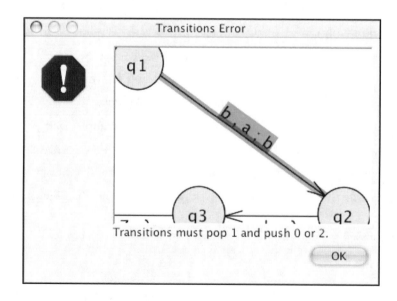

Figure 6.10: Transition not in correct format.

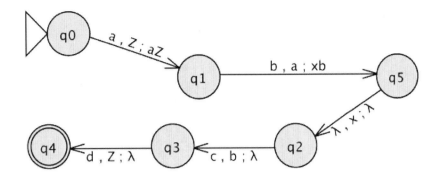

Figure 6.11: The NPDA in the correct format.

the stack, as before. It also pushes the extra symbol x onto the stack, so it is pushing two items on the stack. The second new transition $\lambda, x; \lambda$ pops the extra symbol off the stack.

Fix your NPDA. Now is it in the correct format? It has one start state, one final state, and all the transitions pop one symbol off the stack and push zero or two symbols onto the stack. Again select **Convert : Convert to grammar**. This time there should be no error message.

You will see a view much like that in Figure 6.12, except there is no highlighting yet in the NPDA and there are no productions yet on the right side.

To convert the NPDA $M = (Q, \Sigma, \Gamma, \delta, q_s, Z, F)$ into a CFG $G = (V, T, S, P)$, we must define the parts of the grammar based on parts of the NPDA.

Variables in the grammar will be represented in the form $(q_i A q_j)$ where q_i and q_j represent states from the NPDA and A is a stack symbol. The meaning of $(q_i A q_j)$ is, "if when moving along a path from state q_i to q_j, the stack is exactly the same except that A is removed from the stack."

The start variable S will be represented by our goal, (q_0, Z, q_4). Figure 6.13 illustrates its meaning. We start in q_0 with only Z on the stack; we walk through some path (represented by the

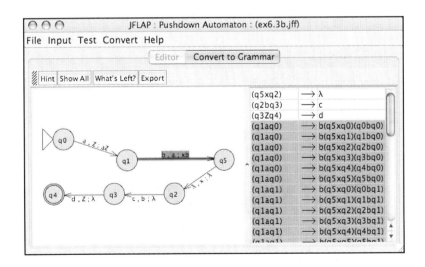

Figure 6.12: Creating the productions.

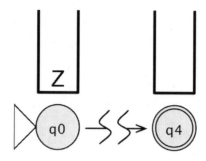

Figure 6.13: Meaning of the start variable.

squiggly lines), pushing and popping symbols off the stack; and eventually arrive in q_4 with nothing on the stack. The stack changes size by decreasing by one between q_0 and q_4. (If other symbols are pushed on along the way, they must be popped off so the overall effect is the stack size decreased by one.)

We now describe how to convert each transition into equivalent productions. There are two types of transitions. First, we will describe how to generate a production for a transition that decreases its size by 1 by looking at the transition from q_5 to q_2, $\lambda, x; \lambda$. Note the stack contents will stay exactly the same except one symbol (x) is popped off the stack, as shown in Figure 6.14

For transitions of this type $\delta(q_i, a, A) = (q_j, \lambda)$, there is one production equivalent,

$$(q_i, A, q_j) \rightarrow a,$$

meaning from q_i to q_j there is one symbol popped (A) and one symbol from the input (a), so we will derive this symbol.

To create the corresponding productions for a transition, click on the transition. Click on the transition $\lambda, x; \lambda$ from q_5 to q_2 and you will see the equivalent production appear on the right side, $(q_5 x q_2) \rightarrow \lambda$. Also click on the other transitions in which the size of the stack decreases by one, $c, b; \lambda$ and $d, Z; \lambda$, and you will see the equivalent productions. These are the first three productions shown in Figure 6.12.

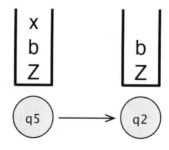

Figure 6.14: When the stack decreases in size by 1.

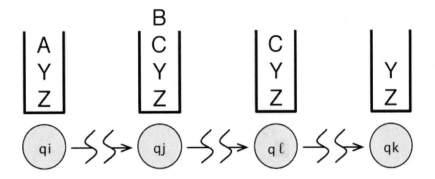

Figure 6.15: Meaning of when the stack increases in size by 2.

Now we will see how to convert a transition in which the size of the stack increases in size by one by looking at the transition $b, a; xb$ from q_1 to q_5. For transitions of this type $\delta(q_i, a, A) = (q_j, BC)$ there are many productions generated. For all possible q_k and q_l we create the productions

$$(q_i A q_k) \rightarrow a(q_j B q_l)(q_l C q_k) \text{ for all } q_k \text{ and } q_l.$$

Figure 6.15 illustrates the meaning of this. In going from q_i to q_k, the symbol A is popped off the stack and the stack is exactly the same as it was in q_i, except the A is no longer on the stack. The symbol Y is shown to illustrate that there might be other symbols on the stack below the A in q_i, and that those symbols should still be on the stack in q_k. Along the path from q_i to q_k there are other symbols that are pushed on (B and C), but they must be pushed off before reaching q_k.

Click on the production $b, a; xb$ and you will see many productions generated and highlighted on the right side. Many of these productions will be useless, but some will be needed to derive a string. For an example, you should see the production

$$(q_1 a q_3) \rightarrow b(q_5 x q_2)(q_2 b q_3).$$

Figure 6.16 illustrates this production. Starting in q_1 the a is on top of the stack. In q_3 the stack is exactly the same, except the a is removed from the stack. Along the way, b and x were pushed onto the stack and removed.

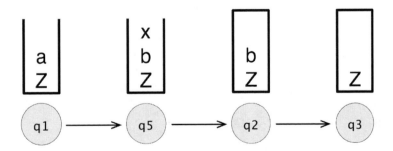

Figure 6.16: Example of when the stack increases in size by 2.

Click on the button **What's left?**. It should show that you have one more transition to convert to productions. Click on that transition and many productions are added to the grammar. You may have to scroll down to see the highlighted block of productions.

If the generated CFG is small enough, then you can can export the grammar to another window. Click on **Export**, and you will see that in this case the grammar is too large to export. Since we cannot see the derivation in JFLAP, a derivation of the string *abcd* follows so you can see that our conversion does accept a string in the language. You can run the same input string on the NPDA to see that it also accepts this string.

$$
\begin{aligned}
(q_0 Z q_4) &\Rightarrow a(q_1 a q_3)(q_3 Z q_4) \\
&\Rightarrow a(q_1 a q_3)d \\
&\Rightarrow ab(q_5 x q_2)(q_2 b q_3)d \\
&\Rightarrow ab(q_2 b q_3)d \\
&\Rightarrow abcd
\end{aligned}
$$

6.3.2   Algorithm

We describe the algorithm to convert an NPDA M into a CFG G.

1. Start with an NPDA $M = (Q, \Sigma, \Gamma, \delta, q_s, Z, F)$.

2. Modify M to have one final state q_f.

3. Modify M such that each transition pops exactly one symbol and pushes either zero or two symbols.

4. Create a CFG $G = (V, T, S, P)$ with $V = \{(q_i A q_j) \mid q_i, q_j \in Q \text{ and } A \in \Gamma\}$ and with the start variable equal to $(q_s Z q_f)$.

5. For each transition $\delta(q_i, a, A) = (q_j, \lambda)$, generate one production

$$
(q_i, A, q_j) \rightarrow a.
$$

6. For each transition $\delta(q_i, a, A) = (q_j, BC)$, generate the productions

$$
(q_i A q_k) \rightarrow a(q_j B q_l)(q_l C q_k) \text{ for all } q_k \text{ and } q_l.
$$

6.4 Summary

In Section 6.1 we learned how to parse strings with a grammar using the brute-force method. A derivation of a string may be visualized either as a derivation table or a parse tree. The derivation table preserves the order the productions are applied; the parse tree does not. We also showed that brute-force parsing can be very inefficient.

In Section 6.2 we learned how to convert a CFG to an equivalent NPDA using the LL parsing method. The NPDA has exactly three states, and starts by pushing the start variable on the stack. Transitions are created that mimic productions by popping the left side of a production and pushing down its right side. Other productions are created to make sure the symbols read in the input string are popped off the stack in the same order.

In Section 6.3 we learned how to convert an NPDA to an equivalent CFG. The NPDA must first be modified to have one final state, and transitions that always pop exactly one symbol and push exactly zero or two symbols. Each transition that pushes zero symbols can be converted into one production in the grammar. Each transition that pushes two symbols is converted into many productions that mimic possible scenarios in which these two symbols can be eventually popped off the stack.

6.5 Exercises

1. For each CFG, list five strings in the language and give a written description of the language.

    (a) `ex6.5cfg-a`

    (b) `ex6.5cfg-b`

    (c) `ex6.5cfg-c`

    (d) `ex6.5cfg-d`

2. For each language listed, the corresponding CFG does not correctly represent the language. List a string that either is in the language and is not represented in the grammar, or is not in the language but is accepted by the grammar. Then modify the grammar so that it represents the language.

    (a) $L = \{a^n b^m c^p \mid 0 < n < m + p, m > 0, p > 0\}$ and file `ex6.5cfg-e`

    (b) $L = \{(ab)^n (ba)^m \mid n > 0, m > 0\}$ and file `ex6.5cfg-f`

3. Consider the ambiguous grammar in file `ex6.5cfg-ambiguous` and the string *ababab*. Run the brute-force parser on this string. Which parse tree does JFLAP produce? Give two different parse trees for this string.

4. Write a CFG for each of the following languages. Create a set of test strings that includes strings that should be in the language and strings that should not be in the language, and verify with JFLAP.

   (a) $L = \{a^n b^m \mid m < n, m > 0\}$

   (b) $\Sigma = \{a, b\}, L = \{w \in \Sigma^* \mid aba$ is a substring and $n_a(w)$ is even$\}$

   (c) $L = \{a^n b^m c^n \mid n > 0, m > 0, n$ is even, m is odd$\}$

   (d) $L = \{a^n b^m c^p \mid p = n + m, n > 0, m > 0\}$

   (e) $L = \{a^n b^m c^m d^n \mid n \geq 0, m \geq 0\}$

   (f) $L = \{a^n b^m \mid 0 < n \leq m \leq 3n\}$

5. Consider the CFG in file `ex6.5-longparse` and the strings of the form $a^n bb$.

   (a) Run the brute-force parser for $n = 2, \ldots, 8$ and record the number of nodes generated. What observation can you make about the time to parse?

   (b) Remove the production $S \rightarrow SS$ and again run the brute-force parser for $n = 2, \ldots, 8$ and record the number of nodes generated. What observation can you make about the time to parse?

   (c) In addition to the previous change, change the production $A \rightarrow AA$ to $A \rightarrow aA$. Run the brute-force parser for $n = 2, \ldots, 8$ and record the number of nodes generated. What observation can you make about the time to parse?

   (d) Is the modified grammar equivalent to the original grammar?

6. Convert each of the following CFGs into an NPDA. Export each NPDA and trace several strings in both the CFG and the NPDA.

   (a) `ex6.5cfg-a`

   (b) `ex6.5cfg-b`

   (c) `ex6.5cfg-c`

   (d) `ex6.5cfg-d`

7. For each of the following NPDAs, list the language of the NPDA and convert the NPDA into a CFG. Export the CFG and trace several strings in both the NPDA and the CFG.

   (a) `ex6.5-toCFGa`

   (b) `ex6.5-toCFGb`

   (c) `ex6.5-toCFGc`

8. Convert each of the following NPDAs into a CFG. You will first have to put the NPDA in the correct format. Once you have, save the modified NPDA and then run several input strings on both NPDAs to make sure that the modified NPDA represents the same language as the original NPDA. Then convert the NPDA to a CFG. The CFG will be too large to export.

   (a) `ex6.5-toCFGd`

   (b) `ex6.5-toCFGe`

   (c) `ex6.5-toCFGf`

Chapter 7

Transforming Grammars

Sometimes it is advantageous to transform a CFG into an equivalent grammar with a simpler format. The Chomsky Normal Form (CNF) for a CFG has a restricted format which has no λ-productions, no unit-productions, and additional restrictions that limit the number of variables and terminals in productions. CNF's restrictions result in many efficient algorithms. For example, the brute-force parsing method in Section 6.1.2 can be slow if the grammar has λ-productions and unit-productions. Transforming the grammar into CNF can speed up the parsing.

In this chapter we will study four algorithms implemented in JFLAP that transform a CFG without changing the language of the grammar. The first three transformations remove λ-productions, unit-productions, and useless productions, respectively, and the fourth transforms the resulting CFG into CNF. JFLAP requires that these four transformations occur in this order. The order is important, as removing λ-productions can generate unit-productions, and removing unit-productions can generate useless productions. JFLAP will skip a transformation if it is not needed.

The empty string in the language would result in special cases in the algorithms, so it is easier to remove λ from the language, and later add λ back into the resulting grammar after the transformation. Thus, JFLAP's algorithms in this chapter only consider CFGs that do not derive λ.

7.1 Removing λ-Productions

In this section we will remove λ-productions from a CFG that does not derive λ. The idea is to identify variables that derive λ, remove all λ-productions, and replace them with equivalent productions. If a λ-deriving variable V appears on the right side of a production, then a new production is created with V missing, as V could have derived λ and thus "disappeared" from the right side. An exception occurs if all of the right side can disappear as a result of removing the λ-deriving variables; you do not add the λ-production with all variables removed in this case.

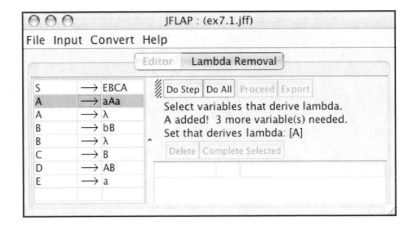

Figure 7.1: λ-production removal.

7.1.1 The Transformation

Start JFLAP and either enter the grammar shown in Figure 7.1 or load the file `ex7.1`. Note that this grammar has two λ-productions, but λ is not a string in the language of the grammar.

Select **Convert : Transform Grammar**. The **Lambda Removal** window appears and should look similar to Figure 7.1. The original grammar appears on the left side of the window for reference. On the right side is where the new grammar will be created in two steps.

The first step is to identify the set of variables that derive λ. To add a variable V to this set, click a V production (a production with V only on the left side) in the left grammar view. For example, A has a λ-production. Click on either of the A productions (either $A \to aAa$ or $A \to \lambda$). On the right side of the window in Figure 7.1, the set of variables that derive λ is shown as [**A**]. A note mentions **3 more variable(s) needed** to complete this set. B also has a λ-production, so click on either of the B productions and B is added to the set.

Can C derive λ? It is not obvious, as C has no λ-production. However, the right side of $C \to B$ has only variables from the set of variables that derive λ, and no terminals, implying that C must also derive λ. Click on the C production to add C to the set.

Can any other variable derive λ? For the same reason above, the right side of $D \to AB$ has only variables that derive λ, and no terminals, so D also derives λ. Click and add D to the set. At this point the set is complete and JFLAP moves on to the next step.

> **Note** ‖ Why were S and E not added to the set? The right side of E's only production has a terminal, so it cannot derive λ. The right side of S's only production has the variable E, which does not derive λ.

The second step is to modify the grammar, resulting in an equivalent grammar with no λ-productions. The original grammar now appears on the right side of the window where we will delete λ-productions and add replacement productions.

To delete the λ-productions, select them on the right side of the window and then click **Delete**. Remove all the λ-productions.

We will add productions by entering them into the grammar on the right side of the window. For each production from the original grammar that has a λ-deriving variable appearing on its right side, we will enter a new production with that variable absent, unless the new production is a λ-production. For the production $A \rightarrow aAa$, enter the new production with the A missing, $A \rightarrow aa$.

Consider the production $D \rightarrow AB$. There are three new productions that could be generated with the A removed, the B removed, or both the A and B removed. But only the first two of these new productions can be added to the grammar, because removing both the A and the B will result in a λ-production. Edit the grammar at the right to add these two new productions $D \rightarrow B$ and $D \rightarrow A$.

An alternative way to add productions is to first select the production in the original grammar on the left side and then click **Complete Selected**. The new productions generated from this production are added to the grammar in the window on the right. Select $B \rightarrow bB$ in the original grammar and then click **Complete Selected**. The production $B \rightarrow b$ is added to the modified grammar.

Now add the remaining productions to the grammar.

Tip	There are three ways to add productions to the new grammar. One is to enter them in the grammar window. A second is to use the **Complete Selected** to add productions based on one production at a time. The third is to show the resulting grammar by using the **Do Step** or **Do All**.

When the λ removal is complete, a message appears in the window. At this point you can either proceed with the next transformation toward converting the grammar into CNF by clicking **Proceed**, or you can export this modified grammar into its own window by clicking **Export**.

Is the new grammar equivalent to the original grammar? Let's compare the two by parsing input strings. Export the new grammar. Start the brute-force parser for both the original grammar and the newly exported grammar. Parse the string a in both. These strings should be accepted by both. What do you observe by looking at the two parse trees? Parse the strings aa and $abaa$. Try several strings that are in the language and several that are not in the language.

7.1.2   Algorithm for Removing λ-Productions.

1. Start with a CFG $G = (V, T, P, S)$; V is the set of variables, T is the set of terminals, S is the start variable, and P is the set of productions.

2. Create the set V_λ, the set of variables deriving λ.

(a) For each variable A, if A has a λ-production, place A in V_λ.

(b) Repeat until no more variables can be added to V_λ.

    i. For each variable A not in V_λ, if there is an A production with a right side composed only of variables in V_λ, then add A to V_λ.

3. Generate the new grammar G'.

(a) Place all non-λ-productions from G in G'.

(b) For each production R in G', if the right side of R contains any variables from V_λ, create new productions with all combinations of these variables missing and place these new productions in G' if they are not λ-productions.

7.2   Removing Unit-Productions

In this section we will remove unit-productions from a CFG. A unit-production in a CFG has only a single variable on the right side. Unit-productions are not helpful in parsing, as they do not add another terminal in a derivation and they do not increase the length of the sentential form. Unit-productions can cause problems with parsing if they create a cycle such as $A \overset{*}{\Rightarrow} B$ and $B \overset{*}{\Rightarrow} A$.

The idea in removing unit-productions is to identify unit-derivations, remove unit-productions, and add productions that replace unit-derivations so the resulting grammar has no unit-productions, but is equivalent to the original grammar. If there is a unit-derivation $A \overset{*}{\Rightarrow} B$, then A productions must be added so A can derive any form that B could previously derive.

We use a variable dependency graph (VDG) to represent all the unit-productions and to derive all the unit-derivations. In the VDG, variables are represented as nodes, and unit productions are represented as directed edges from one variable to another. For example, an edge from node A to node C represents a unit-production $A \rightarrow C$. If there is a path from variable node A to variable node B in the completed VDG, then $A \overset{*}{\Rightarrow} B$.

7.2.1   The Transformation

Start JFLAP and either enter the grammar shown in Figure 7.2 or load the file ex7.2. This grammar has three unit-productions.

Select **Convert : Transform Grammar**. The **Unit Removal** window appears as shown in Figure 7.2. The original grammar appears on the left side of the window. The new grammar will be created on the right side. Above the grammar editor is an incomplete variable dependency graph (VDG).

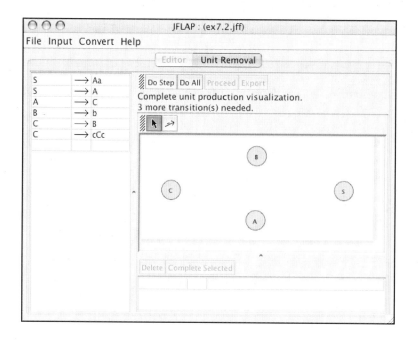

Figure 7.2: A CFG with unit-productions.

Note | Why didn't the Lambda Removal window appear as it did in Section 7.1 when we selected the option **Transform Grammar**? There are no λ-productions in this grammar, so the first transformation is skipped.

The first step is to complete the VDG. For each variable in the grammar, there is a node labeled with that variable in the graph. Since nodes are predetermined, JFLAP has already created the nodes. These nodes can be moved around using the Attribute Editor tool ⬉. A VDG represents the unit-productions in the grammar as transitions so that unit-derivations can be visualized. For each unit-production, an edge should be added between the two labeled nodes in the VDG. For example, for the unit-production $S \rightarrow A$, add an edge from node S to node A. To create this edge, select the Transition Creator tool ⬈. Then press the mouse cursor down on the S node, drag the cursor to the A node, and release the mouse button. Note that in this graph there are no labels on the edges. Add edges for the remaining unit-productions.

Note | How many unit-derivations are there in the completed VDG? There are three unit-productions (these are also unit-derivations), and visually we see three additional unit-derivations $S\overset{*}{\Rightarrow}C$, $S\overset{*}{\Rightarrow}B$, and $A\overset{*}{\Rightarrow}B$.

When the dependency graph is complete, the grammar editor below it becomes enabled and the original grammar appears. The next step is to modify this grammar to delete the unit-productions and add equivalent productions. We will now modify this grammar.

For each unit-production, we will remove it and replace it with equivalent productions. For variables A and B such that $A \overset{*}{\Rightarrow} B$ in the original grammar, for each non-unit-production $B \to w$ we will add the production $A \to w$.

To modify the grammar, we first remove the production $S \to A$, the only unit-production with S on the left side of the production. In the grammar editor window in the right-lower portion of the window, select $S \to A$ and then click **Delete**.

Next add S productions to the grammar by entering them in the grammar editor. Since $S \overset{*}{\Rightarrow} A$, $S \overset{*}{\Rightarrow} C$, and $S \overset{*}{\Rightarrow} B$, all nonunit right sides for A productions, C productions, and B productions are added as right sides of an S production. There are two such new productions. Enter $S \to b$ (due to $B \to b$) and $S \to cCc$ (due to $C \to cCc$).

An alternative way to generate new A productions for a variable A is to select one of the A unit-productions in the right grammar table and then click **Complete Selected**. The A unit-production is deleted and the new A productions are added.

Complete the grammar. A message appears above the VDG when the unit removal is complete. At this point you can either proceed with the next transformation toward converting the grammar into CNF by clicking **Proceed**, or you can export this modified grammar into its own window by clicking **Export**.

Tip	There are three ways to add productions to the new grammar. One is to enter them in the grammar window. A second is to use the **Complete Selected** to replace a unit-production with equivalent productions, one unit-production at a time. The third is to show the resulting grammar by using the **Do Step** or **Do All**, which are the same here, as this is the last step.

Is the new grammar equivalent to the original grammar? Compare the two grammars by parsing input strings. Export the new grammar and start the brute-force parser. Start the brute-force parser for the original grammar as well. Parse the string *cbca* in both. These strings should be accepted by both. What do you observe by looking at the two parse trees? Try several strings that are in the language and several that are not in the language.

7.2.2 Algorithm for Removing Unit-Productions

1. Start with a CFG $G = (V, T, P, S)$; V is the set of variables, T is the set of terminals, S is the start variable, and P is the set of productions.

2. Draw the VDG and determine the unit-derivations. Each variable from the grammar is represented as a labeled node in the VDG. For each unit-production $A \to B$, add a transition from node q_A to node q_B in the VDG. $A \overset{*}{\Rightarrow} C$ if there is a path from A to C in the VDG.

3. Generate the new grammar G'.

(a) Place all non-unit-productions from G in G'.

(b) For each unit-derivation $A \overset{*}{\Rightarrow} B$ from G, for each B production $B \to w$ in G', add the production $A \to w$ to G'.

7.3 Removing Useless Productions

In this section we will remove useless productions from a grammar. A production is useless if no derivation can use it. Removing useless productions is a two-step process. First, find variables that cannot derive any string of terminals and remove productions with those variables. Second, find variables that are unreachable from the start symbol and remove productions with those variables. All remaining productions in the grammar are useful for deriving strings from the grammar's language.

7.3.1 The Transformation

Start JFLAP and either enter the grammar shown in Figure 7.3 or load the file ex7.3.

Select **Convert : Transform Grammar**. Note that this grammar has no λ-productions or unit-productions, so those transformations are skipped. The **Useless Removal** window appears and should look similar to Figure 7.3. The original grammar appears on the left side of the window. The new grammar will be created on the right side. Above the grammar editor for creating the new grammar is an incomplete VDG.

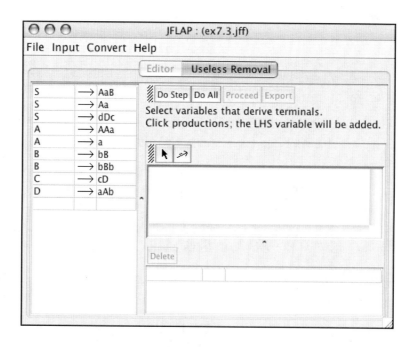

Figure 7.3: Useless production removal.

The first step is to identify those variables that can derive a string of terminals. For example, the production $A \to a$ is an obvious production showing that A can derive a terminal. Click on either of the A productions. On the upper-right portion of the window, the set of variables that derive terminals is shown as [**A**]. A note mentions **3 more variable(s) needed** to complete this set. There are no obvious variables as there are no more right sides that have only terminals.

Can S derive a string of terminals? It is not clear yet. All the S productions have at least one variable on the right side for which we do not know if it derives a string of terminals. Can D derive a string of terminals? Yes, the production $D \to aAb$ indicates it can, as the right side contains only terminals and variables that can derive a string of terminals. Add D to the set and determine the remaining variables.

Once you have identified the variables that can derive terminals, JFLAP presents you with a VDG and a grammar on the right side of the window. Both use only the variables that derive terminals. Productions that contain variables that cannot derive terminals have been eliminated from the grammar shown on the left side of the window.

The next step is to identify those variables that are reachable from the start variable. In the VDG, add an edge from variable A to variable B if there is an A production with B on the right side. At most, one edge is added from A to B and edges are not added for loops, A to A. For example, for the production $S \to AaD$, add the edges S to A and S to D. For the production $A \to AAa$, no edges are added. Add the remaining edges to the VDG.

Note ‖ How are the edges in this VDG defined differently than the edges in the VDG for unit-production removal? In unit-production removal an edge was drawn only for unit-productions.

The final step is to examine the VDG to determine those variables that are not reachable from the start variable. For those variables that are not reachable, remove their productions. For example, in the VDG note that there is no path from S to C. To remove the one C production in the right grammar editor, select it and then click **Delete**.

Does it make sense to compare the modified grammar with the original grammar, as we have done with λ-production removal and unit-production removal? Not really. Our modified grammar is smaller, but derivations will be the same in both grammars. We removed productions that were not useful.

7.3.2 Algorithm for Removing Useless Productions

1. Start with a CFG $G = (V, T, P, S)$; V is the set of variables, T is the set of terminals, S is the start variable, and P is the set of productions.

2. Create the set V_T, the set of variables deriving strings of terminals.

(a) For each variable A, if A's right side has only terminals or variables in V_T, place A in V_T.

(b) Repeat until no more variables can be added to V_T.

3. Let the new grammar $G' = G$. Then remove from G' all productions that contain variables that are not in V_T.

4. Draw the VDG. Each variable in G' is represented as a labeled node in the VDG. For each variable A, add an edge from A to B if B appears on the right side of an A production.

5. Modify G' to remove useless productions. For any variable A in the VDG that is not reachable from S, remove all A productions from G'.

7.4   Converting a CFG to CNF

In this section we will transform a CFG to Chomsky Normal Form (CNF). CNF is a restricted form of a CFG. In CNF, the right side of a production is either a single terminal or two variables. This restricted right side results in faster parsing times.

The idea in transforming a CFG to CNF is to replace each terminal in a right side of length greater than one by a variable, and then to replace each pair of adjacent variables by another variable until all right sides of productions with variables have exactly two variables. Note that λ-productions and unit-productions are not in CNF, so they must be removed.

7.4.1   The Transformation

We have already learned the first three steps in converting a CFG to CNF: removing λ-productions, removing unit-productions, and removing useless productions. This section will focus on the last step in the conversion.

Start JFLAP and either enter the grammar shown in Figure 7.4 or load the file `ex7.4`.

Select **Convert : Transform Grammar**. The **Chomsky Converter** window appears and should look similar to Figure 7.4. The original grammar appears on the left side of the window for reference. On the right side is a copy of the grammar that will be modified. The message **3 production(s) must be converted** appears in the upper right portion of the window.

> **Note** ‖ Which one of the four productions is already in CNF?

We will convert the simpler productions first. All interactions are with the grammar on the right side of the window. Select the production $A \rightarrow Aa$ from this side. This production needs to be replaced by two equivalent productions that are in CNF. Click **Convert Selected**. The production

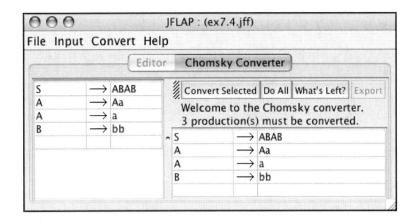

Figure 7.4: Conversion of a CFG to CNF.

is replaced by two equivalent productions. In this case, $B(a)$ is a new variable representing the terminal a, as the new production $B(a) \rightarrow a$ indicates.

> **Note** ‖ In JFLAP each terminal x is replaced with a new variable $B(x)$, with one exception. If
> there exists a production $A \rightarrow a$ that is the only A production, then JFLAP will use A
> for a replacement for a instead of creating a new variable.

Select the production $B \rightarrow bb$ and then click **Convert Selected**. In this case only one new variable $B(b)$ is added in $B \rightarrow B(b)B(b)$.

There is now only one production left to convert, $S \rightarrow ABAB$. Select this production. The right-hand side of this production is too long, so pairs of adjacent variables need to be replaced by new variables until all new productions have the correct length. In JFLAP these new variables will be $D(n)$ where n is an integer starting with 1. Click **Convert Selected** to divide this production into two productions $S \rightarrow AD(1)$ and $D(1) \rightarrow BAB$ with a new variable $D(1)$. The latter production needs further splitting. Select $D(1) \rightarrow BAB$ and click **Convert Selected** to split it into $D(1) \rightarrow BD(2)$ and $D(2) \rightarrow AB$. No further splitting is necessary, since all productions with variables in the right side now have exactly two variables on the right side.

At this point the conversion is complete. The variables of the form $B(x)$ and $D(n)$ are temporary variables used only for the conversion algorithm. When the grammar is exported, they will be replaced with variables allowable in grammars.

> **Note** ‖ If the reformed grammar has more than 26 variables, it cannot be exported in JFLAP.

Export the grammar now and compare it with the original grammar by running the brute-force parser with both of them on the input string *aaabbaabb*. Which one will take longer to parse? Which parse tree will be smaller?

7.4.2   Algorithm for Converting a CFG to CNF.

1. Start with a CFG $G = (V, T, P, S)$; V is the set of variables, T is the set of terminals, S is the start variable, and P is the set of productions.

2. Remove λ-productions.

3. Remove unit-productions.

4. Remove useless productions.

5. For each terminal a that appears in the right side of a production of length greater than one, replace a by the variable $B(a)$ and add the production $B(a) \to a$ to P if it is not already there. There is one exception: This step is not needed if the production $A \to a$ is the only A production.

6. For each production that has more than two variables on the right-hand side, such as $A \to X_1 X_2, \ldots, X_m$ where m is greater than 2, replace the production with two productions $A \to X_1 D(n)$ and $D(n) \to X_2, \ldots, X_m$, where n is an integer and $D(n)$ is a new variable. If there is already a $D(n)$ production for some n with the same right side, use that production instead of creating a new production.

7.5   Summary

In this chapter we learned how to convert a CFG to Chomsky Normal Form (CNF) in four steps using JFLAP. In Section 7.1 we transformed a CFG to a CFG with no λ-productions. We removed the λ-productions, identified the λ-deriving variables, and then added new productions that were copies of the old productions but with combinations of λ-deriving variables missing in the right sides.

In Section 7.2 we transformed a CFG to a CFG with no unit-productions. We identified unit-derivations, removed unit-productions, and then added new productions that were old right sides with new left sides of variables that could derive these right sides.

In Section 7.3 we transformed a CFG to a CFG with no useless productions. We identified variables that do not derive strings of terminals and removed all productions that contain such variables, and then identified variables that are not reachable from the start variable and removed all productions that contain such variables.

In Section 7.4 we transformed a CFG to CNF. After doing the three previous transformations, all terminals in right sides of length two or greater were replaced by a current variable, if possible, or a new variable and production. Then each right side of variables of length greater than two were replaced by a new variable and productions of pairs of variables.

7.6 Exercises

1. For each CFG, remove the λ-productions using JFLAP.

   (a) `ex7.6lambda-a`

   (b) `ex7.6lambda-b`

   (c) `ex7.6lambda-c`

   (d) `ex7.6lambda-d`

   (e) `ex7.6lambda-e`

2. For each CFG, remove the unit-productions using JFLAP. These grammars do not have any λ-productions.

   (a) `ex7.6unit-a`

   (b) `ex7.6unit-b`

   (c) `ex7.6unit-c`

   (d) `ex7.6unit-d`

   (e) `ex7.6unit-e`

3. For each CFG, remove the useless productions using JFLAP. These grammars do not have any λ-productions or unit-productions.

   (a) `ex7.6useless-a`

   (b) `ex7.6useless-b`

   (c) `ex7.6useless-c`

   (d) `ex7.6useless-d`

   (e) `ex7.6useless-e`

4. For each CFG, convert the grammar to CNF. These grammars do not have any λ-productions, unit-productions, or useless productions.

   (a) `ex7.6cnfonly-a`

   (b) `ex7.6cnfonly-b`

   (c) `ex7.6cnfonly-c`

   (d) `ex7.6cnfonly-d`

   (e) `ex7.6cnfonly-e`

5. For each CFG, convert the grammar to CNF. These grammars may have λ-productions, unit-productions, or useless productions.

   (a) `ex7.6cnf-a`

   (b) `ex7.6cnf-b`

   (c) `ex7.6cnf-c`

   (d) `ex7.6cnf-d`

   (e) `ex7.6cnf-e`

   (f) `ex7.6cnf-f`

6. Convert the CFG in `ex7.6cnfNoB` to CNF. Explain why there are no $B(x)$ variables generated.

7. Convert the CFG in `ex7.cnfparse` to CNF. Export the grammar after removing λ-productions, again after removing unit-productions, again after removing useless-productions, and finally after converting to CNF. Start the brute-force parser in each of the three grammar windows and parse the string *aabab*. For each of the four grammars, compare the number of nodes generated for the derivation tree (the number is given beside the **String accepted!** message) and the size of the resulting parse tree.

Chapter 8

LL and SLR Parsing

All the grammars we have parsed thus far have used the brute-force parser. In Section 6.1 we saw that brute-force parsing can be very inefficient. In this chapter we will learn two new parsing methods in JFLAP that are more efficient: LL parsing and SLR parsing. These methods use the symbols in the string and the productions to guide the parsing by incorporating such information in a parse table.

Section 8.1 describes how to compute FIRST and FOLLOW sets, functions that are needed for building both LL and SLR parse tables. Section 8.2 explains LL parsing, and Section 8.3 explains SLR parsing. The latter two sections also explain how to convert grammars into NPDAs that model the method, and how to use and build a parse table for the method.

8.1   Getting Started on Parse Tables: FIRST and FOLLOW Sets

Both LL and SLR parsing methods compute functions called FIRST and FOLLOW to aid in constructing their parse tables.

8.1.1   FIRST Sets

FIRST determines candidates for the first terminal to start a string. The FIRST function is given a string w formed of variables and terminals and returns a set of terminals that begin strings derived from w. Thus a terminal a is in $\text{FIRST}(w)$ if $w \overset{*}{\Rightarrow} av$, where v is a string of terminals and variables. The terminal a is the terminal that begins the derived string. If $w \overset{*}{\Rightarrow} \lambda$, then λ is in $\text{FIRST}(w)$.

Both LL and SLR parsing need to compute $\text{FIRST}(V)$ for each variable V in a grammar, and also $\text{FIRST}(w)$ for some strings w made up of terminals and variables. $\text{FIRST}(V)$ is the union of FIRST applied to all the right sides of V's productions. Let's look at some examples in JFLAP.

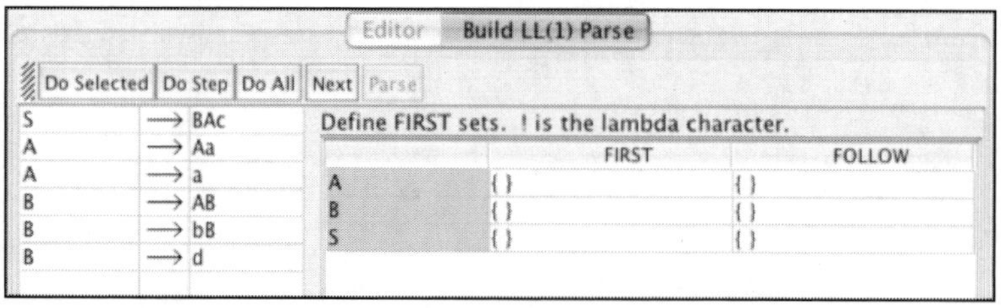

Figure 8.1: Computing FIRST in LL parser Window.

Example of FIRST when grammar has no λ-production

Start JFLAP and either enter the grammar shown in Figure 8.1 or load the file `ex8.1a`. FIRST sets are computed as the first step in both the LL and SLR parsing algorithms. We will select the LL parser and only look at FIRST sets for now. In the next section we will learn more about the LL parsing process. Select **Input : LL(1) Parse**. A message appears stating **The grammar is not LL(1). Continue anyway?** Since we only want to compute FIRST sets, ignore this message for now. Click on **Yes**. In Figure 8.1, the grammar is shown on the left side of the window. JFLAP is waiting for FIRST sets to be entered for each variable.

This grammar does not have a λ-production. The computation of FIRST for the variables in this grammar is simple, as the first terminal of a string will come from its leftmost symbol. Suppose that string $w = Xv$ where X is either a terminal or variable and v is a string of terminals and variables. If the grammar has no λ-production, and thus no variable can derive λ, then $\text{FIRST}(Xv) = \text{FIRST}(X)$.

Let's compute FIRST for all the variables in this grammar, starting with A and applying FIRST to the right sides of all of A's productions. A's production $A \to a$ indicates a is in $\text{FIRST}(A)$. Enter a by clicking on the entry in row A under the FIRST column, typing a, and pressing enter. A's other production is $A \to Aa$. $\text{FIRST}(Aa)$ is equivalent to $\text{FIRST}(A)$, which is redundant. This production does not place anything into $\text{FIRST}(A)$.

> **Note** To enter FIRST and FOLLOW sets, click on the entry and type the items. There is no separator between symbols, e.g., type bcd to enter in b, c, and d in the same entry. Lambda is entered as ! and converts to λ after it is entered.

Now compute $\text{FIRST}(B)$. The production $B \to bB$ clearly derives a string that starts with b, and the production $B \to d$ clearly derives a string that starts with d. Enter both b and d into $\text{FIRST}(B)$ now. No spaces are needed; enter them as bd. The production $B \to AB$ derives a string that starts with symbols from $\text{FIRST}(A)$, so also enter a into $\text{FIRST}(B)$.

> **Note** Since $\text{FIRST}(B)$ depends on $\text{FIRST}(A)$, if any other symbol is added to $\text{FIRST}(A)$ it must also be added to $\text{FIRST}(B)$.

Finish the example by computing FIRST(S) and then click on **Next**. If any of the FIRST sets are incorrect, they will be highlighted. If the message **Define FOLLOW sets** appears, then the FIRST sets are correct.

Example of FIRST when grammar has λ-productions

When a grammar has a λ-production, variables in a sentential form can disappear. FIRST(w), for string w, may have to look at additional symbols to compute all terminals that can start its derivation. Assume the string $w = Xv$, where X is a variable or terminal and v is a string of variables and terminals. If X is a terminal or a variable that does not derive λ, then calculate FIRST as in the previous section. If X derives λ, then FIRST(w) is the union of FIRST(X) $- \{\lambda\}$ and FIRST(v). If w is λ, then FIRST(λ) $= \{\lambda\}$. For example, FIRST(C) would include e if A, B, and C all could derive λ, and thus could disappear.

Let's look at a grammar with several λ-productions and calculate the FIRST sets for its variables. Using JFLAP, either load the file **ex8.1b** or enter the grammar:

$$S \rightarrow ABcC$$
$$A \rightarrow aA$$
$$A \rightarrow \lambda$$
$$B \rightarrow bbB$$
$$B \rightarrow \lambda$$
$$C \rightarrow BA$$

Select **Input : LL(1) Parse**. There are four FIRST sets to compute. Which one do you compute first? There are two easy ones, A and B. The production $A \rightarrow aA$ puts a in A's FIRST set and the production $A \rightarrow \lambda$ puts λ into A's FIRST set. To enter λ, type "!". Enter both A and B's FIRST set. Then click on **Next** to check if they are correct. If you are correct, JFLAP will only highlight the entries FIRST(C) and FIRST(S).

Try to compute FIRST(C) and FIRST(S) on your own now. Then read the explanation for computing them that follows. To begin, consider computing FIRST(C). By the production $C \rightarrow BA$, FIRST(C) is ((FIRST(B) $- \{\lambda\}) \cup$ (FIRST(A) $- \{\lambda\})) \cup \{\lambda\} = \{b, a, \lambda\}$. The symbols minus λ in FIRST(B) are included, as B is the leftmost symbol in BA. FIRST(A) minus λ is included since $B \overset{*}{\Rightarrow} \lambda$. We do a special check at the end to see if $C \overset{*}{\Rightarrow} \lambda$, and add λ to FIRST(C).

Next, consider computing FIRST(S). By the production $S \rightarrow ABcC$, FIRST(S) is ((FIRST(A)$\cup$ FIRST(B) $\cup$ FIRST(c)) $- \{\lambda\}) = \{a, b, c\}$. FIRST($A$) puts a and λ in FIRST(S). FIRST(B) puts b and λ in FIRST(S). FIRST(c) puts c in FIRST(S). Then λ is taken out of FIRST(S). Here, the λ is taken out and not put back in, since S cannot derive λ. Click on **Next** to see if the FIRST sets have been entered correctly.

8.1.2   Definition of FIRST

We give the formal definition of FIRST:

1. $\text{FIRST}(\lambda) = \{\lambda\}$

2. For terminal a, $\text{FIRST}(a) = \{a\}$.

3. For variable A, $\text{FIRST}(A)$ is the union of $\text{FIRST}(w)$ for all right sides w of A.

4. Let every X_i be either a terminal or a variable.

   $\text{FIRST}(X_1 X_2 X_3 \ldots X_N) = \text{FIRST}(X_1)$ if X_1 does not derive λ

   $\text{FIRST}(X_1 X_2 X_3 \ldots X_N) = \text{FIRST}(X_1) - \{\lambda\} \cup \text{FIRST}(X_2 X_3 \ldots X_N)$ if $X_1 \overset{*}{\Rightarrow} \lambda$

8.1.3   FOLLOW Sets

The FOLLOW function applied to variable A returns a set of terminals that can immediately follow A in some derivation. For the termination of a string we introduce an end-of-string marker, \$, and tack the \$ onto the end of any string we are parsing. Now every variable will be followed by some marker, either a terminal or a \$. Suppose S is the start variable. If $S \overset{*}{\Rightarrow} w$, then with \$ tacked onto the end of the string (and thus also tacked onto the end of the start symbol), the derivation is now $S\$ \overset{*}{\Rightarrow} w\$$. Thus, \$ is always in $\text{FOLLOW}(S)$.

Let's look at some examples of computing FOLLOW using JFLAP.

Example of FOLLOW when grammar has no λ-production

The first example is the same first grammar in the FIRST section. If the JFLAP window for file `ex8.1a` is no longer up, then either enter the grammar shown in Figure 8.1 or load the file. Remember that this grammar does not have a λ-production.

FOLLOW sets are computed after FIRST sets are computed in both the LL and SLR parsing algorithms. We will select the LL parser and only look at the FIRST and FOLLOW sets for now. Select **Input : LL(1) Parse**. A message appears stating **The grammar is not LL(1). Continue anyway?** Click on **Yes**. At this point we only want to compute the FIRST and FOLLOW sets, so ignore this message. Click on **Do Step** once to reveal the FIRST sets we already calculated.

To compute the FOLLOW set for a variable A, look at the right side of all productions to see where A appears and what immediately follows A. If the symbol that follows A is a terminal, then place the terminal in $\text{FOLLOW}(A)$. If the symbol that follows A is a variable B, then whatever first terminal B can derive is a terminal that can follow A in some derivation. If A is at the end of a production, say $B \rightarrow cA$, then everything in $\text{FOLLOW}(B)$ is in $\text{FOLLOW}(A)$.

Now we compute FOLLOW for all the variables in this example. FOLLOW(S) always includes the $, so enter $ for FOLLOW(S). Since S does not appear on the right side of any of the productions, FOLLOW(S) is complete.

Next we compute FOLLOW(A). From the production $S \rightarrow BAc$, c is in FOLLOW(A) and from the production $A \rightarrow Aa$, a is in FOLLOW(A). Enter a and c in FOLLOW(A). From the production $B \rightarrow AB$, FIRST(B) are terminals that can follow A in some derivation. Add those terminals to FOLLOW(A). (You do not need to add a again, as it is already in FOLLOW(A).) A does not appear on any other right side, so FOLLOW(A) is complete.

Next we compute FOLLOW(B). B appears on the right side in three productions. In $B \rightarrow AB$ and $B \rightarrow bB$, B appears at the end of a right side, but B also appears on the left side, so this implies that FOLLOW(B) is in FOLLOW(B), which is redundant. No new terminals are added. In the third production $S \rightarrow BAc$, B is followed immediately by A, so all terminals in FIRST(A) are placed in FOLLOW(B); in this case, just a. Enter a in FOLLOW(B) and click on **Next** to see if the FOLLOW sets are correct. If the message **Fill entries in parse table** appears, then the FOLLOW sets are correct.

Example of FOLLOW when grammar has λ-productions

When a grammar has λ-productions, variables may disappear and we may have to look at additional symbols in determining FOLLOW sets. For the production $A \rightarrow vBw$, where v and w are strings of variables and terminals, FOLLOW(B) has FIRST(w) $- \{\lambda\}$ in it. If FIRST(w) has λ in it, then that is the same as B appearing at the right end of the right side, so FOLLOW(A) is in FOLLOW(B).

The next example is the same second grammar in the FIRST section. If the JFLAP window for file `ex8.1b` is no longer up, then load the file. Then enter the FIRST sets. Note this grammar has two λ-productions.

Try now to compute the FOLLOW sets for the variables, and then read the explanation that follows. Since S does not appear on the right side of any production, only $ is in FOLLOW(S). C appears only in $S \rightarrow ABcC$, thus everything in FOLLOW(S) is in FOLLOW(C). B appears in three productions. $S \rightarrow ABcC$ puts c in FOLLOW(B) and $B \rightarrow bbB$ is redundant. $C \rightarrow BA$ puts terminal a from FIRST(A) in FOLLOW(B). Since λ is in FIRST(A), $C \rightarrow BA$ can be viewed as if B is at the end of the production, $C \rightarrow B$, and thus FOLLOW(C) is put into FOLLOW(B). A appears in three productions. $A \rightarrow aA$ is redundant. From $S \rightarrow ABcC$, FIRST(BcC) $= \{b, c\}$ is in FOLLOW(A). From $C \rightarrow BA$, FOLLOW(C) is in FOLLOW(A), thus $ is in FOLLOW(A). Click on **Next** to see if the FOLLOW sets are correct. If the message **Fill entries in parse table** appears, then the FOLLOW sets are correct.

Note ‖ There are some differences between FIRST and FOLLOW. The $ can be in a FOLLOW set, but not in a FIRST set. The λ can be in a FIRST set, but not in a FOLLOW set. FIRST can be applied to a string of variables and terminals, but FOLLOW is only applied to a single variable.

Observing terminals following variables

For each symbol in the FOLLOW sets, there is some sentential form in a derivation that shows that symbol following the variable. We will parse some strings for the preceeding example and see all the cases where a terminal follows a variable.

We want to leave the window with FOLLOW sets showing and start a new window with the same grammar. Load 8.1b-dup, which is a copy of the grammar in 8.1b. In the new window, select **Input : Brute Force Parse**. Click on **Noninverted Tree** and select **Derivation Table**. Move the two windows so that you can see both of them. We will need to examine the parsing of two strings to see all the symbols from the FOLLOW sets.

In the brute-force parser, parse the string *abbcbba* by clicking on **Start**, then follow by clicking on **Step** repeatedly until the derivation is complete. Examine the sentential forms. S, A, and C all appear at the end of some sentential form, thus $ follows the three of them. In some sentential forms, the substrings Bc, Ab, and Ba appear, thus showing a and c follow B, and b follows A. Now parse the string *acbb*. To see that $ follows B, see the sentential form *acbbBA*. Both the A and B are replaced by λ in the next two steps. In the derivation shown, B is replaced first, then A. If A was replaced first, then the sentential form would be *acbbB*. Thus, $ follows B. To see that c follows A, see the sentential form *aABcbbBA*. Again, in the next two steps, the leftmost A and then the leftmost B are replaced by λ. If B is replaced first, then the sentential form would be *aAcbbBA*. Thus, c follows A. We have shown an example for each symbol in a FOLLOW set following its corresponding variable.

8.1.4   Definition of FOLLOW

We give the formal definition of FOLLOW: Let S be the start symbol, A and B be variables, and v and w be strings of 0 or more variables and terminals.

1. $ is in FOLLOW(S).

2. For $A \rightarrow vB$, FOLLOW(A) is in FOLLOW(B).

3. For $A \rightarrow vBw$:

   (a) FIRST(w) $- \{\lambda\}$ is in FOLLOW(B).

   (b) If $\lambda \in$ FIRST(w), then FOLLOW(A) is in FOLLOW(B).

8.2 LL(1) Parsing

The type of LL parsing in JFLAP is LL(1) parsing. The first L means the input string is processed from left to right. The second L means the derivation will be a leftmost derivation (the leftmost variable is replaced at each step). The 1 means that one symbol in the input string guides the parse; that is, the parser *looks ahead* one symbol.

In this section we show how to parse strings with the LL(1) parser, how to compare LL(1) parsing with the LL(1) conversion of CFG to NPDA, and how to build the LL(1) parse table.

8.2.1 Parsing a String with the LL(1) Parser

Before showing how to build the LL(1) parse table, we show how to use the table to parse strings. Start JFLAP and load the file **ex8.1b** if that file is not open. Select **Input : LL(1) Parse**, and click on **Do All** to build the FIRST sets, FOLLOW sets, and the LL(1) Parse Table. Then click on **Parse**. The window should look similar to Figure 8.2, but with no parse tree and the **Input** and **Input Remaining** fields blank.

The LL(1) Parse Table appears in the top left corner of the window. Each row represents a variable in the grammar and each column represents a *lookahead*, the next symbol to match in the input string. A lookahead can be either a terminal in the grammar or the $. Each entry in the table is a right side of a production in which the left side is the variable for that row. For example, BA appears three times in the C row, representing $C \rightarrow BA$.

LL(1) parsing takes a *top-down* approach. That is, the parse tree is built by starting with the start symbol S and repeatedly replacing the leftmost variable in the sentential form until the string

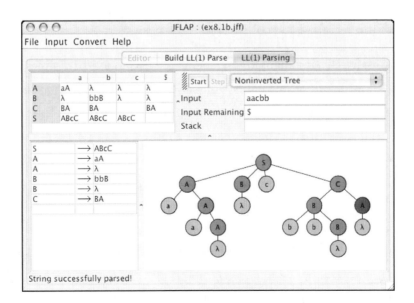

Figure 8.2: LL(1) Parsing Showing a Parse Tree.

has been derived. We will watch the parse tree being constructed for a derivation, starting at the *top* of the tree and building it *down*. Enter *aacbb* in the **Input** field. As this string is parsed and the tree is built top-down, note the highlighted productions in the parse table that are used. Click on **Start** and then click on **Step** repeatedly until the string is derived. The tree should look like the tree in Figure 8.2. Now we will look at the derivation. Click on **Noninverted Tree** and select **Derivation Table**. Examine the sequence of sequential forms under **Derivation** and note that the leftmost variable is replaced at each step.

How does LL(1) parsing work? A stack stores variables and terminals from right sides of productions, processing them by replacing variables with new productions and matching the terminals with corresponding terminals in the input string. The start symbol of the grammar is placed on top of the stack to start. Variables are popped off the stack and replaced by the right side of a production, and terminals are popped off and matched in the order they appear in the string. When the stack is empty and all the terminals in the string have been matched, the string has been derived. How does the LL(1) parser know which production to use? The terminals in the input string are matched from left to right. The part of the string that has not been matched yet is called the *in*put remaining. The leftmost symbol of the input remaining is the lookahead. For a particular variable, the production to use is chosen by comparing the variable's right sides with the lookahead. If all the terminals have been matched, then $ is the lookahead.

We will go through the example again, this time examining more details in the window. First change **Derivation Table** back to **Noninverted Tree**. Click on **Start**. The field **Input Remaining** has the input string followed by $, and the lookahead is *a* (the first symbol in *aacbb*$). All the terminals in the input remaining (except $) must be matched for this string to be derived. Click on **Step** and S is placed on the stack and also placed as the root of the tree. The derivation can now begin. Click on **Step** again. The production $S \rightarrow ABcC$ is highlighted in the table, the message **Replacing S with ABcC** is shown at the bottom of the window, and S has been popped off the stack. Note that the highlighted table entry is in column *a*. Recall columns represent possible lookaheads, and *a* is the current lookahead. Click on **Step** four times and observe the Stack and parse tree. The right side $ABcC$ (with A on top) is placed onto the stack. In the parse tree, the variables in S's right side $ABcC$ become children of S. A is on top of the stack, so A will be replaced by an A production next, but which A production? The lookahead is *a*, so the A production in the *a* column will be chosen. Click on **Step**. The A has been popped off the stack, the production $A \rightarrow aA$ in the *a* column is highlighted, and the message **Replacing A with aA** is shown at the bottom of the window. Click on **Step** twice and the right side aA is pushed onto the stack, with *a* on top. At this point the top of the stack is a terminal and it matches the lookahead. Click on **Step**. The *a* on top of the stack is popped off and the matching *a* is removed from the input remaining. The new lookahead is *a*. Continue stepping through the example. When there is a variable on top of the stack, it will be replaced by the right side that appears in the column of the lookahead. When there is a terminal on top of the stack, it matches the lookahead.

When JFLAP finishes with the example, the message **String successfully parsed!** appears at the bottom of the window. For a string to be accepted, the stack must be empty and all the symbols in the input string must be matched. Examine the stack and input remaining from the example. The stack is empty and the input remaining is $.

What happens when you parse a string that is not in the language? There are different types of errors that can occur. A string is rejected if the top of the stack is a terminal and it does not match the current lookahead, or if the top of the stack is a variable and there is not a rule in the entry for that variable under the column for the current lookahead. Try parsing the strings *bca* and *cca* that should not be accepted and identify the errors.

8.2.2   Comparing with Corresponding NPDA

Section 6.2 showed how to use JFLAP to convert a CFG to an equivalent NPDA that modeled the LL parsing method. Now we will convert the example grammar to an NPDA to see how the LL parsing method works using an NPDA.

Using file **ex8.1b** from the last example, select **Convert : Convert CFG to PDA (LL)**. The NPDA has three states. The transition from q_0 to q_1 pushes S onto the stack. The transition from q_1 to q_2 verifies the stack is empty. Click on **Show All** to complete the NPDA and then **Export** to place it in an NPDA window. The NPDA is shown in Figure 8.3. Note the top six transitions on q_1 are the productions in the grammar, popping the left side and pushing the right side onto the stack. The bottom three transitions are for matching the terminals and removing them from the stack.

This NPDA is nondeterministic. We will parse the same string we did earlier. To simulate the LL parser, you will need to decide which configuration is correct when there are multiple configurations. Select **Input : Step with Closure** and enter the input string *aacbb*. Click on

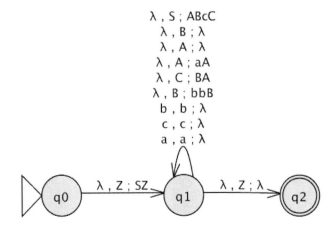

Figure 8.3: CFG to NPDA Using the LL Method.

Step twice. The S is pushed onto the stack, and then S is replaced by $ABcC$ with A on top. Click on **Step** again. Since there are two A productions, both of them were applied creating two configurations. The correct configuration is the one in which aA was pushed onto the stack, as the a in aA is needed to match the a in the lookahead. Click on the other configuration (with stack $BcCZ$) and then click on **Remove**. Click on **Step**. The lookahead a was matched and is now shaded in the input string. The a was removed from the top of the stack. Continue the parsing to derive the string using the LL(1) method by removing configurations whenever more than one occurs, leaving the one that the LL(1) method would choose.

8.2.3   Building the LL(1) Parse Table

Using JFLAP, we will build an LL(1) Parse Table for the grammar in file `ex8.1b`. Recall that the rows in the LL(1) Parse Table represent variables, the columns represent lookaheads, and the entries represent a right side of a production. For each production $A \rightarrow w$, we must decide which symbols could be the lookahead. FIRST(w) are all the terminals that can start a string, and thus are candidates. If λ is in FIRST(w), then candidates include those symbols that can follow A. For $A \rightarrow w$, w will be entered in the A row under the columns that are valid lookaheads.

In the LL(1) parsing window for file `ex8.1b`, dismiss all the tabs until the grammar is shown. Select **Input : LL(1) Parse** and click on **Do Step** twice to list the FIRST and FOLLOW sets.

The production $S \rightarrow ABcC$ should be entered in the S row for all symbols in FIRST($ABcC$) = $\{a, b, c\}$. Enter $ABcC$ in columns a, b, and c. For $A \rightarrow aA$, enter aA in row A under column a. For $A \rightarrow \lambda$, enter λ in row A under columns for symbols in FOLLOW(A) = $\{\$, c, b\}$. Recall that λ is entered by typing !. For $C \rightarrow BA$, FIRST(BA) = $\{b, a, \lambda\}$, so enter BA in row B under columns a and b. Since λ is in FIRST(BA), enter BA in row C under the $\$$ column, as FOLLOW(C) = $\{\$\}$. Continue making entries in the table and click on **Next** when done.

8.2.4   Algorithm for Building an LL(1) Parse Table

Let A be a variable and w be a string of 0 or more variables and terminals. Let T be the parse table, and T[A,a] represent the entry in row A, column a.

For each production $A \rightarrow w$:

1. For each terminal a in FIRST(w), put w in entry T[A,a].

2. If λ is in FIRST(w), put w in entry T[A,b] for each b in FOLLOW(A).

8.2.5   When a CFG Is Not LL(1)

The first grammar in this chapter from file `ex8.1a` was not LL(1). Load the file again in JFLAP and select **Input : LL(1) Parse**. JFLAP informs you that it is not LL(1), but lets you continue anyway. Enter in the FIRST and FOLLOW sets. Try making entries in the parse table and then read the explanation. For $A \rightarrow a$, enter a in the a column. For $A \rightarrow Aa$, FIRST$(Aa) = \{a\}$ so it should also be entered in the a column. Both can be entered in by entering a space between them. This grammar is not LL(1) because there is more than one production for variable A and lookahead a. JFLAP allows the parse table to be built with conflicts, but parsing cannot occur. Note that when the table has been entered, the **Parse** button is disabled.

8.3 SLR(1) Parsing

The type of LR parsing in JFLAP is SLR(1) parsing. The S stands for *simple* LR. The L means the input string is processed from left to right, as in LL(1) parsing. The R means the derivation will be a rightmost derivation (the rightmost variable is replaced at each step). The 1 means that one symbol in the input string is used to help guide the parse. There are several other types of LR parsing.

In this section we will examine how SLR(1) parsing works, convert a CFG to an NPDA using the SLR(1) method, and show how to build the SLR(1) Parse Table. We will look at three example grammars. The first grammar has no λ-production. The second grammar has a λ-production and a more complex structure than the first grammar. In the third example, we will see how to parse a CFG that is not SLR(1).

8.3.1 Parsing a String with the SLR(1) Parser

Before building the SLR(1) parse table, we will show how to parse strings using the table. Start JFLAP and load the file `ex8.3a` or enter the following grammar:

$$S \rightarrow A$$
$$A \rightarrow aaA$$
$$A \rightarrow b$$

Note that this grammar has three productions. Select **Input : SLR(1) Parse**, and click on **Do All**. Ignore all of these items for now and click on **Parse**.

The window should look similar to Figure 8.4, but with no parse tree and the **Input** and **Input Remaining** fields blank. The grammar is in the lower left part of the window. Note that the grammar now has four productions. SLR(1) parsing adds a new variable to the grammar as a new start symbol, S'. It also adds the new production $S' \rightarrow S$. This new production ensures that there is only one production that can start a derivation. The new production is the last production processed in SLR(1) parsing.

SLR(1) parsing works bottom-up, starting with terminals and applying productions in reverse. The right sides of productions are replaced by the left sides repeatedly until the start symbol is

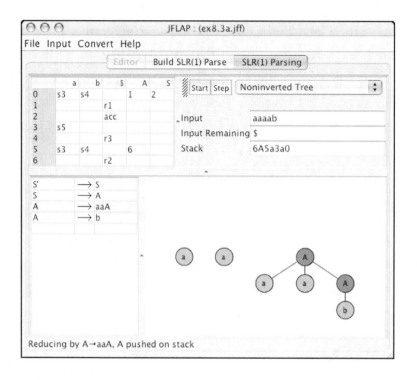

Figure 8.4: Creating the Parse Tree for SLR(1).

derived. The parse tree is thus built from the bottom to the top. We will watch the parse tree being constructed in a derivation. The parse tree will be constructed in the bottom right side of the window. Enter *aaaab* in the **Input** field. As this string is parsed, notice the highlighted productions used. Click on **Start**, and then click on **Step** five times. Five nodes representing the five terminals have been created in the parse tree. Note that there are no right sides in the parse tree until the *b* appears. The *b* is the right side of $A \rightarrow b$. Click on **Step** twice. The *A* node is created and linked to *b*, representing $A \rightarrow b$. This production is also highlighted. Note that there is now another right side appearing in the nodes, *aaA*. Click on **Step** repeatedly until the tree is complete. Note that S' is not part of the tree. The new production was not part of the original grammar, so it does not appear in the parse tree.

Now look at the derivation. Click on **Noninverted Tree** and select **Derivation Table**. The derivation starts with the string and applies productions backward, with the right side of a production replaced by the left side of a production, until the start symbol S' is derived.

8.3.2   Conversion of CFG to NPDA Using the SLR(1) Method

Section 6.2 showed how JFLAP converts a CFG to an equivalent NPDA that models the LL parsing method. There are other methods of conversion from a CFG to an NPDA. We will now convert our example CFG to an NPDA that models the SLR parsing method.

Select **Convert : Convert CFG to PDA (LR)**. The start of an NPDA appears as shown

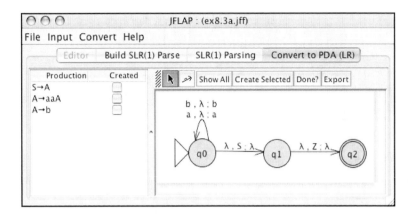

Figure 8.5: Building an NPDA for SLR(1) parsing.

in Figure 8.5. Similar to the NPDA constructed for LL(1) parsing, this NPDA will also have three states, with most of the work done in one state. For SLR(1), most of the work is in the initial state, q_0. In q_0, all the terminals are pushed onto the stack, and the right side of productions is replaced by the corresponding left side of productions until the start symbol S is on the stack. The transition from q_0 to q_1 pops S off the stack, and the transition from q_1 to q_2 ensures the stack is empty.

There are two types of transitions in q_0. First, for each terminal in the grammar, there is a transition on q_0 that reads the terminal and pushes it onto the stack. This is referred to as *shifting* symbols onto the stack. The two transitions for shifting a and b have already been added to the NPDA and are shown on q_0 in Figure 8.5. Second, there is a transition for each production in the grammar that pops the right side off the stack and pushes the left side onto the stack. This is referred to as *reducing* by a production. These transitions must be added. Note that the grammar appears on the left side of the window with **Created** check boxes.

In JFLAP, each production $A \rightarrow BCD$ will be replaced by a loop transition on q_0 with the label $\lambda, DCB; A$. Note the BCD appears backward on the stack (with D on top). The BCD is popped off the stack and replaced by pushing A onto the stack. Select the transition tool and click on state q_0. Add the missing transitions. Each production will be checked off as it is entered. When the NPDA is complete, click on **Export** to put it into an NPDA window.

> **Tip**   Similar to the creation of an NPDA using LL(1) parsing, labels can also be created by
> selecting a production and then clicking on **Create Selected**.

We now parse a string using this NPDA to see how the SLR(1) method works, and to observe the nondeterminism. Select **Input : Step with Closure** and enter the same string we parsed earlier, *aaaab*. Click on **Step** five times and observe that all the terminals are pushed onto the stack. At this point, the right side of $A \rightarrow b$ is on top of the stack. Click on **Step** and observe that the right side b is replaced by its left side A. Now there are two possible right sides on top of the stack, aaA and A. Note that the right side of $A \to aaA$ is on top of the stack backward as Aaa. We will see later that the SLR(1) parse table incorporates information to determine which of these two productions to apply. The NPDA applies both of them. Click on **Step**, and there are two configurations. The configuration with $AaaZ$ on the stack is the correct configuration that replaced aaA by A. The other configuration with $SaaaaZ$ on the stack will lead to rejection. The Aaa on top of the stack should next be replaced with A again. Click on **Step**. The resulting configuration is the one with AZ on the stack. Next, this A should be replaced with S for $S \to A$. Click on **Step**. The resulting configuration is the one with SZ on the stack. Click on **Step** two more times and the string has been accepted. All other configurations generated result in rejection.

8.3.3 Using the SLR(1) Parse Table

At this point go back to the SLR(1) parser window. You will need to select **File : Dismiss Tab** to dismiss the **Convert to PDA(LR)** tab. We will examine the parser stack and parse table as we trace the string $aaaab$ once more. The stack will work similarly to the stack in the NPDA, but will also store numbers between terminals and variables to keep track of which row in the table the parsing action occurred when the symbol was placed on the stack.

The parse table is in the top left of the window, as shown in Figure 8.4. The parse table has rows that are numbered from 0 to 6. Enlarge the window if you cannot see all the rows. The table has two types of columns: lookaheads (terminals and $) and variables. Recall that a *lookahead* is the leftmost symbol in the input remaining and can be used to guide the parsing. For this grammar there are three columns of lookaheads (a, b, and $), followed by two columns of variables (A and S). The parse table has four types of actions in the lookahead columns. Those that start with the letter s are for *shifting* terminals onto the stack. Those that start with the letter r are for *reducing* a production, replacing the right side with the left side. The entry with *acc* means a string is *accepted*. Entries that are blank are errors. The columns for variables either have numbers in them or are blank. The numbers identify the new current row in the table after placing this variable on the stack.

We first describe in general terms how SLR(1) parsing uses the table and then trace through an example using JFLAP. To parse a string using the SLR(1) parse table, row 0 is the initial row, and thus 0 is placed on the stack. The first symbol in the input remaining is the lookahead. Find the column corresponding to the lookahead symbol. If the entry at the current row and lookahead column is a shift, such as $s4$, then shift the lookahead for that column on the stack, set row 4 to the current row and push the current row number, 4, on the stack.

If the entry is a reduce, such as $r2$, then reduce by popping the right side of production number 2 off the stack and pushing the left side back onto the stack. We now describe a reduce in more detail. Each production in the grammar is numbered by JFLAP, starting with 0 for the new production.

When the right side is popped off the stack, note that twice as many symbols as are in the right side are popped off the stack (all the numbers between the variables and terminals must also be popped off). The variable V to push onto the stack is the left side of production number 2. Before pushing V onto the stack, though, examine the number at the top of the stack, say n. To figure out which row in the parse table will be current after the reduce is complete, look up the entry in row n under column V.

Tip	If you hold the cursor over an entry in the parse table, more information about that entry is displayed. For example, hold the cursor over the $r3$ in row 4. The message **Reduce by production 3, A $\rightarrow$ b** is displayed. Hold the cursor over the $s5$ in row 3. The message **Shift current input and state 5 to stack** is displayed.

Now use JFLAP to parse the string *aaaab*. We will use $T[i, j]$ to represent the ith row and jth column of the parse table. Make sure *aaaab* has been entered in the **Input** field and the **Noninverted Tree** has been selected. Then click on **Start**. Note that 0 is on the stack and a is the lookahead (a is the leftmost symbol in the **Input Remaining** of *aaaab$*). Look up $T[0, a]$, which is $s3$. Click on **Step**. The $s3$ in $T[0, a]$ is highlighted and the shift has been performed. The lookahead, the first a in the remaining input, was removed and placed on top of the stack (a shift). The 3 from $s3$ is placed on top of the stack to indicate the current row. The new lookahead is a. The next entry will be at $T[3, a]$. Click on **Step** four more times and observe that *aaab* is placed on the stack along with the current row numbers. Note that 4 is now on top of the stack, followed by b, which is a right side. Also note the lookahead is $. What will happen next? The entry at $T[4, $]$ is $r3$. We will reduce by production $r3$, which is $A \rightarrow b$. Twice the size of the right side will be popped off the stack ($4b$). Then the top of the stack will be 5. Click on **Step** to see $4b$ popped off the stack. The left side of the production is A. The entry at $T[5, A] = 6$ identifies row 6 as the next current row. The A followed by 6 will be pushed onto the stack. Also note in the parse tree view that the A node is added with a link to b. Click on **Step** to see the rest of this reduction.

What will happen next? $T[6, $] = r2$, which means reduce by $A \rightarrow aaA$. Note that aaA is on top of the stack, backward (Aaa) and with numbers between symbols ($6A5a3a$). Those six symbols will be popped off the stack, resulting in five on top of the stack. $T[5, A] = 6$, so A followed by 6 will be pushed onto the stack. In the parse tree view $A \rightarrow aaA$ is added. Click on **Step** twice to see this reduce. Click on **Step** four times and two more reduces occur. The parse tree is complete. The next entry in the table is $T[2, $]$ which contains accept. Click on **Step** and the string is accepted.

8.3.4 Constructing a DFA that Models the Parsing Stack

The SLR(1) parse table knows when the right side of a production is on top of the stack. This information is incorporated into the table when it is built by modeling the parsing stack with a DFA. The states in this DFA have special marked productions called items that identify the part of the right side of productions that are currently on top of the stack. We will define items and then show how to construct the DFA that models the parsing stack.

An *item* is a production with one marker ($\cdot$) placed in the right side of a production. Symbols in the right side of a production that are to the left of the marker are currently on top of the stack and symbols to the right of the marker still need to be placed on the stack. If there are no symbols to the right of the marker, then the right side is on top of the stack and ready for a reduce. For example, $A \rightarrow a \cdot aA$ indicates that a is on top of the stack and that aA must still be placed on the stack before a reduce can occur. $A \rightarrow aaA\cdot$ indicates that aaA is on top of the stack and a reduce can occur.

Each state in the DFA will have a set of items associated with it. For each set of items, a closure operation will be applied to include all related items. The *closure* of a set of items is defined as the items currently in the set plus all items for any variable in one of the items with the marker immediately to its left. Suppose a marker is in front of variable B, as in $A \rightarrow a \cdot BC$. Then every B production, $B \rightarrow w$, should be added to the item set with none of the right side seen on the stack, as $B \rightarrow \cdot w$. To see why the B production is added this way, consider the B production $B \rightarrow Caab$ applied to $a \cdot BC$, resulting in $a \cdot CaabC$. Note that none of the right side of $B \rightarrow Caab$ is on top of the stack, since the B in $a \cdot BC$ was not on top of the stack.

To build a DFA, start with the initial state and the only production with the new start symbol in the grammar. In the initial state, nothing has been pushed onto the stack. The initial state will always have the new production that was added to the grammar marked as not on the stack yet, $S' \rightarrow \cdot S$. The closure will add additional productions to this state.

How are transitions defined between two states in the DFA? We define an operation $goto(I,X)=I'$ that is applied to an item set I and symbol X that is a terminal or variable. If the X immediately follows a marker in any of the items in I, then the item is placed into a new item set I' with the marker moved to the right of the X. The closure is applied to all items in I'. A transition in the DFA corresponding to this goto operation would be a transition labeled with X from the state associated with I to the state associated with I'. When the transition X is processed, the X is pushed onto the parsing stack. For example, if $A \rightarrow a \cdot bC$ is the item in one state, a transition labeled b leaves this state and enters a state that has the item $A \rightarrow ab \cdot C$, representing the b shifted onto the stack. If any state has an item with the marker at the right end, then the state is identified as a final state. Thus, final states represent where reduces can occur.

We will start our example grammar again and show how to build a DFA that models the SLR(1) parsing process. Dismiss all the tabs except the original grammar editor. Then select **Input : SLR(1) Parse**. Enter in the FIRST and FOLLOW sets and click on **Next** after you enter each set. At this point JFLAP asks if you want to define the initial set of the DFA yourself. Click on **Yes**. A window labeled **Initial Goto Set** appears with the productions from the grammar. The placement of the marker must be identified for each production that is in the item set. Click on

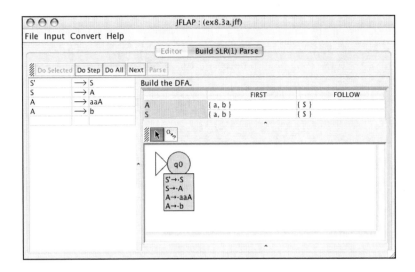

Figure 8.6: Building a DFA for SLR(1) parsing.

the start production of the grammar, $S' \to S$. All possible items derivable from this production appear. Since nothing is on the stack yet, click on $S' \to \cdot S$. This marked production will appear to the right. Since the marker is in front of the S, all S items with the $\cdot$ as the leftmost symbol must be added to the item set. There is only one such item. Add $S \to \cdot A$ to the item set. Since the marker is in front of the A, add all the A items with the $\cdot$ as the leftmost symbol to the item set. Click on **OK** when the item set is complete. The DFA has been started by drawing q_0 and its item set below the FIRST and FOLLOW sets as shown in Figure 8.6.

> **Tip** In the Goto Set window, selecting a production on the right side followed by clicking
> on **Closure** will add the closure of that production to the item set. Clicking on **Finish**
> at any time will complete the item set.

The SLR(1) DFA editor is a modified finite automaton editor. Note this DFA editor has only two tools. The **Attribute Editor** ⭠ tool is very limited. It allows states to be moved around and allows the identification of final states. The **Goto Set on Symbol** ⬏ tool allows one to add a transition and corresponding state at the same time.

> **Tip** In drawing the DFA, make the DFA window as big as possible by resizing the window.
> Click and drag the bar between the grammar and the DFA to increase the amount of
> space for the DFA. Similarly, click and drag the bar between the FIRST sets and the
> DFA to increase the space for the DFA.

We will now complete the DFA. State q_0 has four symbols that can be pushed on the stack: S, A, a and b. We will add a transition for each of these symbols to a new state. Start with the new state for when S is shifted onto the stack. Select ⬏. Click on q_0, drag to the location for the new state, and release the mouse. Enter in S as the grammar symbol and then select the item $S' \to S\cdot$.

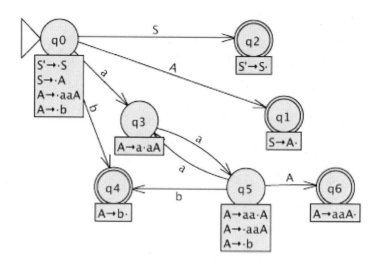

Figure 8.7: Completed DFA.

That is the only production in this item set. Click on **OK** and the transition and new state appear. State q_1 has a production that can be reduced, so use the **Attribute Editor** to make this state final. State q_1 will have no outgoing arcs, as the marker does not appear to the left of any symbols in its item set.

From q_0 add the state for transition A next (the state should be q_2), followed by the state for transition a (the state should be q_3). Next add the state for transition b (state q_4). The order is important, as the discussion that follows will refer to these states.

From q_3 there is only one outgoing arc, on a. Add the transition for this a next (it should be q_5). Note that when you apply the closure, additional items will be added. State q_5 will have three outgoing arcs. Add a transition on A to a new state (it should be q_6). Next add a transition from q_5 on b to a new state. What happened? The state already exists, so the arc goes to q_4. Add a transition from q_5 on a to a new state. Again, the state already exists, so the arc goes to q_3. Click on **Next** when your DFA is complete. The empty parse table appears below the DFA, and may make the DFA smaller. Increase the size of the DFA by moving the horizontal and vertical bars. The completed DFA is shown in Figure 8.7.

8.3.5 Building the SLR(1) Parse Table

The DFA can be used to build the parse table. Note that the DFA has seven states numbered from q_0 to q_6. The parse table has seven rows numbered from 0 to 6. The rows in the parse table correspond to the states in the DFA. Row i represents q_i. For each q_i we add the corresponding actions to row i in the parse table. Again we will use $T[i, j]$ to represent the ith row and jth column of the parse table.

There are three types of actions to enter in the parse table under lookahead columns, and current state numbers to enter under variable columns. Suppose state i has an outgoing arc to state j on lookahead a. This represents a shift. Enter sj in $T[i,a]$. Suppose state i has an outgoing arc to state j on variable A. This represents the end of a reduce, the pushing of a left side of a production onto the stack. Enter j in $T[i,A]$. Suppose a state is a final state, and thus has a reduced item $A \to w\cdot$ for production number k. Enter rk in all lookahead columns in row i for lookaheads that are in FOLLOW(A). There is one exception. If the state has the reduce production that includes the new start symbol, $S' \to S\cdot$, then enter acc in $T[i,\$]$. All entries left blank represent an error.

Start with q_0 and enter the items for each state, clicking on **Next** after each row to see if the row was entered correctly. Then read the discussion that follows.

Tip	To see the production number while building the parse table, place the cursor over the production and the number will appear.

All entries for q_0 are entered in row 0. State q_0 has two outgoing terminals. Enter $s3$ in column a (a is shifted on the stack and enters q_3) and $s4$ in column b. State q_0 has two outgoing transitions with variables. Enter 1 in column A (the A arc goes to q_2) and 2 in column S. There are no reductions, so row 0 is complete. State q_1 has only the reduction $S \to A\cdot$, which is production number 1. FOLLOW(S) = \{$\$$\}, so place $r1$ in $T[1,\$]$. State q_2 has no outgoing arcs, only the reduction $S' \to S\cdot$. Enter acc $T[2,\$]$. State q_3 has only one arc on a to q_5, so enter $s5$ in $T[3,a]$. State q_4 has only the reduction $A \to b\cdot$, which is production number 3. FOLLOW(A) = \{$\$$\}, so place $r3$ in $T[4,\$]$. State q_5 has three outgoing arcs and adds to row 5 an $s3$ in column a, an $s4$ in column b, and a 6 in column A. State q_6 has only the reduction $A \to aaA\cdot$, which is production number 2. FOLLOW(A) = \{$\$$\}, so place $r2$ in $T[6,\$]$. The parse table is complete. Click on **Next**, followed by **Parse**.

Backtracking through the DFA while parsing

At this point, we will trace through the parsing of example $aaaab$ one more time, while looking at both the parse table shown in the window and the DFA in Figure 8.7. Enter in $aaaab$ and click on **Start**. The top of the stack 0 indicates the current state q_0 at the start. The input remaining starts with a (the lookahead), so in the DFA follow the a transition to q_3. Click on **Step**. The current state is q_3 and a is the lookahead. Click on **Step** four more times and follow along in the DFA. The stack tells us the path through the DFA that was taken, $4b5a3a5a3a0$, means $aaaab$ was shifted onto the stack following the path q_0 to q_3 to q_5 to q_3 to q_5 to q_4. When a reduce occurs, steps are retraced (transitions followed backward) as the symbols are popped off the stack. In q_4 a reduce occurs for $A \to b$. The b is popped off and we trace the b transition backward to q_5. Note there are two b transitions into q_4. We know to follow the one to q_5 since 5 appears on the stack after b is popped off. From q_5 we push the A from $A \to b$ onto the stack and in the DFA follow the A transition from q_5 to q_6. We push 6 onto the stack to represent the current state. Click on **Step** twice to see the reduction. In State q_6 a reduce occurs for $A \to aaA$. The top of the stack is

$6A5a3a5$. When the reduction occurs, backtracking occurs in the DFA from q_6 to q_5 to q_3 to q_5. In q_5 push A onto the stack, follow the A transition to q_6, and push 6 onto the stack. Click on **Step** twice now to see the reduction. Again the q_6 reduction occurs, but this time the backtracking leads to q_0, the A is shifted on, and the A transition is followed to q_2. Click on **Step** twice to see the reduction. Click on **Step** three more times and the two final productions are reduced, resulting in acceptance and the DFA finishing in q_2.

8.3.6 An Example Grammar with a λ-production

A λ-production has no symbols to shift onto a stack so it is automatically reduced. The item for the production $A \rightarrow \lambda$ is $A \rightarrow \lambda\cdot$, which is shown in JFLAP as $A \rightarrow \cdot$. We will trace through an example of building the parse table for a grammar that has a λ-production and other differences from the previous grammar.

Start JFLAP and load the file **ex8.3b** or enter the grammar shown in Figure 8.8 (but don't enter $S' \rightarrow S$ as it is added automatically). Note that this grammar has one λ-production. Select **Input : SLR(1) Parse**.

Enter the FIRST and FOLLOW sets, clicking on **Next** after each one, and enter the item set for the initial state. State q_0 and its item set is shown in Figure 8.8. Any state with a λ-production is a final state, thus q_0 is a final state.

How many outgoing transitions will q_0 have? Although q_0 has four items, it will only have two outgoing arcs, for S and A. There is only one arc for A (this is a DFA not an NFA) and no arc for λ. Add the transition and corresponding state q_1 for A. There are two items in q_2 that move the marker over A, both $S \rightarrow A \cdot Bc$ and $A \rightarrow A \cdot a$. A shift of A onto the stack means that one of these two productions is being shifted onto the stack, but we do not know which one yet. Add the transition and corresponding state q_2 for S.

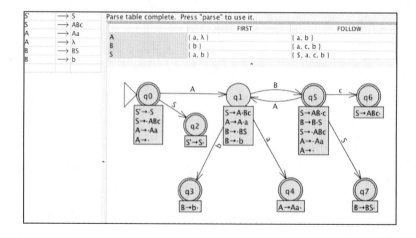

Figure 8.8: Grammar with a λ-production for SLR(1) Parsing.

How many outgoing transitions will q_1 have? It will have three outgoing transitions, for B, a, and b. Add the transition and state for B first, then a, and then b. State q_3 has five items, but only three outgoing arcs. Add the transition and state for A first, then S, and then c. This should complete the DFA, as shown in Figure 8.8. Click on **Parse** and the empty parse table should appear.

Enter the parse table. We will explain only q_3, which is row three in the table. State q_3 has both shifts and reduces. State q_3 has three outgoing arcs, c to q_7 (add $s7$ in $T[3, c]$), S to q_6 (add 6 in $T[3, S]$), and A to q_1 (add 1 to $T[3, A]$). State q_3 has one reduction, $A \rightarrow \lambda$, which is production number 3. Place $r3$ in $T[3, a]$ and $T[3, b]$, as FOLLOW$(A) = \{a, b\}$.

When the table is complete, parse the string *ababcc* while observing the parsing stack. Note the first thing that happens is a reduce of $A \rightarrow \lambda$. In the previous example, all the terminals were pushed onto the stack first, then reduces occurred. In this example, many reduces occur before all the terminals have been pushed onto the stack. Complete the parsing of the string.

Observe the rightmost derivation that SLR parsing produces. Click on **Noninverted Tree** and select **Derivation Table**. Remember that SLR parsing parses in reverse, so start at the bottom of the table with S in the **Derivation** column. Proceed up, observing which production is applied at each step. For each sentential form that has more than one variable, note that the rightmost variable is always replaced next, as in the B in sentential form ABc.

8.3.7 An Example Grammar That Is Not SLR(1)

In JFLAP, if a grammar is not LL(1) we can build the parse table and see the conflicts in the table, but we cannot parse any strings. If a grammar is not SLR(1), we can build the parse table, see the conflicts, select which of the conflicts we prefer, and try to parse strings. We now will go through an example of a grammar that is not SLR(1).

Start JFLAP and load the file `ex8.3c` or enter the grammar shown in Figure 8.9 (but don't enter $S' \rightarrow S$, as it is added automatically). Select **Input : SLR(1) Parse**.

Enter the FIRST and FOLLOW sets, and the initial state of the DFA. State q_0 has three outgoing transitions, a, A, and S. Create the A transition and state q_1 first, followed by the S transition and state q_2 second, and then the a transition and state q_3. (This order is only important for the discussion that follows.) Create the b transition from state q_1 next. State q_3 has three outgoing transitions. Create the A transition and state q_5 first, the b transition and state q_6 second, and then the a transition. Complete the DFA.

Enter actions for the parse table rows 0, 1, and 2. Now consider q_3, which is row 3. There is a b transition to q_6, so enter $s6$ in column b. There is also a reduction of $A \rightarrow \lambda$ (production number 4) and FOLLOW$(A) = \{b\}$. Enter $r4$ also in column b (enter a space between $s6$ and $r4$). When

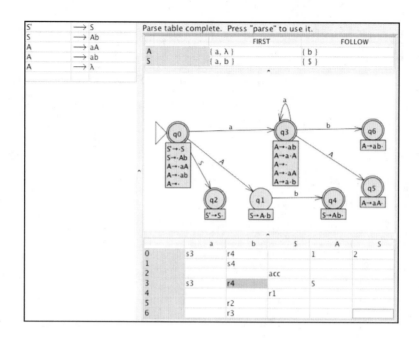

Figure 8.9: Parsing Grammar That Is Not SLR(1).

there is an entry with a shift and a reduce, this means the grammar is not SLR(1) and is called a shift-reduce conflict. Enter the rest of the parse table and click on **Next**.

Before clicking on **Parse** note that row 3, column b is highlighted in orange, indicating a conflict, and only one action appears. Click on the entry and all the actions for this entry appear. Select $r4$. Now click on **Parse** and parse the string aab. It parses fine. Now enter the string abb and parse it. Is abb in the language of the grammar? Yes, but it does not parse successfully. Dismiss the tab, change the conflict in row 3, column b to $s6$ and click on **Parse** again. Now try to parse the string abb. It parses successfully. Try aab. It should be accepted, but fails. When a grammar is not SLR(1), appropriate conflict choices must be made to parse the string.

8.4   Summary

In Section 8.1 we learned the useful functions FIRST and FOLLOW. FIRST is the set of terminals that can start a derivation. FOLLOW is the set of lookaheads that can follow a variable in some derivation. Both of these functions are needed in computing the parse tables for LL and SLR parsing.

In Section 8.2 we learned how the LL(1) parsing method works. A CFG can be converted to an NPDA that uses the LL(1) parsing method. This NPDA is likely to be nondeterministic. The LL(1) parsing method is deterministic by using lookaheads to aid in choosing the next production to apply. This method is a top-down approach, replacing the left side of a production by the right side of a production, and using a stack to apply productions and match the symbols in the input string in the correct order. Not all CFG can be parsed using the LL(1) method.

In Section 8.3 we learned how the SLR(1) parsing method works. A CFG can be converted to an NPDA that uses the SLR(1) parsing method. The SLR(1) parsing method is deterministic by using lookaheads to aid in choosing the next production to apply. This method is a bottom-up approach, replacing the right side of a production by the left side of a production, and using a stack to apply productions and match the symbols in the input string in the correct order. Not all CFG can be parsed using the SLR(1) method, but in JFLAP some CFG with conflicts can be parsed by choosing one of the conflicting actions before parsing.

8.5 Exercises

1. Compute the FIRST and FOLLOW sets for all of the variables in the following grammars.

    (a) `ex8.5FF-a`

    (b) `ex8.5FF-b`

    (c) `ex8.5FF-c`

    (d) `ex8.5FF-d`

    (e) `ex8.5FF-e`

    (f) `ex8.5FF-f`

2. For each of the following grammars, compute the FIRST and FOLLOW sets for all of the variables in the grammar. Then write out derivations of one or more strings that show each of the symbols in the FOLLOW sets following the appropriate variable. In the derivations, circle one instance of a terminal following a variable for each item in the FOLLOW set.

    For example, in `ex8.5showFollow-a` there are five symbols in the FOLLOW sets, so there should be five pairs of terminals following variables circled. Start each derivation with $S\$$ so $\$$ can be shown following variables. You will need to parse several strings to show all pairs. Note that the brute-force parser in JFLAP may not generate all pairs, but there is some string and derivation for each pair.

    (a) `ex8.5showFollow-a`

    (b) `ex8.5showFollow-b`

    (c) `ex8.5showFollow-c`

3. Build the LL(1) parse table for each of the following grammars. Parse the corresponding string in the brute-force parser and the LL(1) parser. Compare the number of nodes in the two parse trees and the running time.

(a) ex8.5llparse-a and *aaacdbb*

(b) ex8.5llparse-b and *aaeaabcdcd*

(c) ex8.5llparse-c and *caabbdaa*

(d) ex8.5llparse-d and *bbaaecaae*

4. Build the LL(1) parse table for each of the following grammars that are not LL(1).

   (a) ex8.5notll-a

   (b) ex8.5notll-b

   (c) ex8.5notll-c

   (d) ex8.5notll-d

5. Load the grammar in ex8.5ll2npda. Compute the FIRST sets, FOLLOW sets, and the LL(1) parse table. Convert the grammar to an NPDA using the LL(1) method.

   In this NPDA, what is on the top of the stack when there is a choice of configurations to go to next? To answer this question, parse the string *aaebccac* in the NPDA using **Input : Step with Closure**. Each time there is a choice of configurations, use the lookahead to determine the correct choice and eliminate the other configurations.

6. Convert the following CFGs to NPDAs using the SLR(1) method.

   (a) ex8.5lrparse-a

   (b) ex8.5lrparse-b

   (c) ex8.5lrparse-c

   (d) ex8.5lrparse-d

   (e) ex8.5lrparse-e

   (f) ex8.5lrparse-f

7. Build the SLR(1) parse table for the following SLR(1) grammars.

   (a) ex8.5lrparse-a

   (b) ex8.5lrparse-b

   (c) ex8.5lrparse-c

   (d) ex8.5lrparse-d

   (e) ex8.5lrparse-e

   (f) ex8.5lrparse-f

8. Build the SLR(1) parse table for the following non-SLR(1) grammars. For each one, give the appropriate conflicts so the given string can be parsed.

   (a) `ex8.5notlr-a` and *aab*

   (b) `ex8.5notlr-b` and *baba*

   (c) `ex8.5notlr-c` and *aabbb*

   (d) `ex8.5notlr-d` and *bbacb*

   (e) `ex8.5notlr-e` and *bbcbaa*

9. Consider the grammar in `ex8.3a` and the DFA that models the SLR(1) parsing process shown in Figure 8.7. Explain why input strings *b* and *aab*, when parsed using SLR(1) parsing, both reach state q_4 in the DFA, but backtrack to different states.

10. Consider the SLR(1) grammar in `ex8.lrcompare`. Compare SLR(1) parsing with brute-force parsing for this grammar using the string $a^{12}b^4c^4 = aaaaaaaaaaaaccccbbbb$.

11. Create a CFG that is not SLR(1), has one to three conflicts in the SLR(1) table, and has a string that cannot be parsed no matter how the conflicts are resolved. Note that a conflict can be resolved only one way for each string.

Chapter 9

Turing Machines

This chapter describes JFLAP's Turing machines (TMs) and multitape Turing machines. We first create a TM and simulate input on that TM. We then show how an alternate multiple simulator may be used to conveniently show the outputs for transducers. We then describe multitape TMs, using as examples a two-tape TM that tests if one string is a substring of another string, and an implementation of the universal TM. We end with JFLAP's formal definition of a TM.

9.1 One-Tape Turing Machines

A TM differs from other automata in its transitions. In a TM, each transition implies reading a single symbol from a tape, overwriting that symbol with a new symbol, and moving the tape head either left, right, or not at all.

A transition for a TM is defined in JFLAP as $r; w, d$. The r is exactly one symbol to read from the tape. If r is read, the w is exactly one symbol to write to the tape over r, and d is the direction to move the tape head after writing w. The symbols r and w must be elements of the tape alphabet Γ, and $d \in \{R, L, S\}$ indicates that the tape head should move **R**ight, **L**eft, or should **S**tay (that is, not move).

9.1.1 Building a Turing Machine

Start JFLAP if it is not already running, or select **File : New** to create a new structure if JFLAP is running. Choose to create a new **Turing Machine**. We will build the TM pictured in Figure 9.1 in stages. This machine accepts the language a^{2^n} and has input alphabet $\Sigma = \{a\}$. In brief, our strategy is to perform a series of passes over the tape from left to right; on each pass half the a's are overwritten with #'s. If the number of a's is a power of two, on one pass there is exactly one a left, at which point the TM accepts.

The automaton editor is now familiar to you. Create the five states q_0 through q_4 with the State

126

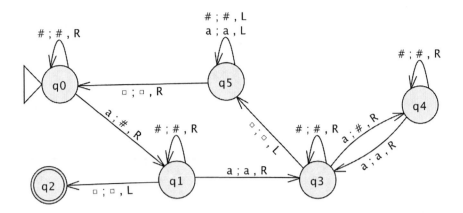

Figure 9.1: A TM That Accepts the Language a^{2^n}.

Creator tool ⊕. With the Attribute Editor tool ↖, make q_0 the initial state and q_2 the single final state. When a TM configuration moves into the final state, the machine unconditionally accepts.

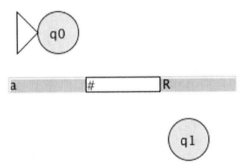

Figure 9.2: An Illustration of Entering
the Transition $a; \#, R$ from q_0 to q_1.

The machine moves into q_2 when the tape has exactly one a remaining. With the Transition Creator tool ↗, create a transition from q_0 to q_1. The transition editor appears in Figure 9.2; the three fields from left to right are the symbol to read, the symbol to write, and the direction to move the tape head. The first two fields are text fields, and editing these is similar to editing the fields for PDA transitions: type "a", type tab, and then type "#", and hit return. We want R as the direction, which it is by default when creating a new transition, so edit only the first two fields. The transition $a; \#, R$ will appear from q_0 to q_1. Also create two $a; a, R$ transitions from q_1 to q_3 and q_4 to q_3, and another $a; \#, R$ transition from q_3 to q_4. The goal of these four transitions is to overwrite every other a with #.

If the machine is in q_1 and has reached the end of the tape, then its last pass encountered a single a. The machine moves from q_1 to q_2 and accepts. Create another transition from q_1 to q_2. JFLAP's TMs have tape infinite to both the right and left, and the input is surrounded in both directions with the blank (empty) tape symbol, □. That is, any string of a's will be prefixed and

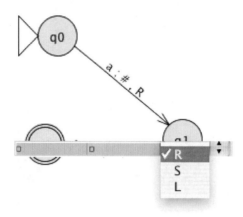

Figure 9.3: An Illustration of Entering
the Transition $\square; \square, L$ from q_1 to q_2.

suffixed with an infinite string of $\square$'s; the machine can detect the end of input when it encounters a $\square$ symbol. To enter $\square$, leave the fields empty as they are now. We want to change only the direction from R to L: click on the R in the rightmost field and you will see the menu pictured in Figure 9.3, with items **R**, **S**, and **L**, respectively. Select **L** to indicate that you want this transition's direction symbol to be L. As always, hit return to finish editing the transition. The transition $\square; \square, L$ will appear from q_1 to q_2.

Tip	When the direction field is selected (as by tabbing to it, for example), you may type "L", "S", or "R" with the shift key down to change the direction field, instead of using the mouse.

9.1.2   Simulation of Input on an Incomplete Machine

We now simulate input on this TM to illustrate what we have so far. (If you no longer have the TM open, it is stored in `ex9-a2n-incomplete`.) Select the menu item **Input : Step** and enter "aaaa". Though *aaaa* is part of the final language we want the TM to accept, right now all the Turing machine will do is perform a single pass on it, and then fail.

The configuration for a TM contains the current state (which should be q_0) and the contents of the tape (which should be *aaaa* with $\square$ symbols stretching to the left and right). The symbol currently under the tape, the leftmost *a*, is shaded red; a small **v** above the tape points to this symbol as well. In JFLAP, the input serves as the tape's initial contents, and the tape head is initially above the leftmost character of the input.

Click on **Step**. From q_0 to q_1 we have the transition $a; \#, R$. JFLAP overwrites the first *a* with #, and moves the tape head right, over the next *a* symbol in the tape. Continue clicking on **Step**, and note that the configurations proceed from q_1 to q_3 to q_4 to q_3 again, overwriting every other *a*

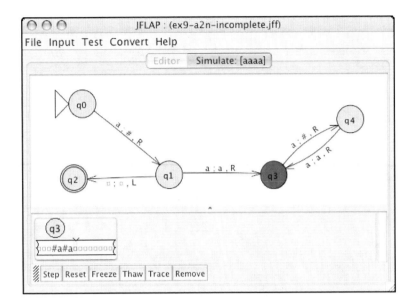

Figure 9.4: After *aaaa* Has Been Rejected By the Incomplete TM.

with #, effectively halving the number of *a*'s. Click on **Step** again, and your window will resemble Figure 9.4, a single rejected configuration; there is no transition that reads the □ symbol. We have yet to add the transitions that enable rewinding.

Dismiss the simulator tab, and simulate the input *a* this time. Again we move from q_0 to q_1, and on the next step we move to q_2 along the $□; □, L$ transition and accept! The goal of the rest of the machine we shall build is to halve the number of *a*'s on each pass so that it is eventually reduced to a single *a* remaining and accepts, as we see here.

9.1.3 Completing the Turing Machine

We will now complete the incomplete Turing machine. (If you no longer have the TM open, it is stored in `ex9-a2n-incomplete`.)

Select the State Creator tool ⑨ and create the last state q_5. Machine configurations in q_0, q_1, q_3, and q_4 have passed over zero *a*'s, one *a*, some even number greater than 0 of *a*'s, and some odd number greater than 1 of *a*'s in the current pass, respectively. When we are at the end of the tape on q_3, we have verified that the number of *a*'s is even, and that we have halved the *a*'s; we should now "rewind" the tape and begin another pass. To do this, create a transition $□; □, L$ from q_3 to q_5 (this will put the machine back on the nonblank portion of the tape), create a transition $a; a, L$ on q_5 (this will cause the machine to backtrack left over the *a*'s), and finally, create a transition $□; □, R$ from q_5 to q_0 (after the tape head backtracks over the *a*'s, we want to be in position for another pass).

The machine is nearly complete, except that during a pass we will overwrite half the *a*'s with #'s, so on all but the first pass the tape head will encounter #'s. These are to be ignored: create loop transitions on q_0, q_1, q_3, and q_4 on $\#;\#,R$ to effectively ignore $\#$'s. We want to ignore $\#$'s when "rewinding" the tape as well, so create a loop transition $\#;\#,L$ on q_5. You now have the TM of Figure 9.1!

9.1.4   Simulation of Input on a Complete Machine

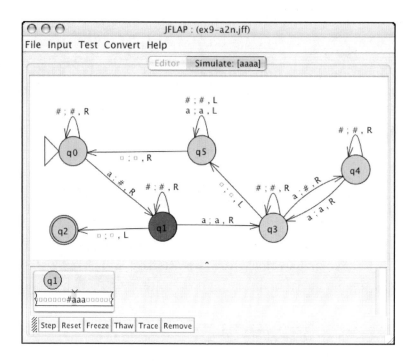

Figure 9.5: In the Midst of Simulation of $aaaa$ on the TM.

We will now simulate input on this completed TM. (If you no longer have the TM open, it is stored in **ex9-a2n**.) Select the menu item **Input : Step** and enter "aaaa", just as you did in Section 9.1.2. The string $aaaa$ is a^{2^2}, so the machine will accept.

Click on **Step**. From q_0 to q_1 we have the transition $a;\#,R$. Again, JFLAP overwrites the first a with $\#$, and moves the tape head right, over the next a symbol in the tape. Your window now resembles Figure 9.5. Click on **Step** repeatedly. Note that a pass halves the number of a's, rewinds, performs another pass to again halve the number of a's, rewinds, and in the next pass detects that there is only one a left. The machine then moves to the final state q_2.

Note If one simulates $a\#\#a\#$ on this machine, it will be accepted, even though this is clearly not in a^{2^n}. JFLAP does not require explicit definition of the input alphabet Σ, and one can abuse this flexibility. Strictly speaking JFLAP is "broken," but requiring explicit specification of Σ is more undesirable than this problem. A simple claim that your machine works as defined only for input under strings of Σ^* suffices. In this case, we specified $\Sigma = \{a\}$, so $a\#\#a\#$ is illegal by fiat.

Rejection

Now simulate *aaaaaa*. This is not in the language, and will be rejected. Click on **Step** repeatedly. Observe how one pass succeeds, and three of the six *a*'s are overwritten. On the next pass over the tape, the machine overwrites what is now the first *a*, skips the second *a*, then overwrites the last *a*. JFLAP should reject this next configuration because the configuration is now in q_4, and is past the end of the tape. No transition that reads □ from q_4 exists. Click on **Step** again: This configuration will be rejected. When no transition from a state reads the symbol under the configuration's tape head, the configuration is rejected. (By comparison, some other definitions of a TM require an explicit reject state q_{reject}, but JFLAP does not.) In this machine, we halve the number of *a*'s; if in a pass the number of *a*'s remaining is not even, the pass fails and the machine halts.

Try simulating some more strings. Is *aa* accepted? What about *aaa*? What about *aaaaaaaa*? What about *aaaaaaa*? Note how the machine accepts or rejects the given input.

Nonhalting machines

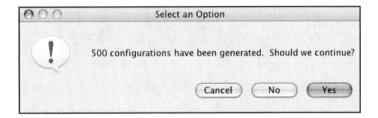

Figure 9.6: The Dialog That Confirms You Want to Continue Simulation.

JFLAP can simulate TMs that do not halt. Open `ex9-infinite`. This machine has a single initial state q_0 and no final state, and has a loop transition on the blank tape symbol. This simple machine will loop forever if its tape head is initially over □. Select **Input : Fast Run**, leave the input field blank, and click on **OK**. Soon, a dialog resembling Figure 9.6 appears. Although JFLAP cannot solve the halting problem, it interrupts a machine after 500 configurations have been generated to ask if you want it to keep searching. If you select **No** or **Cancel** the simulation stops. If you select **Yes** the simulation continues, but JFLAP asks again at 1000 configurations, then at 2000, then at 4000, and so forth until the machine halts or you tell JFLAP to stop. Click on **Yes** a few times to observe this, but click on **No** when you reach 16000 configurations.

9.2 Turing Transducers and the Multiple Simulator

Turing machines differ from other automata in that they do not consume their input as they process it. In this way, they are not limited to giving simple yes or no answers, but may use the tape as output. So far we have examined *Turing acceptors*, which simply produce yes or no answers. An alternate view of Turing machines is as *Turing transducers*, which transform the input into an output, and so may produce more complex outputs than yes or no. For example, a transducer may write as output tape the sum for an input sequence of numbers, or capitalize all the words in a sentence, or perform some other useful modification of the input. We consider the contents of the tape when the machine reaches an accepting configuration to be the output for these transducers.

Note that JFLAP does not distinguish between Turing acceptors and transducers. That distinction lies only in how the user interprets the final result. For the acceptor it is enough that the user knows that the TM accepted, but for a transducer the user is interested in whether the TM accepted and also the final contents of the tape after the acceptance. The simulators are able to display this output after a fashion since they can display the content of a tape for an accepting configuration. However, the multiple-run simulator provides the opportunity to make this output viewing a bit more convenient.

Open the `ex9-adder`. Pictured in Figure 9.7, this TM is given a mathematical expression containing the addition of binary numbers as input and produces the binary sum as output. For example, the input 101+10+100 (five plus two plus four) would produce the output 1011 (eleven), and the input 1011+1 (eleven plus one) produces the output 1100 (twelve). The machine is rather simple, repeatedly summing the two leftmost numbers until exactly one number remains.

You can input a sum in the step simulator to see how it works more fully, and perhaps that would be interesting, but if you're merely interested in whether the machine produces the correct

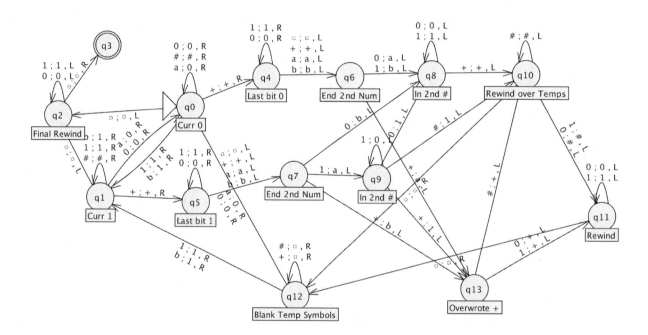

Figure 9.7: A TM That Takes As Input a Mathematical Expression of the Addition of Binary Numbers and Produces the Sum As Output.

answer, clicking on the **Step** button a few hundred times may not be an attractive choice. The fast simulator or multiple simulator may be more appropriate.

In the case of the multiple simulator, you may have noticed during other menu choices simulations that there are two multiple run simulators, **Multiple Run** and **Multiple Run (Transducer)**. This latter option is available only to Turing machines, and is useful in situations where you want to run the Turing machine as a transducer and view the output of multiple runs.

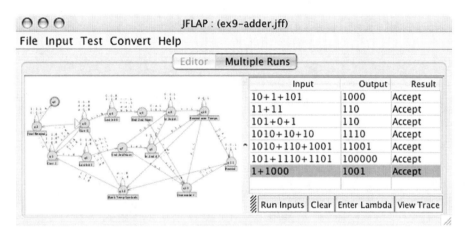

Figure 9.8: The Multiple Simulator with Outputs on the Adding Turing Transducer.

Select **Input : Multiple Run (Transducer)**. Your window should resemble Figure 9.8. This multiple simulator closely resembles the multiple simulator described in Section 1.2.3, except with the addition of the **Output** column between the **Input** and **Result** columns.

In the event that a Turing machine accepts, this simulator will set the corresponding output cell to the output of the tape, as shown in Figure 9.8. JFLAP considers the output of the tape to be the string of symbols from the symbol under the tape head up to but not including the first □ encountered to the right. If the tape head is on a □, the output is considered empty. So, if you build your own transducers in JFLAP, make sure to place the tape head at the leftmost symbol you want in the output.

Try entering a series of additions in the fields of the **Input** column and select **Run Inputs**. The Turing machine should produce the associated sums in the **Output** column. In this way we can conveniently use Turing machines as transducers in the multiple-run simulator.

9.3 Multitape Turing Machines

In this section we introduce JFLAP's multitape Turing machines. JFLAP allows multitape machines with two to five tapes. An n-tape machine requires that each transition read n symbols, one for each of n tapes, each of which has one read-write head; JFLAP progresses a configuration on a transition only if all of the n read symbols match. In this section we give examples of some multitape TMs that solve useful problems.

9.3.1   Nondeterminism and the Substring

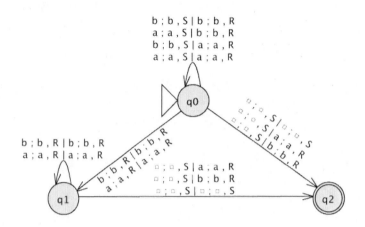

Figure 9.9: A Two-Tape TM That Accepts If the First Tape's String Is a Substring of the Second Tape's String.

We will now build a machine to demonstrate two properties at once: a multitape machine that uses nondeterminism. We will develop a machine with two tapes, T_1 and T_2, with both tapes having input alphabet of $\Sigma = \{a, b\}$ and tape alphabet of $\Gamma = \{\Box, a, b\}$. The machine accepts if the $(a + b)^*$ string in T_1 is a substring of the $(a + b)^*$ string in T_2, and rejects otherwise. Figure 9.9 holds the machine we will build.

Start JFLAP if it is not already running; if it is running select the menu item **File : New**. From the list presented choose to create a new **MultiTape Turing Machine**. Before the editor appears, a dialog asks for the number of tapes for this new TM. The default is **2**; we want two tapes, but nevertheless click on the **2** and see the pop-up menu with integers 2 through 5, allowing choice of the number of tapes for this machine. Select **2** once more, and click on **OK**. A new window with the familiar automaton editor appears.

Create the three states q_0, q_1, and q_2. Make q_0 the initial state and q_2 the single final state, as you see in Figure 9.9. Create a single transition from q_0 to q_2. Instead of a single row as seen earlier for single-tape machine transitions, for an n-tape machine there are n rows as there are n tape heads to read a symbol from, write, and move. The ith row directs what must be read from, written to, and how to move the head of the ith tape.

In the first row, enter $\Box$ as the symbol to be read and written and set the direction symbol to S; recall that to enter $\Box$ you leave a field empty. In the second row, enter b as the symbol to be read and written and set the direction symbol to be R, as shown in Figure 9.10. Finish editing the transition; your transition will appear with the label $\Box; \Box, S | b; b, R$. The n independent controls of

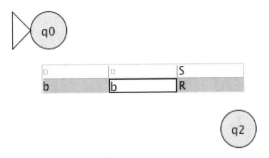

Figure 9.10: Editing the Two-Tape Turing Transition $\square; \square, S|b; b, R$ from q_0 to q_2.

each of the n read-write heads are delimited by the vertical bars |. This transition may be applied if the head of T_1 is over a $\square$ and the head of T_2 is over a b; during simulation, both tape heads will write the same symbol they read, and T_1's head will hold its position while T_2's head will move to the right.

Either enter the remaining transitions shown in Figure 9.9, or open the file `ex9-2tape-substring`. We now describe the meaning of the transitions and states. The loop transitions on q_0 cause T_2's head to move right while T_1's head stays. However, if the two symbols under both heads match, a nondeterministic execution branch is spawned at q_1, where the machine attempts to match T_1's contents as a substring of T_2's contents. The transitions from q_1 to q_2 handle when T_1's head hits $\square$, by which time the entire substring is matched and the machine should accept. The transitions from q_0 to q_2 handle the special case where T_1 is empty, in which case T_1 is always a substring of T_2.

Simulation

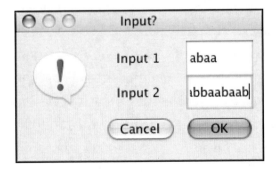

Figure 9.11: Input for Simulation on the Two-Tape Machine, with *abaa* Input for T_1 and *ababaabaab* Input for T_2.

Now, let's simulate input on this multitape TM. Select **Input : Step**. A dialog will appear like the one shown in Figure 9.11. Next to **Input 1** and **Input 2** are text fields for entering the input strings for tapes 1 and 2, respectively. Enter "abaa" and "ababaabaab" in the first and second text fields respectively, and click on **OK**.

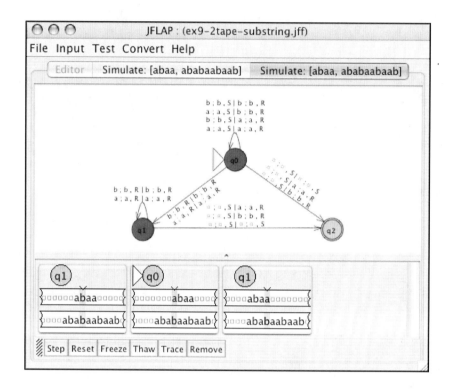

Figure 9.12: In the Midst of Simulation of *abaa* on T_1 and *ababaabaab* on T_2 on the Substring Nondeterministic Two-Tape TM.

The standard step simulator will appear in your window as shown in Figure 9.12. Note a configuration here displays two tapes. Also, you see the workings of nondeterminism in Figure 9.12 with the three configurations: the first configuration, on q_0, is one of the sequence of configurations that simply runs across T_2 and throws off branches of nondeterminism into q_1 as matches occur. Click on **Step** three times to get the configurations shown in Figure 9.12; note that the configurations may be ordered differently than the configurations shown here. The leftmost configuration in Figure 9.12 is part of one of these nondeterministic branches that attempts to match T_1 to part of T_2: the first *a* has already been matched in T_1, and in trying (and succeeding) to match all the remaining symbols, the simulator will eventually reach an accepting configuration! On the other hand, the two right configurations will both next attempt to match an *a* in T_1 to a *b* in T_2, so these configurations will be rejected. Continue stepping to see the acceptance of the first configuration's descendant.

Next, try simulating a few other inputs. Try simulating the inputs *aaa* for tape 1 and *aaabaa* for tape 2; obviously this will be accepted. How about *aaa* for tape 1 and *aabaa* for tape 2? You may, of course, run more simulations until you are satisfied you understand how this two-tape nondeterministic Turing machine works.

9.3.2 Universal Turing Machine

Put briefly, a universal TM is a TM that simulates other TMs. By providing a description of all transitions in some TM M and the initial contents of an input tape for M, U can simulate M. The universal TM U accepts, halts, and does not halt as M accepts, halts, and does not halt.

With three-tape machines, implementations of universal TMs become practical. Here we present an implementation of a universal TM U, explain how to encode a TM M so that M may be input into and processed correctly by U, explain how U works, and as an example encode and run a simple TM on U.

Open the file `ex9-universal`, an implementation of a universal TM. This machine is pictured in Figure 9.13. The universal TM is canonically implemented as a three-tape TM. The first tape T_1 holds a description of M's transitions, T_2 holds M's internal tape, and T_3 holds M's internal state. (Note that T_2 and T_3 together fully describe a simulation configuration.)

The tape alphabet of U is $\Gamma_U = \{\square, 0, 1\}$ and input alphabet of U is $\Sigma_U = \{0, 1\}$. We must have a process to convert any single-tape TM M into input U may process. As a first step, we establish some conditions on M. Suppose M's set of states is $Q_M = \{q_1, q_2, \ldots, q_n\}$ and tape alphabet is $\Gamma_M = \{a_1, a_2, \ldots, a_m\}$. We require M to have initial state q_1, single final state q_2, and blank tape symbol a_1.

As a second step, we describe a method to encode M's tape symbols, states, and transitions as strings of 0's and 1's. Within the context of U each state q_i is encoded as 1^i (for example, q_4 is encoded as 1111), and each tape symbol a_j is similarly encoded as 1^j. Finally, we encode the move symbols L, S, and R as 1, 11, and 111, respectively. The 0 symbol suffixes each string of 1's representing a single element of Γ_M or Q_M or the set of the three movement commands; the exception is in T_3, where only a single element of Q_M is stored. Put another way, if the internal tape of M is $a_{i_1} a_{i_2} a_{i_3} \cdots a_{i_p}$, then T_2's contents are $1^{i_1} 0 1^{i_2} 0 1^{i_3} 0 \cdots 1^{i_p} 0$ (for example, $a_3 a_5 a_2$ is encoded as 1110111110110). As need requires, T_2 may be prefixed and suffixed by repetitions of 10, the representation of a_1, M's blank tape symbol. Similarly, the internal state q_j of M is encoded as 1^j within T_3.

The tape T_1's contents require more explanation. Suppose one of M's transitions is $\delta(q_h, a_i) = (q_j, a_k, d_\ell)$ (where $d_1 = L, d_2 = S, d_3 = R$). This signifies that if M is in state q_h with the tape head

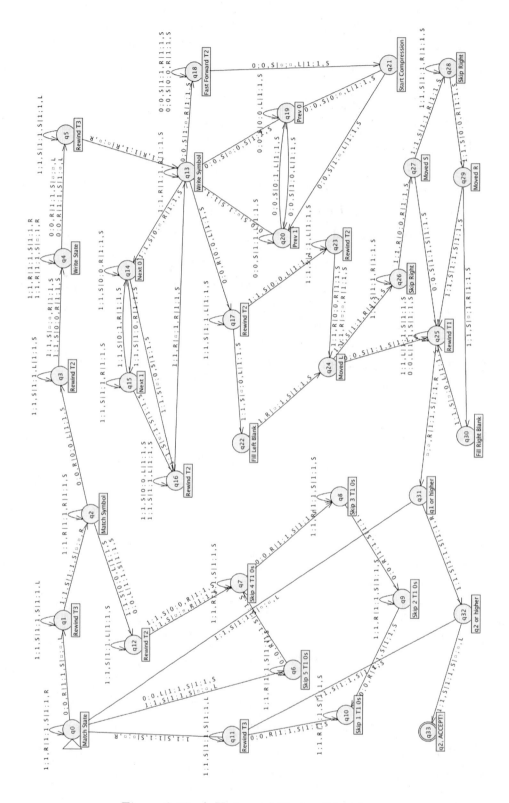

Figure 9.13: A Universal Turing Machine.

on a_i, then M will overwrite a_i with a_k, move the head in the d_ℓ direction, and move to state q_j. Each such transition is encoded as $1^h 01^i 01^j 01^k 01^\ell 0$ with all encoded transitions concatenated together to form the machine description in T_1. For example, one would encode $\delta(q_1, a_3) = (q_2, a_5, S)$ as 101110110110111110110 within T_1.

In brief, U executes a continuous loop. First, U performs a linear search in T_1 for a transition in T_1 that matches the state in T_3 and symbol at the current position of T_2. If the current state and symbol do not match the transition, U proceeds to the next encoded transition in T_1. If the state and symbol match, U changes T_3 to hold the new state and T_2 to overwrite the current symbol with the transition's new symbol, and moves T_2's tape head in the direction indicated by the transition's direction symbol. Then, T_3 is checked to see if T's state q_2 is the current state, in which case U accepts; otherwise, U starts the loop again.

Note ‖ The machine U as implemented does not verify that the initial encodings in T_1, T_2, and T_3 are in accordance with the definitions and restrictions placed on M. If they are not, the results are undefined.

We describe U's run loop in more detail here. The machine in q_0 first compares the state in the current transition of T_1 to the state in T_3. If the states are the same, U proceeds to q_1 to wind T_3 to its beginning; if the states are different, q_6 through q_{11} handle moving T_1's head to M's next transition. Then, in q_2 the machine compares the symbol in the current transition of T_1 to the current symbol of T_2. If the tape symbols are not the same, U proceeds to q_{12}, and q_7 through q_{11} move U to M's next transition.

On the other hand, if the symbols are the same, U moves to q_3 and beyond, where T_2 and T_3 are changed as prescribed by the transition. First, q_4 and q_5 handle writing M's new state to T_3. Then, q_{13} through q_{17} handle writing the new tape symbol to T_2. While writing the new state is trivial, writing the new tape symbol is tricky because encodings of M's tape symbols differ in length and each encoded symbol is put end to end. In overwriting one of M's tape symbols we not only have to overwrite the old encoding, but also shift whatever follows that symbol encoding in T_2 to the left or right depending on whether the new symbol is smaller or larger than the old. The states q_{14} through q_{16} handle the case where the new tape symbol is larger, while q_{18} through q_{21} handle the case where the new tape symbol is smaller. Lastly, U's states q_{22} through q_{30} handle moving the head of T_2 to the start of the encoding of the tape symbol that will now be under M's tape head, depending on the direction symbol; if T_2 is moved past its beginning or end, encodings of M's blank tape symbol 10 are added as appropriate. The state q_{25} handles rewinding T_1 all the way back to its beginning in anticipation of the next search for a transition with the now new symbol and state encoded in T_2 and T_3. Lastly, q_{31} through q_{33} handle the final check of whether

T_3 holds the encoding for M's second state (i.e., M's final state), and if so, U accepts. Otherwise, U goes back to q_0 to start the process all over again.

> **Note** ‖ Keep in mind this machine U will correctly simulate a TM M only if M is deterministic, because for any one state and symbol it will recognize at most one transition encoded in T_1. You will extend U to simulate nondeterministic TMs in an exercise.

Example encoding and run

Figure 9.14: The Simple Transducer We Will Encode and Run on U.

The lengthy encodings make interesting TMs tedious to encode and input. However, a very simple machine, such as the one shown in Figure 9.14, is manageable. This TM is also stored in `ex9-simple`. The Figure 9.14 TM is a trivial transducer: It takes a string in a^*, converts every a to a b, and accepts when it reaches the end of the string. The TM of Figure 9.14 is deterministic, has q_1 as the initial state and q_2 as the single final state, and thus satisfies the requirements of TMs M to encode for U. We encode the tape alphabet $\Gamma = \{\Box, a, b\}$ symbols as $\Box \to 1$, $a \to 11$, and $b \to 111$.

First, we encode the transition $a; b, R$: This is $\delta(q_1, a) = (q_1, b, R)$, encoded as 101101011101110. Remember, the symbols are encoded in the order they appear in the transition function. The $\Box; \Box, S$ transition is formally $\delta(q_1, \Box) = (q_2, \Box, S)$, encoded as 101011010110. Therefore, the machine description is 10110101110111010101101010110, the input for T_1. Suppose we want our initial input for M to be aaa: this we encode as 110110110 as input for T_2. Finally, as always T_3 must hold 1 to signify our initial state q_1.

Select **Input : Fast Run** and enter these values for T_1 through T_3, and click on **OK**. Within a short time the machine will say it accepts. The configuration trace contains a large number of configurations: scroll to the bottom to see the configuration with T_2, with its head on 10 past three 1110 encodings, that is, on the $\Box$ after three b's, and T_3 holds 11, the encoding of q_2, as we would expect.

9.4 Definition of n-tape TM in JFLAP

JFLAP defines a possibly nondeterministic n-tape TM M as the septuple $M = (Q, \Sigma, \Gamma, \delta, q_s, \square, F)$ where

Q is a finite set of states $\{q_i | i$ is a nonnegative integer$\}$;

Σ is the finite input alphabet, where $\square \notin \Sigma$;

Γ is the finite tape alphabet, where $\square \in \Gamma$ and $\Sigma \subsetneq \Gamma$;

δ is the transition function with $\delta : Q \times \Gamma^n \to$ subset of $Q \times \Gamma^n \times \{L, S, R\}^n$;

$q_s \in Q$ is the initial state;

$\square$ is the blank tape symbol; and

$F \subseteq Q$ is the set of final states.

Like FAs and PDAs, in JFLAP TMs do not require explicit definition of Σ or Γ. For each transition on each tape exactly one symbol is read and written under the tape head, and each head is moved either 1 or 0 places to either the left or right. During simulation, the user inputs each tape's initial contents, with $\square$ tape symbols extending infinitely to the left and right of the input string in each tape. The tape head starts over the leftmost character of user input, or over a $\square$ in the tape if the user had input the empty string for initial tape contents.

For example, the TM M of Figure 9.9 is defined as $M = (Q, \Sigma, \Gamma, \delta, q_s, \square, F)$ where

$Q = \{q_0, q_1, q_2\}$

$\Sigma = \{a, b\}$

$\Gamma = \{\square, a, b\}$

$\delta(q_0, \square, a) = \delta(q_1, \square, a) = \{(q_2, \square, a, S, R)\}$

$\delta(q_0, \square, b) = \delta(q_1, \square, b) = \{(q_2, \square, b, S, R)\}$

$\delta(q_0, \square, \square) = \delta(q_1, \square, \square) = \{(q_2, \square, \square, S, S)\}$

$\delta(q_0, a, a) = \{(q_0, a, a, S, R), (q_1, a, a, R, R)\}$

$\delta(q_0, b, b) = \{(q_0, b, b, S, R), (q_1, b, b, R, R)\}$

$\delta(q_0, a, b) = \{(q_0, a, b, S, R)\}$

$\delta(q_0, b, a) = \{(q_0, b, a, S, R)\}$

$\delta(q_1, a, a) = \{(q_0, a, a, R, R)\}$

$\delta(q_1, b, b) = \{(q_0, b, b, R, R)\}$

$q_s = q_0$

$F = \{q_2\}$.

9.5 Summary

Section 9.1 described editing Turing machines (TMs) and simulating input on TMs. The transition format is $x; y, d$ where x is the symbol to read, y is the symbol to write upon x, and d is the direction to move the tape, either L, S, or R. During simulation, input becomes the tape's initial contents, with the tape head at the symbol corresponding to the leftmost character of input.

Section 9.2 described how the multiple-run simulator can be used to conveniently produce outputs of a transducer. A transducer that evaluates mathematical expressions of additions in the input was used as an example.

Section 9.3 described the process for creating and simulating n-tape TMs. With these, the transition format is $x_1; y_1, d_1 | x_2; y_2, d_2 | \cdots | x_n; y_n, d_n$, where each $x_i; y_i, d_i$ section represents the control directives for tape T_i. We built a two-tape machine with multitape and nondeterministic functionality to greatly simplify building a machine that checks if one string is a substring of another string. We also studied and used an implementation of a universal Turing machine, a TM capable of taking a machine description for any one-tape TM M and simulating input on that TM M.

Section 9.4 described the formal definition for a JFLAP TM.

9.6   Exercises

1. Load the following files containing Turing machines. Describe the language that is accepted by each one.

   (a) `ex9.5langacc-a`

   (b) `ex9.5langacc-b`

2. The Turing machine in `ex9.5fix-a` is supposed to accept the language $\{w \in \Sigma^* \mid n_a(w) = 2 * n_b(w)\}, \Sigma = \{a, b\}$. Correct this machine so it does accept this language.

3. The Turing machine in `ex9.5fix-b` is supposed to accept the language $\{ww \mid w \in \Sigma^*, |w| > 0\}$, $\Sigma = \{a, b\}$. Correct this machine so it does accept this language.

4. Write one-tape Turing machines to accept each of the following languages.

   (a) $\{ww^R \mid w \in \Sigma^*, |w| > 0\}$, $\Sigma = \{a, b\}$.

   (b) $\{vwv \mid v, w \in \Sigma^*, |v| = 2\}$, $\Sigma = \{a, b\}$.

   (c) $\{vcw \mid v, w \in \{a, b\}^*$, and v is a substring of $w\}$. For example, $aabcaaaba$, $aacbbbaa$ are accepted and $aabcbaaaa$ is not. This Turing machine may have around 20 states.

5. Load the following files containing Turing machines as transducers. Describe the function they represent.

   (a) `ex9.5trans-a`

   (b) `ex9.5trans-b`

6. The Turing machine in `ex9.5fix-c` is supposed to be a transducer for $f(w) = v$ with $w \in \{a, b\}^*$, and v is w with c added between every pair of a's. For example, $f(abaaaa) = abacacaca$. Correct this machine so that it works correctly.

7. Write one-tape Turing machines as transducers for the following.

   (a) $f(w) = a^m$, where $m = n_a(w) \bmod 3$, $w \in a^*$. For example, $f(aaaa) = a$ and $f(aaaaaaaa) = aa$.

   (b) $f(wvvy) = waay$ where $v, w, y \in \Sigma^*, |v| = 1, |w| = |y|, \Sigma = \{a, b\}$. For example, $f(babbba) = baaaba$ and $f(babaabaa) = babaabaa$.

   (c) $f(w) = w^R$, where $w \in \Sigma^*, \Sigma = \{a, b\}$. For example, $f(aabb) = bbaa$ and $f(baa) = aab$.

8. Load the two-tape Turing machine in `ex9.5ttm-whatlang-a` with $\Sigma = \{a, b\}$. Assume the Turing machine starts with an input string on tape 1 and tape 2 blank. Describe the language that is accepted by this Turing machine.

9. Load the two-tape Turing machine in `ex9.5ttm-whatlang-a` with $\Sigma = \{1\}$. This Turing machine is a transducer that starts with the input on tape 1 and the second tape blank, and produces the output on tape 2. Describe the function for this transducer.

10. Write two-tape Turing machines to accept each of the following languages. Each one starts with the input string on tape 1 and tape 2 blank.

    (a) $\{w \in \Sigma^* \mid n_b(w) = 2 * n_a(w)\}, \Sigma = \{a, b\}$.

    (b) $\{ww^R \mid w \in \Sigma^*\}, \Sigma = \{a, b\}$.

    (c) $\{a^n b^m a^n b^m \mid n > 0, m > 0\}$

11. Write two-tape Turing machines as transducers for each of the following functions. Each Turing machine should start with the input string on tape 1 and tape 2 blank, and produce the output on tape 2 with the tape head on the leftmost symbol.

    (a) $f(w) = w^R, w \in \Sigma^*, \Sigma = \{a, b\}$. For example, $f(abb) = bba$ and $f(ba) = ab$.

    (b) $f(w) = w'$ where w' is w with a b added after each pair of a's, $w \in \Sigma^*, \Sigma = \{a, b\}$. For example, $f(aaa) = aaba$ and $f(aaaaaba) = aabaababa$.

    (c) $f(x\#y) = 3x + 2y$ where $x, y \in \{1\}^+, \Sigma = \{1, \#\}$. Here x and y represent unary numbers and the result is also a unary number. For example, $f(1\#11) = 1111111$ and $f(11\#1) = 11111111$.

12. Consider the universal Turing machine U of Section 9.3.2 pictured in Figure 9.13.

(a) Provide a brief functional description of what happens within U when there is not a transition encoded in T_1 for M's current internal state and tape symbol, and why.

(b) A TM M simulated on U must be deterministic. What nondeterministic transition can we add to U to remove this restriction, so that M may be nondeterministic? Many answers are possible. Answers for which every *single* acceptance path for any input on any M will result in a single acceptance path within U are preferred.

(c) Remember, the restrictions on M imply T_3 must initially hold 1. However, no enforcement makes sure this is so: T_3 can *really* hold any state encoding you want initially. Suppose that we lift the requirement that T_3 initially hold only q_1's encoding, so that T_3 may hold the encoding of any state (that is, not just 1, but 11, 111, and so forth). With U unmodified and this restriction lifted, U no longer simulates M correctly. Why not? *Hint: U simulates M correctly for all but one state.*

(d) How can we modify U so that U simulates M correctly no matter the initial state in T_3?

Chapter 10

L-systems

In this chapter we describe L-systems, an alternative type of formal language structure. Like grammars, L-systems generate a language of strings. Unlike grammars, L-system derivations are often interpreted as graphical rendering instructions, and have been used to generate fractals and simulate plant growth. This chapter describes how L-systems work and how JFLAP interprets derivation strings to produce graphics.

10.1   L-system Creation and Display

L-systems are similar to context-free grammars (CFGs) in that they generate strings of symbols from a finite alphabet Σ through the application of a finite set of rules. In this section we create a series of L-systems, and with them first explore the definition of L-systems within JFLAP and then intersperse this with examples of how JFLAP uses symbols in L-system derivations to create interesting graphics.

Start JFLAP and choose to create an **L-System**. You will see a window similar to Figure 10.1, though with blank fields and tables.

In JFLAP, symbols in the L-system are strings of characters space-delimited from other symbols. For example, the string $g + gg - f$ consists of five symbols: g, $+$, gg, $-$, and f. This possibility of multiple character symbols differs from JFLAP's CFGs, where every single character is considered a symbol. On the one hand this allows some flexibility and power, but on the other this can lead to confusion: Sometimes one forgets spaces, and it is odd to think of gg as being a single "letter" in an alphabet, but it is. In all cases, if one wants JFLAP to interpret two strings of characters as two alphabet symbols, the symbols must be separated by a space or JFLAP will consider the two as a single alphabet symbol.

145

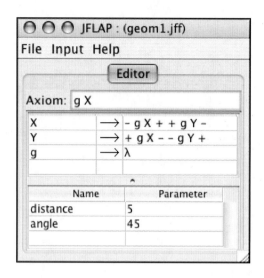

Figure 10.1: An L-System Editor, with the L-System for a Dragon Fractal.

10.1.1   Turtle Symbols

An L-system's mathematical definition calls for a finite alphabet Σ, an *axiom*, and a collection of *rewriting rules*. L-systems share similarities with CFGs: Like CFGs, L-systems all have a starting point, called an *axiom*, which is analogous to a start variable in a CFG in that it is the start of any series of derivation strings, but differs in that an axiom is a finite string in $\Sigma+$ so may hold one or more symbols. An L-system's *rewriting rules* are analogous to the productions in a CFG, but for now we limit our discussion to the axiom without any rewriting rules.

Start editing the **Axiom** text field at the window's top, and enter the string "g + g + f - g - g". (Remember to separate adjacent symbols with spaces.) Then, select the menu item **Input : Render System**. A new tab **L-S Render** will appear. When rendering an L-system as a graphic, JFLAP considers symbols of the derivation (in this case, the axiom itself) to be a sequence of directives to a *turtle*. We use turtle in the sense of LOGO: an object that stores a position and heading, and to which one may send commands to move and draw lines to new positions, to turn in different directions, and to perform other commands. The rest of the chapter is largely an exposition of the use of turtle commands.

The majority of the window shows a large canvas where turtle commands are rendered. A simple crooked line broken in the middle as shown in Figure 10.2 will appear on the canvas, the

Figure 10.2: The Result of Rendering $g + g + f - g - g$.

turtle's rendering to the $g + g + f - g - g$ string. How does this string result in that graphic? In JFLAP, the L-system renderer turtle starts pointing upward. A g tells the turtle to move forward with the pen down (that is, to move and draw a line in its wake). By default the g causes the turtle to go forward 15 pixels. A + tells the turtle to turn to its right; the default turn angle/indexL-systems!parameter!angle is 15°, so + causes a 15° turn. The f symbol tells the turtle to move forward with a pen up (that is, to move and *not* draw a line in its wake). The − symbol tells the turtle to turn to its left, again by 15°. Therefore, with the turtle starting at the bottom of the lower line, the $g + g + f - g - g$ string of symbols tells the turtle to draw forward (g), turn to the right (+), draw forward (g), turn to the right (+), go forward without drawing (f), turn to the left (−), draw forward (g), turn to the left (−), and draw forward once more (g).

The commands g, f, +, and − are four of many turtle commands. More are exhibited throughout this chapter. Appendix A and the help provided in JFLAP for the L-system renderer are both references of all turtle commands.

When you are done, dismiss the **L-S Render** tab, or close the L-system entirely.

10.1.2 Rewriting Rules

Now we will write an L-system with a *rewriting rule*, a mapping from a particular symbol to a string of replacement symbols. Grammar productions that map variables to a string of replacement grammar symbols is a close analogy: As in a grammar derivation, subsequent L-system derivations will see symbols rewritten (that is, replaced) with other symbols according to rewriting rules. We enter rewriting rules in the grammar production editor directly below the axiom field. The symbol to rewrite appears on the left side, and the string of replacement symbols appears on the right side.

We now write an L-system that results in a sequence of g symbols that doubles in length with every step of derivation. As you may recall, g causes the turtle to go forward and draw a line in its wake, so graphically this sequence will be represented as a line that doubles in pixel length with every derivation. Since g goes forward by 15 pixels, we will first have a line of pixel length 15, then 30, then 60, and so forth.

Create a new L-system, and enter the single symbol g as the axiom. Then, in the rewriting rules section, enter the rewriting rule $g \rightarrow g\ g$, entered just as if you were entering a grammar production. Remember, the g symbols on the right side must be space-delimited!

You have finished the L-system. Select **Input : Render System**. This time we will describe the **L-S Render** tab's components. Along the window's top are three components. The top-left component is a progress bar that shows the progress of rendering, which is useful in very large L-system derivations that may take a while to process and display the turtle commands; it is less useful in this simple case. The top component in the center displays the derivation itself; it now displays **g**, the axiom. The top-right component lets us set the number of derivation steps: It displays **0**, or the derivation after 0 steps, i.e., the axiom. Note that below all of these we again see the canvas, and far to the left we see a single small vertical line, the graphical result of the turtle interpreting g. Ignore the controls along the window's bottom for now.

The control in the upper-right is a *spinner*, and with it we can adjust how many derivation steps the current derivation is removed from the axiom. We adjust a spinner by pressing the up and down arrows along its right side. Press the up arrow to increase the derivation steps. When it shows **1** in its display, note that the derivation field now shows **g g**, and that the line is twice as long as before! The axiom was g, and with one derivation step the g was rewritten with the rule $g \to g\ g$, so we get $g\ g$. Increase to 2 derivation steps. The derivation is now $g\ g\ g\ g$: the first and second g symbols were rewritable according to the rule $g \to g\ g$, so both were rewritten as $g\ g$.

CFGs differ. Each grammar derivation step involves expanding a *single* nonterminal in the previous derivation string. We see that each L-system derivation step involves rewriting *every* rewritable symbol in the previous derivation string. If we rewrote symbols as we would in a CFG, four successive derivation steps would produce g, $g\ g$, $g\ g\ g$, and $g\ g\ g\ g$, in that order. On the other hand, four successive L-system derivation steps would produce g, $g\ g$, $g\ g\ g\ g$, and $g\ g\ g\ g\ g\ g\ g\ g$, in that order, as all symbols are rewritten in parallel.

Increase to seven derivation steps with the spinner. Note that with each derivation the line's length doubles. We may also press the down arrow on the spinner to undo a derivation step. If we set the control to 0 again, JFLAP displays the axiom and its rendering.

> **Tip** Depending on the window's size, the line will at some point grow too large to be held: When an L-system rendering grows too large to be displayed in the window, scroll bars appear to allow you to view hidden portions of the image.

> **Note** Note that the with seven derivation steps, the derivation field now displays **Suffice to say, quite long**; most interesting L-systems have exponential growth in the number of symbols in a derivation with respect to the number of derivation steps. When there are very many symbols it does not display the derivation, but rather that message. In such circumstances it is unlikely that a symbol-by-symbol showing of the L-system would be enlightening to a human. Additionally, on a more practical note those strings quickly reach sizes of many megabytes, and attempting to display strings of such size in text fields reveals interesting performance characteristics of Java.

When you are done, dismiss the **L-S Render** tab.

As a final step, it helps to emphasize that we must insert spaces between rules: Change $g \to g\ g$ to $g \to gg$. Render the system again. We start with g, but on the next derivation get gg and the graphic vanishes. Why? Because $g \to gg$ replaces the g with the gg, which the turtle does *not* interpret as two move forward commands, but simply as gg, which is nothing. Furthermore, attempt more derivations: The derivation remains *gg*, and does not grow, because, again, *gg* is its own symbol, and while there is a rewriting rule for *g* there is not one for *gg*. Remember those spaces! You may close this L-system when you are done.

Non-Turtle symbols

The turtle may not recognize some symbols in a derivation; unrecognized symbols are ignored. For example, the turtle does not recognize any uppercase letters, so a derivation $g + A\ g\ B\ C - g$ would produce the same graphic as the string of symbols $g + g - g$. Very often we want a symbol to be used exclusively for rewriting and to not produce a visual artifact, so this is useful.

Create a new L-system. Enter "X" into the axiom field; as an uppercase letter, the turtle will not recognize it. It is conventional to use uppercase letters for symbols that are meant to be only rewritten. Enter the rewriting rule $X \to g\ f\ X$. Select **Input : Render System** once again, and perform a few derivations.

The derivation starts with X, proceeds to $g\ f\ X$, and then to $g\ f\ g\ f\ X$. The L-system will be rendered as a dashed line, first with no dashes (i.e., nothing) with the rendering of X, then one for $g\ f\ X$, then two, then three, and so forth.

When you are done, dismiss the **L-S Render** tab, or close the L-system entirely.

10.1.3 Pushing and Popping Turtles

L-systems can model organisms with modular growth characteristics, like plants. We shall use L-systems to draw a mighty tree! Our tree is very simple: It starts with a branch, and from each branch grow two branches, and from each of those branches grow two more branches, and so forth, for each derivation step.

Create a new L-system. Suppose we use the symbol B to represent the "seed" of a branch. The tree trunk itself is one branch, so our axiom is B. Enter the rewriting rule $B \to g\ -\ B\ +\ +\ B$. When we rewrite a B with this rule, we first get a line representing a branch segment (g). Second, we get a slight turn to the left ($-$) and the seed for a branch (B). Third, we get an equal turn to the right (one $+$ to undo the $-$, and another $+$) and the seed for another branch (B). That seems plausible.

Try rendering it. The eighth derivation step is shown in Figure 10.3; the eagle-eyed will see it is not a tree. The problem is that for $g\ -\ B\ +\ +\ B$, the second branch B will draw in the manner we desire only if the turtle still has the position and heading it had when starting the first branch B. However, once the first of the two B's is expanded on the next derivation, the turtle is put somewhere entirely different.

Dismiss the **L-S Render** tab. We have two choices: we can either put the turtle back ourselves with a series of turtle commands, or we can save the turtle's state before we draw a branch, and

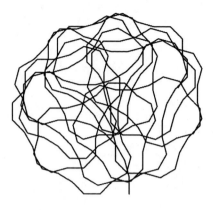

Figure 10.3: This Is Not a Tree.

Figure 10.4: This Is a Tree.

retrieve it when we are finished. The former option is often preferable. To accomplish this, prefix and suffix the rewriting rule's right portion with the bracket symbols [and], respectively, that is, change the $B \rightarrow g \ - \ B \ + \ + \ B$ rewriting rule to $B \rightarrow [\ g \ - \ B \ + \ + \ B \ ]$. When the turtle encounters a [, it saves itself and its attributes (position, heading, and other attributes you have not learned yet) to a stack. When the turtle encounters a], it pops that stack, and sets its attributes to those popped from the stack. In this case, we used the bracket symbols so that every time a B is expanded, the turtle state is saved and retrieved, so that the $- \ B \ + \ + \ B$ string of symbols works in a fashion more in line with our original intentions!

Render the L-system with this change. Successive renderings of derivations should resemble a tree! The eighth derivation is shown in Figure 10.4.

Change the derivation spinner so that the second derivation is rendered: It should look like the letter Y, and the derivation is $[\ g \ - \ [\ g \ - \ B \ + \ + \ B \ ] \ + \ + \ [\ g \ - \ B \ + \ + \ B \ ] \ ]$. Figure 10.5

Figure 10.5: This Is the Second Derivation.

shows this derivation's turtle rendering. Taking this one symbol at a time, the [preserves the turtle state, *g* goes forward (producing the bottom vertical line in Figure 10.5), then − turns the turtle to its left. We now have a [*g* − *B* + + *B*] block resulting from the rewriting of a *B*. This preserves the turtle state on [, goes forward on *g* (producing the top-left line in Figure 10.5), performs some currently useless turns of −, +, and +, and then restores the turtle state with]. With that], the turtle is moved back to the point it was when just [*g* − had been interpreted by the turtle, that is, the symbols just before the last [. Now we encounter two more +'s, and draw another [*g* − *B* + + *B*] block that draws the top-right line in Figure 10.5, and on] delivers the turtle to the point where it was before it drew the *g* of that block. Finally, the last] delivers the turtle to the point where it was before the first *g* ever was drawn, so the turtle is at the base of the trunk again, pointing up. Note once again that] restores from the last unpopped [(in this case the first [ever), not the last [. As we have seen in Figure 10.4, this preservation of state continues recursively through *B* with subsequent derivations.

10.1.4 Polygon

Load the file **ex10-tree-growing**. This is a slight modification to the tree built in Section 10.1.3, so that not only are new branches added, but existing branches are continually elongated: Each new branch starts small, but with each derivation step each branch increases in length, with the effect that the new branches are shortest, and the "trunk" is the longest branch of all. It differs from the previous L-system in that *T* has replaced *g* in the *B* rewriting rule, and there is a rewriting rule $T \rightarrow T\,g$ which serves to add a *g* after *T* with each derivation step. Render the L-system to see the effect of this modification.

It would be nice if our tree could grow leaves as well as branches. JFLAP's turtle has the ability to draw filled-in polygons as well as lines, so we can draw some odd sort of leaf. Our leaves will be diamond-shaped.

Consider the rewriting rule $L \rightarrow [\,\{\,-\,g\,+\,+\,g\,\%\,-\,-\,g\,\}\,]$. We see a few new symbols here that we have not encountered. First we have the brace symbols { and }; these indicate that we should start and end a polygon, respectively. The { symbol causes the turtle to enter *polygon mode*, and the first point of the polygon is set to the turtle's current location. Whenever a *g* is encountered in polygon mode, instead of drawing a line, the turtle is moved forward, and the turtle's new location is added as the polygon's next vertex. When } is encountered, the polygon is filled with red and we exit polygon mode. As one last note, % will turn the turtle 180° in the same axis as + and − turns. When *L* is rewritten, it will produce a polygon in a spearhead or diamond shape. We have the [and] symbols surrounding the polygon to preserve the state.

Figure 10.6: Our Tree with Leaves, After Six Derivations.

Add the $L \rightarrow [\{ - g + + g \% - - g \}]$ rewriting rule to the L-system. Also, in the B rewriting rule, put an L after the T; a leaf shall grow on the tip of each branch! Render this L-system. The graphical representation of the sixth derivation step is shown in Figure 10.6.

> **Note** ‖ In polygon mode, the f turtle command will move forward, but unlike g, the move's
> endpoint will not become a polygon vertex! Lines are not drawn in polygon mode.

10.1.5   Parameters

Continue with the now leaved tree from the previous section; if you have closed the file, load the file `ex10-tree-leaves`. Recall the rendering of the tree, and its bright red leaves. The leaves' red color may seem odd (unless your favorite tree is the Japanese maple, though strictly speaking it is a shrub, not a tree). Therefore, a conventional leaf color like green is more appropriate.

Dismiss the renderer tab to return to the editor for the tree L-system. Below the section for rewriting rules, there is the *parameter table* with two columns, **Name** and **Value**. Each row in the table corresponds to the identifying name of and value of a parameter. In the first row of this table, in the left cell enter "polygonColor" and in the right cell enter "green". (Note that the table grows to accommodate more values as you edit the bottom row.) Re-render the L-system; it will resemble the same leafed tree from Figure 10.6, except the leaves will be green, not red!

Dismiss the renderer tab. The fill color of polygons is just one of many configurable parameters. We will set other parameters now. Just as you set *polygonColor* to *green*, on the next line set *angle* to 30; render again, and you will see that the $+$ and $-$ turtle commands will turn 30° instead of the default 15°. The tree will be more squat and have fatter leaves, as shown in Figure 10.7.

Dismiss the renderer tab. Lastly we want to set a value for the parameter *color*, which specifies lines' color. In the parameter table's upper-right corner (to the right of the **Parameter** heading and above the space for the scroll bar) there is a small rectangular region. Click on it; a pop-up menu of many choices for parameter names will appear. Choose **color**, and type "brown" for the

Figure 10.7: The Tree with 30° Turns Instead of 15° Turns, After Six Derivations.

tree's trunk: The choice of **color** will create a new entry for the parameter *color* in the table and start the user in editing a value, so that we merely have to choose a name, then type the value. This little menu is useful if we forget the exact parameters' names that the turtle recognizes.

In addition to setting parameters in the parameter table, the turtle will interpret certain symbols in a derivation as a command to change a parameter. If we want a parameter's value to vary throughout the rendering, we can insert a symbol *name = value* where *name* is the parameter name and *value* is the value we want assigned to that parameter. For example, insert *angle = 15* after the [in the *L* rewriting rule. (Remember, L-systems considers spaces as the delimiter for separate symbols, so when you enter *angle = 15* do not use spaces!) Render the L-system again: Note that, though the branches have retained their sharper turns as shown in Figure 10.7, the leaves are as thin as they were before we set the *angle* parameter to 30. Nonnumerical parameters may be set as well. For example, if the symbol *color = red* is encountered, all lines created with *g* afterward will be drawn in red.

> **Note** ‖ Though we set *angle = 15*, − and + turns when turning to produce new branches still turn with 30°. This is because the *angle = 15* symbol appeared within [and] turtle push and pop symbols, so the turtle's state, including the turn angle, is preserved on [and restored on].

When you are satisfied, dismiss the renderer tab.

10.1.6   Increment/Decrement Parameter Commands

In addition to setting parameters manually as described in Section 10.1.5, special turtle symbols exist for incrementing and decrementing some turtle parameters: the line's width, the line color's hue, and the polygon color's hue.

If you do not have the L-system from the previous section open, open `ex10-tree-green-leaves`.

First we are going to use turtle commands that change the polygon fill color's *hue angle*. Informally speaking, the hue angle is the color's angle within a color wheel: reddish colors hover around 0°, green-ish colors are around 120°, and blue is at 240°. For example, any color of hue 60° would be a shade of yellow.

We want leaves on the new peripheral branches to still appear green, but we also want leaves that have already been drawn to appear to grow more red over time. Two turtle symbols will help us here: The symbol ## increments the polygon color's hue angle, and @@ decrements the polygon color's hue angle. (The symbols # and @ are similar, but increment and decrement the *line* color.)

> **Note** ‖ The symbols ## and @@ are each single symbols within JFLAP, so do not insert a
> space between the #'s or between the @'s. If you do, # # will be recognized as #
> then #, not ##.

Change the axiom from *B* to *R B*. This *R* is going to be a symbol at the root of our tree (so to speak) before any branches are rendered. Create the rewriting rule $R \rightarrow$ @@ *R*. During each derivation step, the hue angle will be decremented, causing the leaves to appear more and more yellow, then orange, then red as the tree grows. Try rendering a few derivations to confirm that the leaves change color. However, we want newer leaves to retain the green color: in the *B* rewriting rule, insert a ## symbol after the [symbol. The newest branches will have encountered as many ## symbols as @@ symbols, thus nullifying the "reddening" effect and leaving them green, while the progressively more interior leaves have had their hue angle more decremented than incremented. Render the L-system and observe how leaves on the interior become slightly yellower with each derivation!

There is one small cosmetic problem: The outermost leaves are not really green. This is not evident now: The parameter *hueChange*—the amount colors' hue angles are incremented or decremented—is 10° by default. A mere 10° does not make the problem obvious. Return to the editor, and set the parameter *hueChange* to 60! Render the L-system again. Note that the peripheral leaves start out yellow, not green! That is because the last ## symbol appears before an unexpanded *L*; the outermost rewritten *L* appears before the last ##, so at that point the hue angle decrements and increments are not yet balanced. Change the axiom to *R ## B* before you continue. Render again, and note that the outer leaves now appear green, as they should!

Delete your change to *hueChange* now. To do this, it suffices to delete the contents of the **Name** and **Value** cells of a row. Blank rows are ignored.

In addition to leaves yellowing and turning red, it would be nice if, when our tree grew taller, its trunk would also grow wider near its base. We will use the commands ! and ~, which increment and decrement the line width, respectively. Modify the *R* rewriting rule so that it reads $R \rightarrow$! @@ *R*. Before, this rule made the polygon color increasingly red with each derivation. Now it will also serve to make lines increasingly thicker. To balance it, in the *B* rewriting rule insert a ~ after the [.

Figure 10.8: The Tree L-System Rendering with a Thicker Trunk and Apparently Wintering Leaves, After Six Derivations.

(Also, for reasons similar to the cosmetic problem with polygon fill colors described, insert a $\sim$ in the axiom to make the axiom $R \sim \#\# B$.)

Render the L-system. Your tree will resemble Figure 10.8, with leaves growing more yellow and red, and with branches growing thicker, toward the tree's interior!

10.1.7 Stochastic Rules

If you do not have the tree L-system from the previous section, open `ex10-tree-thick-fall-leaves`. Look again at Figure 10.8. There is nothing wrong with the tree except its eerie perfection. That shall soon be amended.

This time, the modifications are quite short: Add the rewriting rule $T \rightarrow T$. Also, in the parameter table change the parameter *angle* to 15, as this tends to yield more aesthetic results. Re-render the L-system a few times. You may encounter a tree like the tree in Figure 10.9, or you

Figure 10.9: One of Many Possible Renderings with the Addition of the $T \rightarrow T$ Rewriting Rule.

may encounter something that looks entirely different, but you almost certainly will not encounter the exact same tree!

The growth of branches was steady and predictable, but is now uneven and inconsistent. It has a more natural feel that previous renderings' perfect symmetry lacked. This is because in adding the $T \rightarrow T$ rule, we made the L-system *stochastic*, that is, under the effect of a random variable!

When rewriting any symbol, the rewriting rule used is uniformly randomly chosen from the rewriting rules that may legally rewrite the symbol. In this case, since we have two rewriting rules for T, it is even money whether a T shall be rewritten as T (not growing the branch) or $T\ g$ (growing the branch).

We are now completely finished with the tree example! You may close the window.

10.1.8   Mathematical Expressions

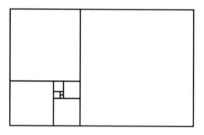

Figure 10.10: The Golden Rectangle, the Rendering of the Ninth Derivation Step of the Fibonacci L-System.

In addition to assigning simple numerical values to parameters as in section 10.1.5, parameters may be set to a value determined by a mathematical formula! This allows some graphics that are otherwise difficult or impossible to render to be produced fairly easily.

Figure 10.10 shows a geometric figure called the *golden rectangle*. Put informally, the golden rectangle is an arrangement of squares, where each square's sides are the length of one of the numbers of the Fibonacci sequence (the unit is undefined but is uniform across all squares). The Fibonacci sequence is defined by $f_0, f_1, f_2, \ldots$, with $f_0 = f_1 = 1$, and $f_i = f_{i-1} + f_{i-2}$ for $i > 1$. In the middle you see the two smallest squares corresponding to 1 and 1, then a square four times the area corresponding to 2, and so forth.

Open the file `ex10-fibonacci`. Render a few derivations of this L-system; the rendering will resemble the golden rectangle of Figure 10.10.

Dismiss the renderer and examine the L-system. First, note the list of parameters and values. While *angle* and *distance* are parameters that directly affect the way the turtle draws, the parameters a and b are not: The parameter list accepts values for parameters that are used in mathematical expressions as variables and are not necessarily consulted by the turtle. In this case,

a and b are variables that hold two Fibonacci values f_{i-1} and f_i as the rendering progresses; as we shall see, these parameters are updated through the course of rendering.

Note the S rewriting rule. Ignoring the apparent complexity and whatever meaning the symbols hold to the turtle, the L-system itself is incredibly simple: The only symbol that is rewritten is S, and there is always only one of them in every derivation, and it always occurs at any derivation's uttermost right. The ending string of symbols $g + g + g \% f + S$ will create a small three-sided box, and then put the turtle in position to create the next three-sided box, which is slightly larger.

This raises the question of how the squares get slightly larger at each derivation step. Note now the string of symbols in the rewriting rule before the first g symbol. During rendering, when the turtle encounters a $c = a + b$ symbol, at that point the parameters a and b hold the last value and current value respectively of the Fibonacci sequence. The $c = a + b$ symbol sets the parameter c to the value of $a + b$, which is the next Fibonacci number after b. Then, a is set to b in $a = b$, and b is set to c in $b = c$. This collection of symbols changes a and b from holding f_{i-1} and f_i to holding f_i and f_{i+1}. Then, we encounter the symbol $distance = a * 3$. As you may expect, this sets the *distance* parameter to $a * 3$, or three times every successive Fibonacci number. The *distance* parameter is what the turtle consults when deciding how far the g and f parameters travel; this is why the rectangles get larger and larger. With each box drawn, *distance* is changed to a constant multiple of successive Fibonacci numbers.

Mathematical expressions in JFLAP must obey some guidelines:

- Just as we had *parameter* = *value*, we now have *parameter* = *expression*. The *expression* is evaluated to a numerical value and assigned to the *parameter*. Indeed, *value* is also a mathematical expression, though one consisting of a single numerical operand and no operator!

- There are addition $(+)$ and multiplication $(*)$ operators, and there are also subtraction $(-)$, division $(/)$, and power $(\char94)$ operators. The expression $x\char94 y$ signifies x raised to the yth power. The $+$ and $-$ operators have lowest precedence, $*$ and $/$ operators have next to lowest precedence, and $\char94$ has highest precedence. Parentheses may also be used to control the order of evaluation.

- The expression's operands must be either parameter values or numbers. If an operand does not map to a numerical value, then 0 is assumed.

- If an assignment commits a mathematical no-no, e.g., division by zero, the results are undefined. In the current version of JFLAP, the entire rendering is invalidated and nothing appears.

- As with any L-system symbols, mathematical expressions cannot have spaces in them. Notwithstanding their significance to the turtle, any single mathematical assignment expression, no matter how complex, is simply a "letter" in the L-system's alphabet.

- Mathematical expressions obey infix notation. The expression $a + b * c$ is an example of infix notation, which is called infix because operators come between operands.

10.1.9   Turtle Commands with Arguments

Figure 10.11: The Rendering of an L-System That Uses Command Arguments.

Mathematical expressions are not used just for the simple setting of parameters. Open the file `ex10-command-arguments`. Like the golden rectangle L-system described in Section 10.1.8, this L-system is simple, and the form of most of these symbols should look familiar except for $g(a)$ and $g(a*a)$. Render this L-system. A few derivation steps should produce an image like that shown in Figure 10.11.

The string of symbols responsible for the drawing of a single blue line are $[+ color = blue \; g(a * a) \;]$. The turtle draws the line when it encounters $g(a * a)$. This is an example of an *argument command*, a turtle command that takes an argument. In this case, the g command draws a line the length of its argument, in this case a^2. The first blue line is of length $1^2 = 1$, the second of length $2^2 = 4$, the third of length $3^2 = 9$, the fourth of length $4^2 = 16$, and so on. Argument commands take the form *command(argument)*, where *argument* is a value or mathematical formula as described in Section 10.1.8. Many of the commands that we have used so far can be used as argument commands. For example, we use g here with an argument: Instead of g going forward *distance* pixels, g will go forward by the number of pixels equal to the numeric evaluation of its argument. A command like $+(50)$ will cause the turtle to turn $50°$ to the right instead of the default *angle°* to the right. Similarly, $\#(30)$ will "turn" the line color's hue angle by $30°$ instead of *hueChange°*. A $+(-angle)$ symbol would produce the same graphical result as a $-$ symbol! Appendix A describes argument commands and the significance of their arguments.

> **Note** ‖ Notwithstanding $g(a)$'s and $g(a*a)$'s special relevance to the turtle, both are still single symbols in the L-system alphabet. If a rule rewrites g, it will not rewrite $g(a)$ or $g(a*a)$; to rewrite either of these symbols you must construct rules to rewrite either $g(a)$ or $g(a * a)$ specifically.

10.1.10   3D L-Systems

When we spoke of turns via $+$ and $-$ symbols, we always spoke of the turtle turning "to its right" or "to its left," but clearly what is happening from our perspective is that the turtle is turning

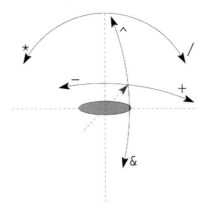

Figure 10.12: An Illustration of Turtle Turns and Movement In 3D.

clockwise and counter-clockwise. Create a new L-system, and enter the axiom $g + g + g + g + g$. Render this system, and you will see an arc curving to the right, as though the turtle were making gentle clockwise turns as it moved forward; this fits expectations. So, why do we not say clockwise, and not describe turns from the turtle's point of view?

Return to the editor, and prefix the axiom with the symbol $*(180)$. Render again, and note that now the arc curves to the *left*, as though all the +'s had been turned to −'s! The + no longer appears to turn the turtle clockwise!

No, we did not flip the image. Rather, we flipped the turtle! By default we are looking down at our turtle from above; its head initially points toward the top of the screen and its shell faces outward toward us. The $*(180)$ symbol is the argument command version of the $*$ turtle command. The $*$ command tells the turtle (loosely speaking) to roll onto its left side. With $*(180)$, we tell the turtle to turn 180° onto its left side, that is, to roll onto its back so its belly faces us! The + commands still turn the turtle to *its* right, though to us the turtle seems to bend counter-clockwise.

This has applications beyond confusing people; with these and other turns, the turtle is not limited to movement in the two-dimensional plane that we have seen up until now. It may travel in any direction in three dimensions. The turtle moves only with the f and g commands, that is, it may only go forward, but the meaning of forward changes with every turn. These 3D turns allow the turtle to travel anywhere in three dimensions without movement commands other than f and g!

Up until now we have seen + and − turns, two turns in opposite directions on the same axis. When moving in three dimensions, we turn around three axes, and so require six turn commands. Examine the diagram of Figure 10.12 as we explain turtle turn commands. This diagram is meant to express a three-dimensional world, where the dashed gray lines represent orthogonal axes in 3D space. The direction the turtle goes forward on f or g is in the arrow's direction on the dashed gray diagonal line. We are looking down in the same direction as the turtle moves, more or less. The solid black lines show the direction in which a turn will swivel a turtle; think of these black lines as being on the face of a globe in which the turtle is embedded, and those arrows as showing the direction one may rotate the globe by dragging one's hand across it. Next to each black arrow head is the turtle command to effect each of these turns.

Think of the turtle as a trained circus dog. With the + and − turns, the turtle is simply turning in place to its right and its left, respectively, as even a wild dog will when changing direction. With / and *, we have a trained dog, capable of rolling over onto its back by either its right or left side, respectively (as we made the turtle do in the example). However, with the ^ and & commands, we have a trained circus dog that does back-flips and somersaults!

On top of these wonders, our turtle-dog has the ability to not only do these incredible turns, rolls, and flips, but to stop in the middle of a turn and go forward as if it were swimming. We may also think of the turtle as a sea turtle for this reason!

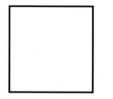 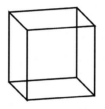 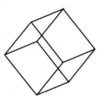

Figure 10.13: Renderings of the Same Cube with Various Angles for Pitch, Roll, and Yaw, the First with 0°, 0°, and 0°, Respectively; the Second with 15°, 75°, and 0°, Respectively, and the Third with 45°, 30°, and 45°, Respectively.

It is often useful to view a 3D L-system from different angles. Open the file ex10-cube. Render it. You need not perform any derivation steps as the string of turtle symbols to render the desired graphic are contained within the axiom itself. The name suggests this produces a cube, but right now we are looking down one of its axes so it appears to be a square, as shown in the left shape of Figure 10.13.

Note the three controls at the window's bottom, labeled **Pitch**, **Roll**, and **Yaw**. Intuitively, these controls allow us to turn our rendering of the L-system in various directions so that even with an orthogonal 2D rendering of the L-system we may get a sense of its 3D shape by looking at the rendering from different directions. These are spinners like the control that allows us to change the number of derivation steps.

Using these spinners, change the pitch to 15° and roll to 75°; leave the yaw unchanged at 0°. Your cube will look like the middle shape of Figure 10.13. Next, change the pitch, roll, and yaw to 45°, 30°, and 45° respectively. Your cube will look like the right shape of Figure 10.13! In this way we see that it is a cube, and not a simple square.

Note	Functionally, setting the pitch, roll, and yaw to p, r, and y degrees, respectively, is the same as if the turtle, prior to rendering the derivation, accepted the argument commands $\&(p)$, $*(r)$, and $-(y)$, in that order, to turn the turtle ahead of the rendering.

10.1.11 Contextual Rules

Ignore the turtle's graphical nicety for a moment; concentrate only on the L-system as a generator of a formal language. We can add all the turtle commands we want, and the power of L-systems as a generator of formal languages remains the same as it was through Section 10.1.2 where we introduced rewriting rules. However, with a slight extension of rewriting rules, the power of L-systems can be increased.

If Σ is the L-system's alphabet, we know that rewriting rules have the form $b \to d$ where $b \in \Sigma$ and $d \in \Sigma^*$, and during each derivation step any symbol b in the derivation string is rewritten with the string of symbols d.

We extend this now to rules of the form $(a, b, c) \to d$, where $b \in \Sigma$ and $a, c, d \in \Sigma^*$. This differs in that b will be rewritten as d only if it is immediately prefixed by the string a and immediately suffixed by the string c! We call these *contextual rewriting rules*, or simply contextual rules, since they are sensitive to the context in which a symbol appears.

By now you are familiar with how to enter the $b \to d$ rewriting rules, but how do we enter these new $(a, b, c) \to d$ rewriting rules in JFLAP? The form of the right side remains unchanged: It is, as ever, a string of symbols JFLAP rewrites another symbol with. However, the left side changes. Instead of a single symbol, we now have a space-delimited string of symbols of the form $k\ s_0\ s_1\ \cdots\ s_{k-1}\ s_k\ s_{k+1}\ \cdots\ s_{n-2}\ s_{n-1}$. The first symbol, k, is an integer between 0 and $n-1$, inclusive, and the following n symbols, s_i for $i \in [0, n)$, are in Σ. The k specifies which s_i element is the symbol this rewriting rule is meant to rewrite, which is the b in our $(a, b, c) \to d$ notation. The s_i preceding s_k compose the a prefix list, and the s_i succeeding s_k compose the c prefix list. For example, suppose in JFLAP we enter "3 a b c d e f" in the left side, and "g h i" in the right side. This represents the rule $abc, d, ef \to ghi$, that is, the symbol d would be rewritten with $g\ h\ i$ if the d were preceded by $a\ b\ c$ and succeeded by $e\ f$ in the current derivation string.

Open the file `ex10-simple-context` in JFLAP. This is a very simple example of contextual rules. Render the system. It does not render a graphic; our interest is in the derivation strings, so keep an eye on the derivation strings shown at the window's top. Perform many derivation steps. Note that the > symbol appears to move to the right, bounce off the right # symbol, turn around (now as a < symbol), move to the left, bounce off the left # symbol, and repeat.

How does the > travel to the right? Take a look at the two rules $0\ \ >\ \ -\ \to\ -$ and rule $1\ \ >\ \ -\ \to >$. The first rule says whenever > is followed by a $-$, rewrite the > with $-$. The second rule says whenever $-$ is preceded by a >, rewrite the $-$ with >. Since these rewriting rules are applied in parallel, this provides the appearance that the $>$ is moving to the right with each derivation. How does the $>$ bounce off the $\#$? Take a look at the rule $0 \ > \ \# \ \to <$. This will rewrite $>$ as $<$ whenever it is followed by a $\#$, providing the appearance that $>$ is bouncing off the right $\#$. The remaining three rules that we have not described perform similar operations with the $<$ traveling to the left and bouncing off the left $\#$, and are nearly of the same form; we do not describe them in detail here, since they work under the same principle as the previous three commands.

10.2   Definition of an L-System in JFLAP

JFLAP's formal definition of an L-system presented here includes the contextual rules described in Section 10.1.11.

In JFLAP an L-system is defined as the triple (Σ, A, R), where

Σ is the finite alphabet of the L-system;

$A \in \Sigma+$ of finite length is the axiom; and

$R = \{(a, b, c) \to d | a, c \in \Sigma^*, b \in \Sigma, d \subset \Sigma^*\}$ is the set of rewriting rules. The sets d and R have a finite number of elements.

For any $(a, b, c) \to d \in R$, if $|d| > 1$ the L-system is a stocastic L-system, and if $a \neq \lambda$ or $c \neq \lambda$ the L-system is a contextual L-system.

This definition of L-systems is considerably more broad than most definitions due to the inclusion of the stocastic and contextual rewriting rules defined in sections 10.1.7 and 10.1.11. Nonstocastic, noncontextual L-systems are typically more common than their stochastic, contextual variants.

The user does not explicitly define Σ; rather, Σ is implicitly defined through the space-delimited symbols present in the rewriting rules and axiom.

> **Note** ‖ Although you can define parameters in JFLAP that are saved with the L-system for convenience, the formal definition of an L-system has absolutely nothing to do with how derivations manipulate a turtle to produce a graphic. Parameter values are not included with the formal definition. Remember always that L-systems and turtle graphics are intertwined only by an accident of history, and are otherwise separate subjects!

10.3   Summary

L-systems are a breed of formal languages. They are often used to generate graphics of fractals and organisms with modular growth characteristics. L-systems are reminiscent of CFGs in several respects. Similar to how CFGs derive strings through expansion of variables in successive derivation steps, L-systems derive strings through *rewriting* of symbols in successive derivation steps. L-systems have a collection of rewriting rules that describe how symbols are rewritten from one derivation step to the next, similar to a CFG's productions.

L-systems differ from CFGs, of course. A CFG always starts with a single symbol, the start variable; the axiom of an L-system may consist of multiple symbols. CFGs generate strings by replacing all variables, so only the end result of all derivation steps is considered as part of the CFG's language; in an L-system every derivation step's string is considered part of the L-system's language. CFG string derivation involves expanding a single variable from one derivation step to the next; L-system string derivation involves rewriting every symbol that can be rewritten from one derivation step to the next. CFGs maintain a distinction between terminal and variable; in an L-system no such distinction is made. Lastly, there is a characteristic particular to JFLAP's L-systems: Although symbols and single characters are one and the same in a CFG, all distinct symbols in an L-system must be space-delimited.

After defining an L-system, we may perform derivation steps. The first derivation string is always the axiom. A turtle interprets each derivation string, and produces a graphic from the symbols in the string. The turtle considers each symbol in the derivation string as a command (except those symbols it does not recognize, which it ignores). There are many commands, but most interesting renderings can be produced with only six commands and some cleverness: g and f, which tell the turtle to move forward with the pen down and up, respectively; $+$ and $-$, which turn the turtle to its right and left, respectively; and [and], which push and pop a turtle state (including its position and heading), respectively.

We can also set parameters the turtle consults when drawing. Some parameters accept numeric values; for example, *distance* holds the pixel length, and g and f consult *distance* to determine how far to move forward. Others accept color values; for example, *color* holds the line color. Some turtle symbols can be used to change the value of a parameter in the middle of a render, of the form *parameter* = *expression*, where *expression* is an infix mathematical expression involving numeric values and numeric parameters, or a color. Alternatively, we may use a turtle command with an infix mathematical expression argument to customize drawing; for example, $g(2 * distance)$ will cause the turtle to drawn a line twice the length of *distance*.

If a symbol can be rewritten with more than one rule, the L-system becomes stochastic. During derivation, the single rule chosen to rewrite a symbol is chosen uniformly randomly from all rules that may rewrite that symbol. This allows the L-system to model quasi-chaotic systems!

L-system rules may also be context-sensitive, that is, they will rewrite a symbol only if it is prefixed and suffixed with defined strings of symbols. This addition makes L-systems suitable as a general model of computation!

10.4   Exercises

1. Create an L-system to generate the picture in Figure 10.14. The only symbols needed are
   g, $+$, and one variable. The distance of the line is 100. Rendering at 1 draws the first line.
   Each additional render draws another line.

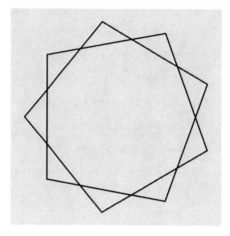

Figure 10.14: A Nine-Point Star.

2. Create an L-system to generate the smiling face Figure 10.15. Symbols you might need are g,
   f, $+$, $-$, and %. The angle is set to 90 and the distance is set to 25. The first rending should
   draw the outline of the face, the second rendering should add one eye, the third rendering
   should add the second eye, and the fourth rendering should add the mouth.

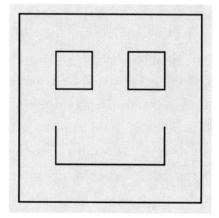

Figure 10.15: A Smiling Face.

3. Create an L-system to generate the squares pictured in Figure 10.16. Symbols you might
   need are g and $+$. The angle is set to 90 and the distance is set to 10. The first rending
   should draw the smallest square, and each additional rendering should add the next larger
   square. The picture is shown after the tenth rendering.

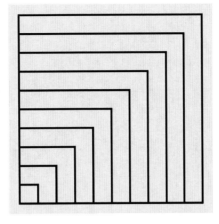

Figure 10.16: Squares.

4. Create an L-system to generate the squares on the diagonal picture in Figure 10.17. Symbols you might need are g, %, and +. The angle is set to 45 and the distance is set to 15. The side of a square is of length 30, and the first diagonal line is of length 60. The first rending should draw the picture on the left, the second rendering should draw the picture in the middle, and the sixth rendering should draw the picture on the right.

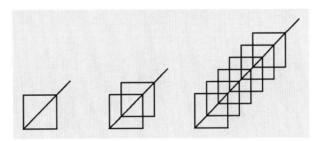

Figure 10.17: Squares on the Diagonal.

5. Create an L-system to generate a tree that has three branches, as shown in Figure 10.18. Symbols you might need are g, +, −, [, and]. The angle is set to 30 and the distance is set to 20. The picture shows the third rendering.

Figure 10.18: A Tree with Branching of Three.

6. Create an L-system to generate lots of squares in the pattern shown in Figure 10.19. Symbols you might need are g, $+$, $-$, [and]. The angle is set to 90 and the distance is set to 15. The picture shows the first, second, and third renderings.

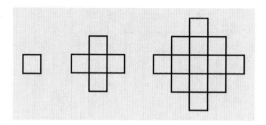

Figure 10.19: Multiplying Squares.

7. Create an L-system to generate a tree with six-sided leaves, as shown in Figure 10.20. Symbols you might need are g, $+$, $-$, [,], {, and }. The angle is set to 30 and the distance is set to 15. The picture shows the fifth rendering.

Figure 10.20: A Tree with Six-Sided Leaves.

8. Create an L-system to generate a tree with two adjacent diamond-shaped leaves extending from each branching point, as shown in Figure 10.21. Symbols you might need are g, $+$, $-$, [,], {, and }. The angle is set to 20 and the distance is set to 15. The picture shows the fifth rendering.

Figure 10.21: A Tree with Adjacent Leaves.

9. Create L-systems to generate the following.

   (a) A fruit tree with leaves and some type of fruit.

   (b) A tree in autumn with leaves of different colors ranging from yellow to orange.

   (c) A decorated tree with ribbons and/or ornaments, such as a Christmas tree.

   (d) A broken tree chewed by a beaver, which has fallen over where the beaver chewed it.

   (e) A wreath of green leaves.

   (f) A wreath of leaves and decorations.

   (g) A spirograph shape, i.e., lines drawn repeatedly in variations of a circle.

   (h) Geometric shapes, such as a triangle filled with triangles, or a square filled with squares.

10. Consider the tree-drawing problem presented in Section 10.1.3. Load the file `ex10-failed-tree`, which holds the broken L-system we started with in that section.

    (a) The fix presented in the text that resulted in the graphic of Figure 10.4 involved the addition of two symbols. Give an alternate modification of the B rewriting rule that produces the same graphic as the fixed version, but has only one more symbol than the original rule!

    (b) The use of pushes and pops is significantly more expensive, computationally, than simple moves and turns. The other option of manually moving the turtle back to its original position and heading was mentioned but not explored. Modify the rule again so that the bracket symbols [and] are not used, but so that the L-system generates the same graphic as Figure 10.4. Remember, the % symbol will turn the turtle 180° around the same axis as the + and − turn commands.

11. We saw how to use mathematical expressions in Section 10.1.8, and with this power we drew the golden rectangle shown in Figure 10.10. Often, results we achieve with mathematical expressions can be achieved more conventionally. Produce an L-system where successive derivation steps produce the golden rectangle as in Section 10.1.8, but without using mathematical expressions, argument commands, or contextual rules. Successive rendering steps should produce an image recognizable as successive golden rectangles, similar to what is shown in Figure 10.10. *Hint: First try creating a line that increases in proportion to the Fibonacci sequence.*

Chapter 11

Other Grammars in the Hierarchy

This chapter describes JFLAP's ability to parse strings using unrestricted grammars and context-sensitive grammars. The first section describes how to define unrestricted grammars in the grammar editor, and shows how to use the brute-force parser to parse strings with unrestricted grammars. The second section is similar to the first section, except it covers context-sensitive grammars instead of unrestricted grammars.

11.1 Unrestricted Grammars

In this section we define an unrestricted grammar, and how to produce an unrestricted grammar within JFLAP. We then use the brute-force parser to parse strings using an unrestricted grammar that generates a fairly complex language. A different equivalent grammar is used as a point of comparison to discuss some practical advice in constructing unrestricted grammars for use with JFLAP's brute-force parser.

11.1.1 Introduction

An unrestricted grammar is similar to a context-free grammar (CFG), except that the left side of a production may contain any nonempty string of terminals and variables, rather than just a single variable. In a CFG, the single variable on the left side of a production could be expanded in successive derivation steps. In an unrestricted grammar, in addition to expanding a single variable, we may "expand" multiple symbols.

Taking lower- and uppercase letters to be terminals and variables, respectively, an example production in a CFG could be $A \rightarrow aaBa$. An expansion using this production replaces the variable A with the string $aaBa$. For example, the sentential form $aAtwf$ could lead to the sentential form $aaaBatwf$.

On the other hand, an example production in an unrestricted grammar could be $AaC \rightarrow aaBa$. An expansion using this production replaces the three symbols AaC with $aaBa$. For example, the sentential form $atAaCqx$ could lead to the subsequent sentential form $ataaBaqx$.

As you might expect, unrestricted grammars are more powerful than CFGs: You may construct an unrestricted grammar to generate any recursively enumerable language.

11.1.2 Simple Grammar

We shall enter a simple unrestricted grammar and use JFLAP's brute-force parser to parse strings using this unrestricted grammar.

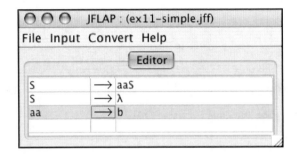

Figure 11.1: Editing a Simple Unrestricted Grammar.

Start JFLAP. When the list of choices for a structure appears, select **Grammar**. When the empty window pops up, enter the grammar pictured in Figure 11.1.[1] The first two productions are acceptable for use in a CFG. However, the two a symbols in the left side in the last production makes this an unrestricted grammar, not a CFG. This grammar generates any string consisting of a's and b's, where there is an even number of a's and any number of b's.

The brute-force parser described in Section 3.2 can also parse strings using an unrestricted grammar. Once you have created the grammar of Figure 11.1, select the menu item **Input : Brute Force Parse**. In the **Input** field, enter aba and click on **Start**.

Click on **Step** twice. In two derivation steps, the production $S \rightarrow aaS$ is used twice to produce the sentential form $aaaaS$. However, after the third click on **Step**, the production $aa \rightarrow b$ is used to produce the sentential form $abaS$ from $aaaaS$. Figure 11.2 shows the parse trees before (left) and after (right) this last derivation. The parse tree here differs from those generated by CFGs; note that the two middle a nodes have been grouped into a single "bracketed" aa node, and this bracketed node is expanded to a single b child node. In this way, JFLAP is able to visually represent the replacement of multiple symbols with a single production using the familiar parse-tree paradigm.

---

[1]If you have forgotten how to enter grammars, see Section 3.1.

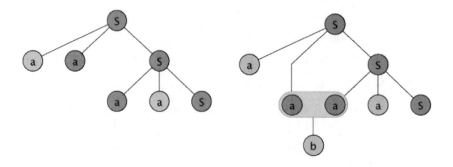

Figure 11.2: The Parse DAG Before and After the Expansion Using the $aa \rightarrow b$ Production.

> **Note** ‖ In a context-free grammar, each production replaces one symbol, so each node except
> the root has exactly one parent. However, since an unrestricted grammar can replace
> multiple symbols when applying a single rule, a node may now have multiple parents.
> For this reason, the unrestricted parse "tree" representation is not a tree, but a directed
> acyclic graph (DAG). So, though we will continue to refer to this structure as a parse
> tree, it is more properly called a parse DAG.

There is one last minor point to explain: In the parse trees shown in Figure 11.2 and in JFLAP, the middle two a nodes with a b child node have the darker green color, and not the lighter yellow color we have previously seen for terminal nodes. Previous parse trees generated from CFGs had green nodes corresponding to variables, and yellow nodes corresponding to terminals; a variable would always be replaced, and a terminal could never be replaced. However, unrestricted grammar productions may replace variables *and* terminals, and nodes containing replaced terminals are green.

> **Note** ‖ With CFGs, JFLAP considers the variable on the left side of the first production to be
> the start variable for the grammar. While an unrestricted grammar may have "unre-
> stricted productions" with multiple symbols on the left side of a production, unrestricted
> grammars in JFLAP continue to require that the first production be in the restricted
> form; the single variable on the left side of this first production provides the start
> variable.

11.1.3   Complex Grammar

The simple example of Section 11.1.2 illustrates how JFLAP handles unrestricted grammars, but the language the grammar generates is hardly interesting: A two state finite automaton could recognize the language. However, unrestricted grammars have equivalent power to Turing machines. The more complex example in this section exercises more of that power.

Open the file `ex11-composite-fast`. (Alternatively, you could enter the productions listed in Table 11.1.) This unrestricted grammar generates the more interesting language of all strings a^n, where n is a composite number.[2] This grammar is fairly lengthly with fourteen productions, but it is quite simple.

1.	$S \to HaC$	6.	$aZ \to ZAa$	11.	$T \to X$
2.	$C \to aC$	7.	$HZ \to HY$	12.	$aX \to Xaa$
3.	$C \to aT$	8.	$YA \to AY$	13.	$AX \to Xa$
4.	$T \to ZU$	9.	$Ya \to aY$	14.	$HX \to \lambda$
5.	$AZ \to ZA$	10.	$YU \to T$		

Table 11.1: The Productions of `ex11-composite-fast`.

Briefly, the strategy of the grammar is to generate a string of a's of length two or longer. Then, the grammar "multiplies" that string of a's two or more times. In this way, this grammar generates strings a^n where n is a product of any two integers greater than one. That is, n can be any composite number, and cannot be a prime number.

Select **Input : Brute Force Parse** from the menu. Enter the string $aaaaaaaaa = a^9$ into **Input** and click on **Start**. Since 9 is a composite number (3×3), the parser will accept the string. It is more helpful for this grammar to view it as a derivation table rather than a parse tree: click the pop-up menu currently displaying **Noninverted Tree**, and select **Derivation Table** instead.

The following few paragraphs will explain the ideas behind what is happening in successive steps as the grammar generates a^9. The productions in `ex11-composite-fast` are displayed and enumerated in Table 11.1 for easy reference.

Productions 1–3 generate an initial string of two or more a's, in this case of the form $HaaaT$. The a's are the initial string of a symbols that will be multiplied by another number. Once this string is generated, production 4 turns the "tail" T into ZU, where the Z will move across the string copying existing a's, and the U is a placeholder for the right end of the string. In production 6, $aZ \to ZAa$, whenever Z encounters an a symbol, it moves over the a symbol and generates a new A symbol, which is a placeholder for a duplicated a. We cannot simply write another a, since in subsequent passes *that* duplicate a would itself be duplicated, and we only wish to duplicate the original a's. So, we use A to denote an a that should not be duplicated in subsequent passes. Production 5, $AZ \to ZA$, moves Z across A symbols without duplicating. For production 7, when Z runs into the "head" of the string H, the Z is turned into a Y, which is meant to travel harmlessly to the right across a and A symbols with productions 8 and 9. The Y is soon delivered next to the U variable generated by production 4: production 10, $YU \to T$ effectively destroys the Y, and

---

[2]Composite numbers are nonprime integers greater than 1.

turns the U into a T so that the cycle defined by productions 4–10 can start over again to perform another duplication of a's.

This cycle *can* run multiple times, ignoring A's and producing another A for every a encountered. However, for this string, only one Z/Y cycle is necessary, and a "finishing" sequence involving X starts. Production 11 turns the T symbol into an X. Productions 12 and 13 help this X sweep across the a and A symbols, converting the A's into a's, and converting every a into two a's, duplicating the a's one last time. When X encounters the head symbol H, production 14 annihilates both, leaving a pure string of a's behind.

In brief, we started with three a's, did one pass using Z to "duplicate" the a's with placeholder A symbols, and did a second pass to again duplicate the a's and convert the placeholder A symbols into a's. This effectively copies a twice, leading to a string of a's three times as long as the original string of three a's. The grammar multiplied three times three to generate the target string of nine a's.

Note that the grammar approaches its problem similarly to how we might design a Turing machine. X, Y, and Z symbols with their "sweeping" behavior act in a fashion very reminiscent of the heads of Turing machines. In a sense, each letter X, Y, and Z corresponds to a different state. Z makes a pass to the left over the symbols, inserting symbols as necessary. Y rewinds the "tape head" to the right after the Z pass is complete, so that another Z pass or the final X pass may be attempted. X finishes by moving left, overwriting placeholder symbols to produce the pure string of a's. Lastly, in a Turing machine there is always a single tape head, and in the grammar at most one of X, Y, or Z may exist at any particular time. It is unnecessary to have an unrestricted grammar form such a close analogy to a Turing machine, but it is often a useful paradigm.

11.1.4   Slow Complex Grammar

The grammar of Section 11.1.3 has a fairly straightforward approach that closely mirrors how we might approach the problem of recognizing the language within a Turing machine. However, it is not necessary to adopt such a limited approach.

1.	$S \rightarrow HaC$	5.	$AZ \rightarrow ZA$	9.	$aX \rightarrow Xaa$
2.	$C \rightarrow aC$	6.	$aZ \rightarrow ZAa$	10.	$AX \rightarrow Xa$
3.	$C \rightarrow aT$	7.	$HZ \rightarrow H$	11.	$HX \rightarrow \lambda$
4.	$aT \rightarrow ZAaT$	8.	$aT \rightarrow Xaa$		

Table 11.2: The Productions of `ex11-composite-short`.

Open the file `ex11-composite-short`. This unrestricted grammar generates the same "composite length" language as the grammar of Section 11.1.3, and is quite similar, but has a few subtle differences. The productions of this grammar are listed in Table 11.2. Start the brute-force parser for this grammar, and start the parser working on the *aaaaaaaaa* string again (that is, a^9).

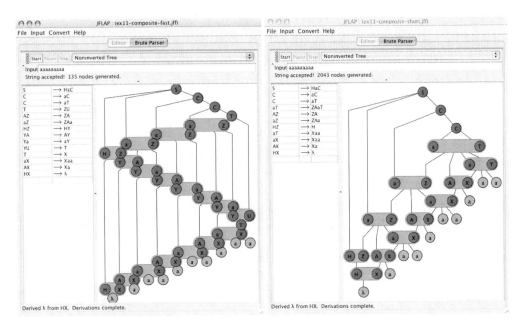

Figure 11.3: The Parse Tree for a^9 Generated by `ex11-composite-fast` Is On the Left and `ex11-composite-short` Is On the Right.

After some time, the parse tree will complete. If you expand the parse tree completely, you will see a tree similar to that shown to the right in Figure 11.3; the parse tree to the left shows the parse tree generated by the grammar of the previous section. The parse tree generated by the new grammar is considerably shorter, though it took far longer to generate.

The `ex11-composite-short` grammar utilizes the same strategy as the `ex11-composite-fast` grammar, with some exceptions. In the `fast` grammar, though making out the details of the parse tree is perhaps slightly difficult, it is extremely easy to see the back and forth "sweeping" action of the X, then Y, then Z symbols. However, consider Table 11.2's production 4, analogous to Table 11.1's production 4: In the new grammar, the T symbol is *not* turned into a U, so that this T symbol can continue generating multiple concurrent X and Z symbols that run at the same time. The Y symbol is no longer necessary: Nothing needs to travel to the right to "inform" the U symbol that it can turn back into a T symbol and generate more Z's or the final X.

As one last enhancement, in the old grammar's productions 4 and 11, the X and Z symbols are generated without processing any symbols. In the new grammar's productions 4 and 8, when the X and Z symbols are first generated, the grammar not only generates these symbols but has them process an a symbol.

As we see in Figure 11.3, the new grammar yields a smaller parse tree. However, parse tree generation takes *far* longer with the new grammar versus the old grammar.

Why is the old grammar faster? It has to do with how JFLAP performs searches. In the old grammar, except during the generation of an initial string of a's (productions 2 and 3), and the choice between whether to perform an X or Z sweep (productions 4 and 11), there was always at most one production that could ever be applied for each sentential form.

However, in the new grammar, since multiple X and Z symbols can concurrently exist within the same sentential form, there is also a question of whether we progress the X or the Z at each particular stage. The brute-force parser works through exhaustive search, and each "choice" creates a new branch that the parser must explore, resulting in a far larger search space. Obviously, we can tell that it makes no difference which X or Z symbol it progresses: However, JFLAP does not possess this human insight.

JFLAP does use some aggressive pruning strategies in order to keep brute-force parsing from becoming too difficult; this form of exhaustive search is still intractable, but not hopelessly intractable. Unfortunately, these strategies have limits. For example, since multiple Z symbols can concurrently exist, in the event that this is a^n where n is prime, the parser might never "reject" the string since it can simply keep adding Z symbols to the sentential form in a search. That is why productions 4 and 8 in the new grammar also process an a symbol: JFLAP can detect that an A symbol or another a symbol will never "go away" and so cause successive sentential forms to shrink; JFLAP therefore detects at some point that the sentential form is getting too large to successfully generate the target string as new Z's (and also A's) are generated. However, JFLAP can also tell that Z symbols can go away (because of production 7), so if production 4 were $T \to ZT$, JFLAP would keep adding Z's, and would not know to prune a branch even if there were thousands of Z's doing nothing.

The new grammar is a more clever construction, but the old grammar works better due to how JFLAP attempts to parse strings with unrestricted grammars. A clever, concise solution is appealing, but using JFLAP's brute-force parser often requires a solution where there is not too much choice in how to progress the expansion. Otherwise the search space may become enormous.

11.2   Context-Sensitive Grammars

This section describes context-sensitive grammars, a subset of unrestricted grammars. Context-sensitive grammars are essentially unrestricted grammars with one important difference: Each production in the grammar must have at least as many symbols in the right side of a production as in the left side. Productions of this type are called *noncontracting productions*, as sequential sentential forms never decrease in size. To allow context-sensitive grammars to derive λ, the definition of a context-sensitive grammar is expanded to allow the production $S \to \lambda$, where S is the start variable. This special case may be used only in the event that the start variable S never appears in the right side of any other production in the grammar.

Unrestricted grammars have the same power as Turing machines. Context-sensitive grammars, with their noncontracting productions, have power equivalent to *linear-bounded automata* (LBA). An LBA is a Turing machine restricted to use at most kn tape for input of size n, where k is a constant noted in the machine specification. The set of context-sensitive languages is a subset of recursively enumerable languages, and a superset of context-free languages.

Note	JFLAP does not distinguish between unrestricted and context-sensitive grammars. The methods for editing and parsing are the same. There will be no error message if a user intends to enter a context-sensitive grammar, but uses a contracting production.

11.2.1 Simple Grammar

In this example we will edit a simple context-sensitive grammar that generates the language $a^n b^m c^n d^m$, where n and m are positive integers. Either create the grammar that appears in Figure 11.4, or open the file **ex11-anbmcndm**. The procedure to enter a context-sensitive grammar is no different from entering an unrestricted grammar, or any other grammar.

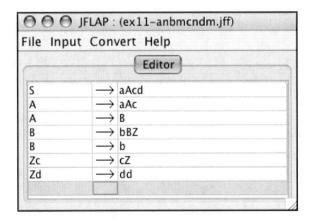

Figure 11.4: Editing a Grammar That Generates the $a^n b^m c^n d^m$ Language.

Parse the string *abcd* with the brute-force parser. The parse tree is pictured to the left in Figure 11.5. This is the shortest string that this grammar can produce. Now parse the string *aabbbccddd* with the brute-force parser. The parse tree is pictured to the right in Figure 11.5. The grammar first generates an equal number of a's and c's using the productions $S \rightarrow aAcd$ and $A \rightarrow aAc$. The grammar then moves to generate b's with $A \rightarrow B$. Then, for each b generated, produce a Z with $B \rightarrow bBZ$. Move the Z's harmlessly across the c symbols with production $Zc \rightarrow cZ$. Then whenever the Z runs into a d symbol, turn the Z into a d with production $Zd \rightarrow dd$. At some point the B will be turned into a b with production $B \rightarrow b$.

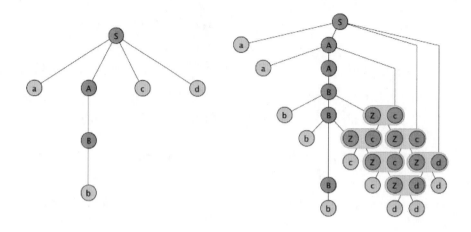

Figure 11.5: The Parse Trees for $a^1b^1c^1d^1$ (left) and $a^2b^3c^2d^3$ (right).

11.2.2   Complex Grammar

In this example we will revisit the example unrestricted grammar of Section 11.1.3. This example grammar generated the language a^n, where n is composite. Though it was phrased in the context of an unrestricted grammar, this is a context-sensitive language, and it is possible to generate this language with a context-sensitive grammar.

1.	$S \rightarrow HC$	5.	$AZ \rightarrow ZA$	9.	$aX \rightarrow Xaa$
2.	$C \rightarrow aC$	6.	$aZ \rightarrow ZAa$	10.	$AX \rightarrow Xa$
3.	$C \rightarrow aT$	7.	$HZ \rightarrow HA$	11.	$HX \rightarrow aa$
4.	$aT \rightarrow ZAaT$	8.	$aT \rightarrow Xaa$		

Table 11.3: The Productions of `ex11-composite-cs`.

Open the file `chap12-composite-cs`. The productions for this grammar are listed in Table 11.3. This grammar is essentially identical to that of Table 11.2, except for a slight change in strategy: In this new grammar, H not only denotes the head of a sentential form, but also acts like a placeholder for an a symbol. A way to interpret the new strategy is that the new production 7 does in one production what the old productions 6 and 7 did. Similarly, the new production 11 does in one production what the old productions 9 and 11 did. Additionally, production 1 has changed: Since H now also acts like a placeholder for an a, the new grammar generates one fewer a than the old grammar.

Open the old grammar in file `chap12-composite-short` again, and attempt to parse $aaaaaaaaa$. Now attempt to parse the same string in the new grammar. Though the grammars take essentially the same strategy, the brute-force parser can generate the target string in the new grammar using only a small fraction of the time and space used for the old grammar when parsing strings. Why is JFLAP more efficient with the new grammar?

Section 6.1.4 gave details about how JFLAP's brute-force parser works. Particularly, the parser detected which variables are part of contracting productions. When all variables are in noncontracting productions, JFLAP is certain that any sentential forms longer than the target string cannot derive the target string. In the old grammar, variables H, Z, and X are part of contracting productions; JFLAP cannot rule out as many sentential forms. In the new grammar, there are no contracting productions; JFLAP can therefore prune the search tree more aggressively.

Unrestricted grammars can be more expressive, and even when the extra expressive power is not being used, unrestricted grammars often are more intuitive than equivalent context-sensitive grammars. However, within JFLAP, a context-sensitive grammar has an advantage over an unrestricted grammar: The brute-force parser tends to find parsing using a noncontracting grammar easier, since JFLAP is able to more effectively limit the search space.

11.3 Summary

Unrestricted grammars allow multiple symbols on the left side of productions, not just a single variable. Instead of using a production to replace a single variable, JFLAP can use an unrestricted production to replace multiple symbols. This flexibility gives unrestricted grammars the power to generate any recursively enumerable language.

When parsing a string using an unrestricted grammar with the brute-force parser, when multiple symbols are being replaced, the multiple nodes for those symbols are bracketed into a supernode, with replacement symbols as children nodes of the supernode. This allows users to visualize unrestricted parses as familiar parse tree-like structures.

For the brute-force parser, a grammar with sentential forms that leave little ambiguity about what expansion should be attempted next tends to be more efficient. If a sentential form allows a large choice of what expansion to attempt, each choice will give another branch in the search tree. A large choice makes brute-force parsing very inefficient. As with any search tree, a tree with a lower branching factor will tend to be more efficient.

Context-sensitive grammars are a special case of unrestricted grammars. A context-sensitive grammar must have productions where the right side of a production is at least as long as the left side of a production; in other words, productions must be noncontracting. To allow context-sensitive grammars to generate λ, a special case production $S \to \lambda$ is allowed if the start variable S does not appear on the right side of any production. Context-sensitive grammars have equal power to linear-bounded automata.

One of the nice things about context-sensitive grammars and the brute-force parser is that noncontracting productions allow JFLAP to make tighter assumptions about what sentential forms are valid, and perform a more aggressive pruning of the search tree of sentential forms, leading to quicker parses. All else being equal, JFLAP will tend to parse strings slowly using a grammar with contracting productions (unrestricted but not context-sensitive), and quickly using a grammar with non-contracting productions (context-sensitive).

11.4   Exercises

1. For the unrestricted grammar in `ex11.4a`, list four strings in the language and give a written description of the language.

2. Write an unrestricted grammar for the following grammars. Create a set of test strings that include strings that should be in the language and strings that should not be in the language and verify with JFLAP. *Hint: Be careful that your grammar does not have too many choices for selecting the next production in a parse, or the parser will run slowly. Use several symbols on the left side of a production to help in restricting the number of choices. If there is any choice, then you will probably only be able to test short strings.*

   (a) $L = \{a^n b^m c^n d^m \mid n > 1, m > n\}$

   (b) $L = \{a^n b^m c^p \mid 0 < n < m < p\}$

   (c) $\{w \in \Sigma^* \mid n_a(w) = n_b(w) = n_c(w), |w| > 0\}, \Sigma = \{a, b, c\}$

   (d) $\{a^n b^{n^2} \mid n > 0\}$

3. Write a context-sensitive grammar for the following grammars. Create a set of test strings that include strings that should be in the language and strings that should not be in the language and verify with JFLAP.

   (a) $L = \{a^n b^m c^n d^m \mid n > 1, m > n\}$

   (b) $L = \{a^n b^m c^p \mid 0 < n < m < p\}$

   (c) $\{w \in \Sigma^* \mid n_a(w) = n_b(w) = n_c(w), |w| > 0\}, \Sigma = \{a, b, c\}$

   (d) $\{a^n b^{n^2} \mid n > 1\}$

Appendix A

L-System Quick Reference

This is the quick reference for L-System turtle commands and parameters used in drawing. These commands are discussed in more depth with examples of use throughout Chapter 10.

A.1   Turtle Commands

Command	Description
g or $g(value)$	Move forward *distance* or the evaluation of *value* pixels in the y direction. If not building a polygon, the pen is down, producing a line of width *lineWidth* and color *color*. If building a polygon, no line is drawn, but the end-point of the move is added to the polygon.
f or $f(value)$	Move forward *distance* or the evaluation of *value* pixels in the y direction. This only moves the turtle. No line is produced, nor points added to a polygon.
+ or +(*value*)	Yaw the turtle right by *angle* or the evaluation of *value* degrees. (A clockwise turn in 2D.)
− or −(*value*)	Yaw the turtle left by *angle* or the evaluation of *value* degrees. (A counter-clockwise turn in 2D.)
& or &(*value*)	Pitch the turtle down by *angle* or the evaluation of *value* degrees.
^ or ^(*value*)	Pitch the turtle up by *angle* or the evaluation of *value* degrees.
/ or /(*value*)	Roll the turtle to the right by *angle* or the evaluation of *value* degrees.
* or *(*value*)	Roll the turtle to the left by *angle* or the evaluation of *value* degrees.
%	Yaw the turtle by 180°.
[or]	Push or pop a turtle from the stack, respectively.
! or !(*value*)	Increment *lineWidth* by *lineIncrement* or the evaluation of *value*.
∼ or ∼ (*value*)	Decrement *lineWidth* by *lineIncrement* or the evaluation of *value*.
{	Begin a polygon. The current turtle position is the first point in the polygon.
}	End a polygon. The current turtle position is not added to the polygon. The polygon is filled with *polygonColor*.
# or #(*value*)	Increment the hue angle of *color* by *hueChange* or the evaluation of *value* degrees.
@ or @(*value*)	Decrement the hue angle of *color* by *hueChange* or the evaluation of *value* degrees.
## or ##(*value*)	Increment the hue angle of *polygonColor* by *hueChange* or the evaluation of *value* degrees.
@@ or @@(*value*)	Decrement the hue angle of *polygonColor* by *hueChange* or the evaluation of *value* degrees.
param = *value*	Sets the parameter *param* to the evaluation of *value*.

A command with multiple characters must not have spaces anywhere in the text of the command.

A.2 Parameters

Name	Default	Description
distance	15	The *g* and *f* commands move the turtle forward by length *distance*.
color	*black*	Lines are drawn with the color specified by *color*. Colors may be specified by name. Color names are case sensitive! The acceptable color names are: *black*, *blue*, *brown*, *cyan*, *darkGray*, *darkOliveGreen*, *darkOliveGreen2*, *dukeBlue*, *forestGreen*, *goldenrod*, *gray*, *green*, *lightGray*, *magenta*, *maroon*, *oliveDrab*, *orange*, *orangeRed*, *pink*, *purple*, *red*, *springGreen*, *violetRed*, *white*, and *yellow*.
		Additionally, one may specify a given color according to three numbers of the form a, b, c. If a, b, and c are all within the range of $[0.0, 1.0]$, they are interpreted as hue, saturation, and brightness values, respectively (where the hue range of 0 through 1 represents a full tour around the color wheel), and are used to define a color appropriately. If any of those values is outside of that range they are treated as standard *red, green*, and *blue*, respectively, with each channel value ranging in increasing intensity from 0 to 255. For example, blue may be defined either as an HSB color by $0.667, 1, 1$, or as an RGB color by $0, 0, 255$.
polygonColor	*red*	Polygons are filled with the color specified by *polygonColor*. This parameter accepts the same value types as the *color* parameter.
angle	15	Whenever the turtle is turned, pitched, or rolled, it does so with *angle* degrees.
hueChange	10	When the command to increment the hue of the current drawing color is given the degrees the hue is turned is *hueChange*.
lineWidth	1.0	Lines are drawn with a pixel-width of *lineWidth*. This parameter accepts real number values greater or equal to zero (e.g., 4, 1.5, 0).
lineIncrement	1.0	When the line width (the parameter *lineWidth*) is incremented or decremented, it is incremented or decremented by this amount.

Appendix B

JFLAP .jff File Format

This appendix describes the .jff format that JFLAP uses to save structures to files. The .jff format uses XML, a simplification of SGML that is currently used for a variety of applications for storing and transmitting structured data. This appendix assumes basic familiarity with XML[1], and instead focuses on how JFLAP encodes a structure as XML.

After a brief review of basic XML terminology, the appendix describes how the .jff format is used to define automata, grammars, regular expressions, and L-systems.

B.1 Brief Review of XML Terminology

We now briefly review some XML-related terminology to establish some common nomenclature.

A *tag* refers to either a start tag of the form `<example>`, or an end tag of the form `</example>`.

Sometimes start tags have *attributes*, where `<person name="Bob">` is a `<person>` start tag with the attribute named `name` with value `Bob`. Values of attributes must appear in double quotes, as shown.

The text after a start tag and before the corresponding end tag is called *data*, which may contain more tags, or strings, or other markup. The start tag, data, and end tag are collectively referred to as an *element*. In the event that the data for an element is empty, one can use an element of the form `<example/>`, which is shorthand for the equivalent `<example></example>` (that is, an `<example>` element with empty data). If the data for an element `<super>` contains another element `<sub>`, then there is a `<sub>` *subelement* to the `<super>` element. If an element `<B>` is a subelement of another element `<A>`, then the start and end tags for the element `<B>` must be contained wholly within the data for `<A>`.

To avoid confusion, in most XML literature, a subelement of another element need not be the *direct* child element; that is, a subelement is not necessarily a child, but perhaps a child of a child.

---

[1] A full, formal treatment on XML may be found at `http://www.w3.org/xml/` or `http://www.xml.org/`.

```
<?xml version="1.0"?>
<structure>
    <type>fa</type>
    <state id="0">
        <x>100</x>
        <y>200</y>
        <initial />
    </state>
</structure>
```

Table B.1: A Simple Example of XML Syntax As It Is Used in a `.jff` File.

For the convenience of this discussion, however, a subelement always refers to a direct child within this appendix. In Table B.1, for example, `<x>` is a subelement of `<state>`, which is a subelement of `<structure>`, but `<x>` is not a subelement of `<structure>`.

In XML there is exactly one *root element*. All other elements are subelements of the root element, or subelements of those subelements, and so forth.

Table B.1 shows a simple example of a JFLAP saved file. It is of a finite automaton, with a single initial state and no transitions. It has a `<structure>` root element, which contains `<type>` and `<state>` subelements. The latter contains `<x>` and `<y>` subelements. The `<state>` start tag has the attribute `id` with value 0. We will go over the meaning of this markup shortly: The point now is not to understand the semantics, but rather the general structure of XML.

The leading `<?xml version="1.0"?>` "tag" is actually not a tag, but a processing instruction. This identifies the document as a document conforming to XML version 1.0. Applications other than JFLAP often use more sophisticated processing instructions, but JFLAP uses only this one instruction to identify that this is indeed XML markup. One may consider this simply as a required prefix, and otherwise ignore it. Processing instructions are not discussed further.

B.2 Elements Common to All Structures

Throughout this manual, the term structure has referred to any sort of formal language structure that may be defined in JFLAP. Correspondingly, the root element of any `.jff` file is a single `<structure>` element.

Every `<structure>` element requires a `<type>` subelement to identify the type of structure. The data of this `<element>` must be one of `fa` (Finite Automaton), `pda` (Pushdown Automaton), `turing` (Turing Machine), `re` (Regular Expression), `grammar` (Grammar), or `lsystem` (L-System). For example, a `<type>fa</type>` element denotes a finite automaton.

Other elements required vary according to the type of structure. The sections that follow describe other subelements of `<structure>` required for various structures.

B.3   Automaton

This section describes the elements used to define an automaton. The elements used to define the states and transitions are discussed, in that order.

B.3.1   Defining States

Elements and subelements to define states are the same for every type of automaton. For every state in the automaton there must be a corresponding `<state>` element that is a subelement of the `<structure>` element. The `<state>` start tags require an `id` attribute whose value may be any string. No two `<state>` tags may have the same string value for the `id` attribute.

To define the position of a state, give `<x>` and `<y>` subelements for the `<state>` element. The data for these elements defines the x and y coordinates of the state, respectively, and must be a real number. Position $x = 0$, $y = 0$ corresponds to the upper-left corner of the automaton editing window, and the data for the `<x>` and `<y>` elements indicate how many pixels to the right and down the state is offset from this position, respectively. JFLAP will use its graph layout algorithm to position any states whose corresponding `<state>` element did not come with the positional subelements.

To define that a state is an initial state or final state, give a `<state>` element either an `<initial>` or `<final>` subelement respectively. The data for these elements are ignored, so one may as well use the abbreviated `<initial/>` and `<final/>` form. If either element is not included, then that state is either not initial or final respectively. Only one `<state>` element should contain the `<initial>` subelement.

To define the label for a state, provide a `<label>` subelement. The data for this element is the text of the label. If there is no `<label>` subelement, the state has no label.

For example, the state defined by the `<state>` element in Table B.1 is placed 100 pixels to the right and 200 pixels down from the upper-left corner of the automata editing window. It is an initial state, not a final state. Its state ID is "0". It has no label.

B.3.2   Defining Transitions

For every transition in the automaton there must be a corresponding `<transition>` element that is a subelement of the `<structure>` element.

Every `<transition>` element requires two subelements `<from>` and `<to>` that specify the states a transition comes from and goes to respectively. The data for each of these elements must be *exactly* the same as the value for some `id` attribute of a `<state>` start tag.

Unlike states, there are also subelements of `<transition>` that differ among the types of automata.

The `<read>` element can occur in FA and PDA transitions. The data of this element indicates the input the transition reads.

The `<pop>` and `<push>` elements can occur in PDA transitions. The data of these elements indicate the symbols the transition pops off and pushes onto the stack, respectively.

If a transition in an FA or PDA omits any of the `<read>`, `<pop>`, or `<push>` elements, the blank string λ is assumed for the corresponding aspect of the transition.

The `<read>`, `<write>` elements can occur in TM transitions. The data for these must be a string of length at most one that indicates the character to read from or write to the tape respectively. The blank tape symbol □ is represented with empty data. If a transition omits a `<read>` element or a `<write>` element, the transition is assumed to read or write the blank tape symbol □ respectively.

The `<move>` element can occur in TM transitions, and the data must be one of the single character strings L, S, or R. If the `<move>` element is omitted, the transition is assumed to move the tape head right.

For Turing machines, `<read>`, `<write>`, and `<move>` start tags have an attribute `tape` whose value must be some integer between 1 and the number of tapes inclusive to indicate which tape this read, write, or move will apply to. The `tape` attribute has a default value of 1 for all of these elements.

The following is a portion of a `.jff` file that defines a transition within a two-tape Turing machine. The transition is from the state with ID 3 to the state with ID 5. On tape 1, the transition reads the blank tape symbol, writes a, and moves the tape head to the left. On tape 2, the transition reads b, writes c, and the tape head stays.

```
<transition>
    <from>3</from> <to>5</to>
    <read tape="1"><read>  <write tape="1">a<write> <move tape="1">L</move>
    <read tape="2">b<read> <write tape="2">c<write> <move tape="2">S</move>
</transition>
```

B.3.3   Tapes for Turing Machines

In addition to these elements, if a Turing machine has multiple tapes it must define a `<tapes>` subelement of the root `<structure>` element, whose data is a positive integer indicating the number of tapes. For example, the element `<tapes>3</tapes>` signifies that a Turing machine has three tapes.

B.4   Grammar

The tag structure for grammars is the same for all types of grammars. For every production in a grammar, there must be a `<production>` subelement of the `<structure>` root element.

The `<left>` and `<right>` elements can occur as subelements of each `<production>` element. The data for these elements define the left side and right side of a production, respectively. The `<left>` subelement must exist and have nonempty data. If a production omits a `<right>` subelement, the production is assumed to be a λ-production.

The following is a portion of a `.jff` file that defines the production $S \rightarrow aaB$ within a grammar.

`<production> <left>S</left> <right>aaB</right> </production>`

Productions will appear in the JFLAP grammar editor table in the same order that their corresponding `<production>` elements are defined within the loaded save file.

B.5   Regular Expression

The tag structure for regular expressions is simple. There can be a single `<expression>` subelement of the `<structure>` element, whose data is the string containing the regular expression. If this `<expression>` element does not exist, then JFLAP assumes the regular expression is the empty string.

B.6   L-System

The tag structure for an L-system requires elements to specify the axiom, the rewriting rules, and any drawing parameters.

The axiom for an L-system is defined with a single `<axiom>` subelement of the root `<structure>` element. The data of the `<axiom>` element holds the axiom. For example, `<axiom>g + + G</axiom>` defines an axiom $g + + G$. The `<axiom>` element must exist.

The rewriting rules for an L-system are defined with `<production>` subelements of the root `<structure>` element. These differ from a grammar's `<production>` elements in some respects. A `<production>` element must have one `<left>` subelement to define the symbols to rewrite; the data for the `<left>` subelement must be in the same format as we would type it into the L-system editor. A `<production>` element must have zero or more `<right>` subelements. For each `<right>` subelement, a rewriting rule is added to the L-system where symbols in the data of the `<right>` element rewrites the symbol in the `<left>` element. This means that in the case of stochastic L-systems, a `<production>` element may contain multiple `<right>` elements to define multiple rewritings for the symbol in the `<left>` element's data. Correspondingly, if a `<production>` element does not contain any `<right>` elements, no rewriting rules are added.

The following is a portion of a `.jff` file that defines two rewriting rules $g \rightarrow g\,g$ and $g \rightarrow +\,f\,g$ for an L-system.

```
<production>
    <left>g</left>  <right>g g</right>  <right>+ f g</right>
</production>
```

Drawing parameters are defined with `<parameter>` subelements of the root `<structure>` element. A `<parameter>` element has two subelements `<name>` and `<value>`. The data for these elements hold the name and the value for a parameter, respectively.

The following is a portion of a `.jff` file that defines two parameters, *distance* with value 5, and *color* with value *green*. For example, this L-system will draw green line segments of length 5 when the *g* turtle command is encountered.

```
<parameter> <name>distance</name> <value>5</value>     </parameter>
<parameter> <name>color</name>    <value>green</value> </parameter>
```

If a `<parameter>` element does not contain a `<name>` subelement, the `<parameter>` is ignored. If the `<parameter>` does not contain a `<value>` subelement, it is assumed that the parameter value is an empty string.

Index